Toxic Wealth

Toxic Wealth

How the Culture of Affluence Can Harm Us and Our Children

Orla Cashman and James A. Twaite

PRAEGER

An Imprint of ABC-CLIO, LLC

A B C 🔻 C L I O

Santa Barbara, California • Denver, Colorado • Oxford, England

Copyright 2009 by Orla Cashman and James A. Twaite

Library of Congress Cataloging-in-Publication Data

Cashman, Orla.
   Toxic wealth : how the culture of affluence can harm us and our children /
   Orla Cashman and James A. Twaite.
      p. cm.
   Includes bibliographical references and index.
   ISBN 978–0–313–35991–0 (hbk. : alk. paper) — ISBN 978–0–313–35992–7
   (ebook : alk. paper)
1. Wealth—Moral and ethical aspects. 2. Wealth—Psychological aspects. 3. Rich people—
Psychology. 4. Children of the rich—Psychology. I. Twaite, James A., 1946– II. Title.
HB835.C37   2009
178—dc22   2009009900

13 12 11 10 09 1 2 3 4 5

This book is also available on the World Wide Web as an eBook.
Visit www.abc-clio.com for details.

ABC-CLIO, LLC
130 Cremona Drive, P.O. Box 1911
Santa Barbara, California 93116-1911

This book is printed on acid-free paper (∞)

Manufactured in the United States of America

Contents

The American Dream and the Myth that Wealth Brings Happiness

THE MYTH

We all know the script for the "American Dream." It goes like this: You study hard, get your degree, work hard in your chosen field, achieve success, and become wealthy. Then you live happily ever after. The essential element of the American Dream is wealth, and the reason why wealth is essential to the dream is the belief that wealth brings happiness.

People who are not affluent already tend to accept the proposition that if only we had enough money, all of our problems would disappear. If we were rich, we could live where we wanted to live, do what we wanted to do, and buy whatever toys we thought might amuse us. If we were rich, we could travel to exotic places, stay in exclusive resorts, and attend exciting and fashionable cultural events. As a result of these wealth-related outcomes and activities, we would necessarily become interesting, attractive, and desirable. We would attract interesting and attractive partners, have beautiful children, do good works, feel good about ourselves, and be recognized for our accomplishments. If we had enough money, everyone would love us, and life would be good.

And the myth continues: If we were rich, the few people who did not love us would nevertheless still respect us. Salespeople and service workers would treat us with deference, because they would know that their liveli-hood depends on satisfying our wishes. Business associates would take care not to harm us, cheat us, or take advantage of us, because they would know that we have advisors and attorneys to safeguard our interests. Professionals would give us special access to their time and expertise, because we can afford to pay their fees. We would have the most inspiring personal trainers and the most knowledgeable physicians to see to our health. We would have the most brilliant therapists to insure that we can handle life's little ups and downs with grace and skill, all the while maintaining our positive outlook.

THE REALITY

But it is not true. The idea that wealth solves all problems is a myth. The reality is that being wealthy certainly does *not* solve all your problems. In fact, being wealthy actually creates some problems of its own. One of the major points that we will make in this book is that the *culture of affluence* that exists in the United States imposes unique stresses on the affluent that sometimes make the pursuit of wealth seem like a hollow and even misdirected goal. We speak from experience. We have been psychotherapists for many years in two of the wealthiest suburban communities in the United States, and we have worked with countless men and women who have all the money they could possibly want, but have nevertheless been just about as miserable and unhappy as anyone could possibly imagine.

Not too long ago, we attended a cocktail party, and the topic of treating affluent clients came up (which tends to happen quite frequently when we are around). One of us made the point that the affluent face significant stresses associated particularly with the culture of affluence. In response, a number of the therapist types present at the party expressed what we believe is a very common sentiment among professionals, i.e., "I only wish I had their problems." In fact, many of our colleagues unabashedly acknowledged that they had a really hard time even listening to the complaints of many of their wealthy clients. They expressed the belief that the wealthy naturally expect life to be perfect, the idea that the wealthy complain too much when life is not perfect, and the conviction that the wealthy generally fail to effec-tively use their financial resources and social connections to deal with the issues that they face.

Before we could begin an argument by assailing our colleagues for their lack of empathy, an obstetrician friend of ours, speaking from a more objec-tive perspective, related an event that he had witnessed that probably made our point as well as it could be made, without the necessity of the argument. Our friend asked if any of us had seen the press conference held the day before by a very famous baseball pitcher who had just signed an extremely lucrative contract with the Boston Red Sox. We think it was Curt Schilling. In any event, our friend said that a reporter at the conference asked the pitcher a question that suggested the money the pitcher would be making ought to leave him "set for life," "free from concerns," and "able to focus 100 percent on baseball."

The pitcher's response to this question was thoughtful and relevant well beyond his personal circumstances and his baseball career. He acknowledged that he would indeed be making a great deal of money, and that this was a good thing. However, he pointed out that all of us have a great many areas of concern in our lives that are relatively unrelated to money. He noted that we are also concerned with our personal health and the health of our loved ones, with the quality of our relationships with our family members, friends, and colleagues, and with the satisfaction we derive from our work and our other interests and activities. On a broader scale, we are also concerned with the state of the world locally, nationally, and globally, matters over which we as individuals have very little control. He concluded that his new contract had freed him from worrying about *exactly one* of the areas that most people worry about on a daily basis, i.e., the financial area. In every other area, he was not necessarily any better off or any worse off than the reporter who had asked the question, or anyone else in the room.

The athlete's response to the reporter's question certainly makes it clear that having money is, in and of itself, no guarantee of happiness. We all tend to think that being wealthy should solve all our problems, but the reality is that it does not. There are too many other potential problems in life for that to be true. Viewing wealth as the answer to just one of a long list of concerns we all face in life, it would be far more logical to conclude that the wealthy are actually only slightly more likely to be satisfied with their lives than individuals of more modest means. This logic would imply that their wealth guaranteed the affluent greater satisfaction than the rest of us in this one area, but that in all of the other important aspects of life, the wealthy have the same chance of happiness as anyone else.

THE AFFLUENT MAY HAVE MORE PROBLEMS THAN THE REST OF US

Actually, however, even this view that the affluent should be only a little better off than the rest of us by virtue of their wealth may be overstating the value of affluence. The reality that we have seen in our work with the wealthy is that, in more cases than not, the affluent are actually *less* satisfied with their lives and *more* likely to experience psychosocial adjustment difficulties than the average person on the street. In fact, recent research confirms that affluent individuals and their children actually experience greater psychological stress and more frequent and serious psychiatric symptoms than individuals of more modest income levels.[1]

The Culture of Affluence

In order to understand why the affluent may actually experience greater stress and lower levels of satisfaction than less affluent individuals, we need to understand a number of aspects of American society and the culture of affluence. These include the pressure to achieve and succeed experienced by the affluent, the impact of extreme achievement-oriented behavior on family life, and specific aspects of wealth itself that are problematic from the point of view of personal development, including widely held negative attitudes toward the wealthy, the potential impact of affluence on personal motivation, and the difficulties created by wealth with respect to the development of a sense of purpose in life. In the following sections of this chapter, we consider each of these issues briefly. We conclude this chapter with a review of the most important recent studies that document the psychosocial problems that tend to be experienced disproportionately by affluent individuals.

The Intense Pressure to Achieve Faced by the Affluent

The affluent experience intense and continuing pressure to achieve. The pressure begins with parental expectations that their children will do well in school and move on to respected and lucrative careers, but by the time these high-achieving children reach adulthood, they have often so thoroughly internalized this pressure that they are self-motivated workaholics. These adults are never satisfied with what they have accomplished. No matter how great their objective success, they are driven to pursue higher and higher goals, acquire greater and greater wealth, and garner more and more honors and other forms of recognition. Life becomes a contest, and money is valued less for what it can buy than as a means of keeping score.

These affluent high-achievers are masters at viewing the glass as half empty. They do not compare themselves to the population at large and recognize that they are indeed very successful. Instead, they compare themselves to those who are most like themselves: their friends from school, their colleagues at work, their neighbors, and those in their close social circles. Within this highly selected subset of the population, their accomplishments may seem relatively unimpressive. A $200,000 year-end bonus may be viewed as a sign of failure by an investment banker who is aware that his colleagues did better. The million-dollar home in Westchester can actually be a source of embarrassment if most of one's friends have $3 million homes.

Due to their intense focus on success, affluent adults tend to work harder than they should. They do not allow themselves the opportunity to relax, to pursue leisure and recreational activities, to enjoy life. They tend to spend too much time away from home. They become strangers to their spouse and their children, thus denying themselves still another important source of life satisfaction. Ultimately, their driven lives can lead to internalizing physical complaints and to psychological depression.

THE TOLL ON CHILDREN

The children of high-achieving parents are under similar pressure to achieve.[2] The pressure they experience comes from parents, teachers, and sometimes from peers. Academic and social successes are simply taken for granted, and any failure to measure up is viewed as both inexplicable and inexcusable.[3] Good grades are expected. High SAT scores are expected. Even excellence in extracurricular activities is expected. It is not enough for the children of the affluent to go to college. It had better be a highly prestigious college.

The affluent tend to spend too little time with their children. In many affluent families, both spouses are pursuing high-level business or professional careers. Child care is likely to be delegated to nannies, housekeepers, coaches, and trainers. Research indicates that adolescents from affluent families are more likely to be unsupervised after school than adolescents from poor and middle-class families.[4] Although high-achieving parents expect their children to succeed, they often fail to provide them with the support and guidance that the children need to develop good values and a strong work ethic. As a result, the children of affluent families sometimes fail to respond as expected to achievement expectations. Instead, they withdraw, rebel, or act out. They may screw up in school, use substances, engage in premature sexual activity, or otherwise self-destruct.

THE DOWNSIDE OF AFFLUENCE

Apart from the effects of the pressure to achieve that pervades the culture of affluence, several aspects of wealth itself may have a negative effect on personal development and adjustment. These include personal experiences related to being on the wrong end of negative cultural stereotypes of the affluent—the experience of being envied, the fear of being approached socially for the wrong reasons, and (for the children of the affluent) possible inability to develop an adequate sense of self apart from the family's economic circumstances, and possible failure to experience normative achievement strivings.

Investigators have shown that just as the poor in our society are often viewed as dishonest, indolent, promiscuous, and uninterested in education, so the affluent are often viewed as unethical, entitled, arrogant, superficial, and narcissistic.[5] We have had many affluent patients complain that they have had people make such assumptions about them. We have also had many patients who seem to have implicitly accepted these stereotypes as valid descriptions of their personalities, capabilities, and behavior. In some cases, the acceptance of these stereotypes has had the effect of placing limits on personal development, ultimately resulting in lowered self-esteem. For example, we have seen patients ignore obvious areas of interest and select educational and career paths that were less interesting than other possible courses, but deemed more appropriate or acceptable. In many instances, the negative fall-out from such choices does not fully manifest itself until midlife, when the individual suddenly realizes that he has not done with his life what he or she really ought to have done to be true to the self.

Affluent individuals whose associates include people of more modest means are frequently the victims of simple envy. Wealthy women who choose to have a career may find that they are never fully accepted by their colleagues, who regard her decision to work as a frivolous choice rather than a serious professional commitment. Affluent men and women who enter the helping professions are often viewed by colleagues as being totally incapable of understanding the worldview and experiences of clients who are poor or middle class. The affluent may, in fact, be the victims of fairly direct social exclusion on the part of less affluent colleagues, who may give vent to their jealousies by excluding the affluent coworker from their on-the-job social circles. More subtle forms of exclusion may result from the reluctance of an affluent worker to share with his or her colleagues experiences that reflect his or her financial situation, such as expensive vacation trips or invitations to exclusive social events. Thus, even if coworkers are not actively hostile to an affluent colleague, the differences in their respective financial situations can represent a barrier to the development of close relationships.

On the other hand, when affluent individuals are approached socially by colleagues, the receptiveness of the affluent person may be influenced by the perception that "He only likes me for my money," or "They are only friendly toward us because they realize that we are powerful and influential people whose connections could some day be of use to them." The extent to which such suspicions are valid is not clear, and perhaps some wealthy individuals tend to be more concerned about this possibility than is really warranted. However, consider an affluent person who is basically somewhat unsure of himself and just how attractive he might be. When an attractive woman shows an interest in him, he must experience at least a seed of doubt as to her motivations. Once again, this possibility represents a barrier to the creation and development of meaningful social interaction, and thus an obstacle to the development of gratifying social relationships and social supports.

Finally, it has been suggested simply that "wealth is not good for children" because "it belittles their own achievements, distorts their relationships with their peers, and increases their sense of what is enough."[6] If the children of affluent parents grow up primarily in the company of similarly affluent peers, they may have difficulty developing an accurate sense of the real world. They may come to assume that wealth is a given, and they may never have the occasion to work hard to obtain some desired goal. They may lose that portion of the motivation to excel in school that is predicated on the necessity of obtaining a good job. Therefore, at the same time that their academic success is taken as a given, their motivation to actually succeed may well be cut in half.

To this we must add the problems associated with the perception that rich kids are not supposed to have any problems.[7] This is another negative stereotype that the affluent are likely to internalize. They may come to believe that if they do experience any sort of difficulty in school, socially, or on the athletic field, there must be something *seriously* wrong with them. They must be weak. They must lack talent. These perceptions are quite likely to lead the children in affluent families to deny any problems that they are having, and perhaps to fail to seek out or to take advantage of available sources of support.

STRESS-RELATED PROBLEMS OF THE AFFLUENT

As a result of these stresses, the affluent experience higher levels of psychosocial adjustment difficulties than the population as a whole. A growing body of data on affluent youth indicates that the children of the affluent manifest rates of clinical depression up to three times higher than the national norms, and substance abuse is significantly higher among young people in affluent suburbs than it is among their less affluent inner-city age group peers. Research also shows a significant relationship between internalizing symptoms and substance abuse, suggesting that the affluent youth may be self-medicating their depression.[8]

In addition to the data suggesting elevated rates of specific psychosocial symptoms among affluent young people, there is considerable evidence that affluent youth are simply not very happy. Research indicates significant negative relationships between income level and measures of subjective well-being and self-esteem.[9] These investigators followed some 2,000 teenagers through high school and beyond, periodically measuring indicators of subjective well-being and self-esteem. They found that teens from affluent communities had lower self-reported happiness and lower self-esteem than their middle-class and low-income counterparts.

Diener and Seligman[10] reported that over the past 50 years, the Gross National Product of the United States has more than tripled in real (inflation-adjusted) terms. However, over the same period of time, measured life satisfaction has not changed at all. Furthermore, evidence suggests that residents of economically developed nations manifest higher levels of depression[11] and lower subjective well-being than individuals living in underdeveloped nations.[12]

On the other hand, Sherman suggested that "before we conclude that wealth breeds unhappiness and depression, we must consider other factors that may mediate the relationship between financial success and poor psychological functioning."[13] Luthar has suggested that "It is not the surfeit of riches in itself, but rather an overemphasis on status and wealth that is likely to compromise well-being."[14] Whybrow[15] compared the affluent individual's internalized drive to amass greater and greater material wealth to an addiction in which the psychological need to get more and more has "high-jacked" the normal economic reward system. Other research has shown clearly that once survival needs are secured, the affluent become focused on relative wealth. In other words, wealth is simply a means of keeping score in the competition to achieve more than everyone else, and the one who dies with the most money wins.[16]

Nickerson, Schwarz, Diener, and Kahneman[17] reported the results of a study in which the results of a survey of incoming college students carried out in 1976 were compared with the results of a follow-up survey of the same cohort of students administered 19 years later. In the first survey, students were asked to rate the importance of achieving financial success in their life-times. In the follow-up survey, the researchers asked the respondents to indicate their actual earnings at the time, and in addition the investigators measured overall life satisfaction as well as satisfaction in specific domains, including family, job, and health. The investigators found that the initial rating of the importance of financial success was correlated negatively with overall life satisfaction at the time of the follow-up. In contrast, actual income at the time of the follow-up was correlated positively with overall life satisfaction. These findings suggest that it is not wealth per se that is the problem, but rather the value placed on achieving wealth. Furthermore, these investigators found that the specific domain of life satisfaction that was most strongly related to the value placed on achieving wealth was that of family life.

SUMMARY

Taken together, these findings support the conclusion that affluent individuals tend to experience unique stresses that can interfere with good psychosocial adjustment, positive self-regard, and overall satisfaction with life. A major purpose of this volume is to explain these stresses and provide guidance to readers who are affluent or trying to become affluent on approaches that can be employed to cope effectively with these stresses.

Summing the positive aspects of wealth with the documented negative effects of affluence, we can safely conclude that, on the average, the affluent are at least as likely as anyone else to experience psychosocial adjustment difficulties. They are therefore as much in need of the services of mental health professionals as poor or middle-class individuals. However, the affluent are likely to feel that seeking professional help is an admission of failure and an indication that they are defective individuals. They may reason that if you cannot be happy when you are rich, you must really be messed up. Therefore, paradoxically, the segment of the population that is most able to afford the services of mental health professionals may be the least likely to actually use these services. Another purpose of this book will be to consider relationships between affluent clients and the professionals they may call upon for help with their problems.

2

The Culture of Affluence and the Unrelenting Pressure to Achieve

In the previous chapter, we pointed out several aspects of the culture of affluence that tend to create stress and therefore threaten healthy psychosocial adjustment. In this chapter, we want to consider in some detail one of these problematic elements of the culture, i.e., the unrelenting pressure to achieve that is experienced by affluent adults and their children.

At the risk of confirming some of the negative stereotypes of affluent individuals that we seek to dispel in this book, we present the following case example to illustrate the negative impact on our values and behavior that may result from the extreme pressure to achieve.

THE PRESCHOOL OF BARBARA'S CHOICE

Barbara came to me (JT) with her daughter Heather, who was just three years old. Barbara asked if I could give Heather an IQ test to determine whether she was "gifted." I remember feeling a little put off by the request. The sarcastic comment that ran through my mind was, "Couldn't she wait until the kid was a little older, like maybe five?" I told Barbara that I certainly could evaluate Heather, but I also asked why she thought it was important to get Heather involved in formal testing at this point in her life. I said that it looked pretty obvious to me that Heather was a bright young child, and I asked if she had observed anything about Heather that led her to believe that her daughter required extraordinary educational interventions. I also asked if she had any concerns regarding Heather's psychological well-being or social adjustment.

In response to my inquiries, Barbara said that of course Heather was happy, bright, and perfectly well-adjusted. She simply wanted to see where her daughter "stacked up" in comparison to her peers. Barbara also mentioned that Heather would be starting school the following year, and she and her husband needed to know where she should be applying. Barbara also mentioned that she wanted to get an idea regarding what their chances might be that Heather would be accepted into the preschool program at a particularly prestigious Manhattan private school that they were considering.

I thought to myself that Heather was potentially in for a very difficult childhood, since parental expectations were obviously so high. I toyed with the idea of discouraging Barbara from having Heather evaluated formally, but then I realized that if I did so, Barbara would simply ignore my advice and go somewhere else to get the testing done. I thought that the more prudent course of action with respect to Heather would be for me to do the testing, making every effort I could to make the experience enjoyable and stress-free for Heather. I agreed to do the evaluation.

I explained to Barbara that three 60-minute sessions would be required to conduct the actual testing, and that we would also need to meet for me to explain the results to Barbara. I mentioned that I would be using several different tests, and I explained how long each test took and how I would break them up into manageable time periods so as not to overburden Heather. At this point, Barbara nodded in agreement, but when I had finished, she stated that it was very important to her that I use a particular intelligence test, the Wechsler Preschool and Primary Scale of Intelligence. This request for a specific test surprised me, and I asked why that test. Barbara explained that a friend had recommended that test as especially useful for predicting academic performance, as well as for identifying children's areas of strength and weakness. I took this response at face value and said that I could certainly use that test.

Over the course of working with Heather and Barbara, I learned a lot about the background of the family. Barbara was 26 years old, and she worked as a marketing executive for a well-known international retail chain that specialized in high-end and designer women's wear. Her husband, Josh, had just become a partner in a major New York investment bank. Barbara and Josh were each independently wealthy, based on trusts derived from their respective families, both of whom were involved in manufacturing enterprises in the Midwest. They had been married for four years. They married the year Barbara received her BA from the University of Pennsylvania, which was two years after Josh had received his MBA from Wharton. They had just the one daughter, three-year-old Heather.

Despite their lifelong financial security, both Barbara and Josh were driven to make their own marks on the world. Both Barbara and her husband came from the Midwest. They had both been very hard-working and excellent students from the time they started elementary school. Barbara had long envisioned an executive career that did not involve the day-to-day management concerns that she had observed in her family's manufacturing firm. She wanted something that she perceived as glamorous, and she wanted to get out of the Midwest and live and work in New York City. Josh had worked toward a career in finance since the age of 11, when he overheard his father complaining to friends about how difficult it was to deal with bankers.

Barbara and Josh also had high hopes for Heather. They planned on her attending the best private schools and eventually going to the University of Pennsylvania, as they had done. In fact, it became clear that they were focused on this outcome to the point that it really became an obsession.

The testing showed that Heather was indeed a very bright child whose academic future should not be limited in any way. In discussing the results with Barbara, I offered that Heather was clearly intelligent enough to succeed academically and go to any college she wanted, provided of course that she was appropriately motivated and that she applied herself to her studies and did not become distracted as some children do. To this observation, Barbara responded that motivation had never been a problem in their families, and that she and Josh would make certain that Heather understood the importance of performing well in school and going to Penn. Again I felt an unpleasant visceral response, and I thought to myself that Heather was going to be under a great deal of pressure, not just to be a good student, but to follow along a very narrow path of acceptable educational and vocational alternatives. I remember wondering what would happen if she came home in 11th grade and suggested that she might like to study art at the Rhode Island School of Design or creative writing at Bard.

In these discussions, Barbara also pressed me with questions on things that she and her husband might be able to do to improve Heather's chances of getting accepted by the fancy preschool program they had their eyes on. I said that I really did not know what they could do other than follow the application procedures (which was simply the truth). At this point Barbara offered spontaneously that she was quite certain that this would not be enough, and that in fact she had already begun to do research on the school's board members, administrators, and faculty, in hopes of arranging to meet them and develop personal relationships that might facilitate Heather's admission. Here again, I had a bad feeling. I suggested to Barbara that it could not hurt to know people, but I would be careful about being too heavy-handed in her efforts to become familiar, because such efforts could potentially backfire if some of the people at the school saw her as being pushy or attempting to be manipulative. It was quite clear to me that this suggestion did not register with Barbara.

As it turned out, Heather was not admitted to the school in question, although she was admitted to the preschool programs at several other equally prestigious schools. I found out about this outcome because Heather's rejection by the school that Barbara and Josh had chosen was such a blow to Barbara that she came back to me to discuss her disappointment and her apprehensions regarding possible problems that Heather might have with making a good impression during interviews. Barbara told me that Heather had performed very well on the school's admission tests, but had been rejected nevertheless. Barbara also told me that Heather had been rejected in spite of the fact that Barbara and Josh had hired a professional dress consultant and coach to prepare Heather for her interview, and in spite of the fact that they had entertained several members of the school's board of directors at a dinner party they threw just before the applications were due.

At this time also, Barbara inadvertently let it slip that the school administered the Wechsler intelligence test as part of the admission process. Thus, it turned out that Barbara's whole motivation in bringing Heather to me to be tested in the first place was not to find out "where she stacked up," but rather to give the child an advance exposure to the test that she would be given by the school in the course of the admissions process.

I was distressed to learn that I had unwittingly contributed to this effort to give Heather an unfair advantage. I told Barbara this. I also asked her whether Heather might not have said something to the person who administered the test at the school about having seen the test before. I suggested that if she had made such a comment, that might explain why she had not been admitted to the program. To my surprise, Barbara said that this could not have happened, because she had told Heather specifically not to mention to anyone at the school that she had ever seen the test before! Wow! Not only had Barbara been willing to act unethically to get Heather admitted to the school, but she was willing to enlist the child herself in the deception.

Even worse, however, I realized that Barbara viewed the whole experience as a failure on the part of Heather. Barbara was convinced that she and Josh had done their part genetically to give Heather the "right stuff." They had also gone out of their way to "prepare" her for the admissions test and the interview. And they believed that they had made all the right moves socially and politically with respect to courting the favor of any individuals who might be influential at the school. The only conclusion they could draw was that Heather must be somehow lacking in social skills or that she did not "interview well." I felt that the poor kid was at risk for being labeled as a poor performer or even a failure before she ever set foot in a school.

I shared these feelings with Barbara. She gave them lip service and reassured me that she did not feel that way at all. She said that she knew Heather was a very bright kid, and she still expected great things from her. But Barbara never acknowledged that she might have done some things that were counterproductive to the goal of getting Heather admitted to the school of her choice, or to Heather's moral development, or to Heather's self-esteem.

Barbara and Josh certainly appear to be very foolish in this case study. They even come off as parents with flawed values who may potentially damage their daughter psychologically and socially as a result of their expectations regarding her future and the extraordinary lengths to which they are willing to go to achieve their goals. But we choose to view Barbara and Josh as themselves the victims of an insidious aspect of the culture of affluence that exists in America and throughout the Western world (and increasingly the rest of the world as well). This aspect of the culture of affluence is the unrelenting pressure to compete, succeed, and achieve.

ACHIEVEMENT PRESSURE

Both Barbara and Josh were born into affluent families, families in which the parents had worked hard to succeed and to build wealth. But their parents had never allowed their children to forget how hard they had worked to achieve this success, and the parents made it very clear to Barbara and to Josh as children that they expected no less hard work from them. Of course, Barbara and Josh would have the advantage of attending the best schools, an advantage their parents did not have. But their parents always made it very clear to them that they were expected to do much more than simply go to these schools. They were expected to compete successfully against their classmates, and they were expected to carry on the family legacy of achievement to the next level. This expectation was manifested in Barbara's goal to get out of manufacturing and the Midwest and into a successful career of her own in a glamorous industry in New York. It was manifested similarly in Josh's goal to become a successful financier. He saw himself as having moved one step higher in the economic pecking order of the society, having gone beyond his father's need to negotiate financial backing to assume the position of the banker who makes the decisions regarding the allocation of financial resources.

It is clear that Barbara and Josh had completely internalized the value of hard work and the importance of success. They had not rebelled when their parents communicated these values and expectations. Rather, they took these values to heart and did their best to live up to them. In fact, they sought to exceed their parents' accomplishments and expectations. They completely bought into the idea that an individual is measured by his or her academic and career success, and they believed that they would be worthy human beings only if they were successful human beings.

Furthermore, Barbara and Josh fully expected their daughter to do the same. They actually demanded more from Heather than their parents had demanded from them. Whereas their parents expected them to work hard, go to college, and be successful, they expected Heather to work hard, have an IQ of 130 and perfect college board examination scores, go to Penn, and then go on to a prestigious business or professional school. Note that we used the word "expected." Barbara and Josh considered these achievements to represent only the minimum acceptable levels of accomplishment.

The truth is that for Heather to accomplish anything "less" would be considered a failure. God forbid that Heather should be comfortable with a modest effort in school. Suppose she ended up with a B-plus average in preparatory school, went to Villanova because she liked basketball, and decided to major in physical education. These outcomes would not be acceptable to Barbara and Josh, no matter how comfortable Heather might be with these choices. In fact, on some level, such outcomes would be viewed as less acceptable than major psychological difficulties like depression or anorexia. Part of the culture of affluence suggests that it is acceptable (if suboptimal) to be miserable, as long as you are not mediocre.

THE PROBLEMATIC ASPECTS OF THE ACHIEVEMENT PRESSURE

There are obviously many problems with the inordinate emphasis that the culture of affluence places upon competing and succeeding. These include: (1) the loss of freedom to choose what one wants to do with one's life;

(2) the loss of the ability to derive an authentic sense of accomplishment from one's efforts; (3) the tendency to succumb to the temptation to do whatever it takes to succeed, even if it involves the use of inappropriate or even unethical tactics; and (4) the inability to take time off to simply relax.

THE LOSS OF THE FREEDOM TO CHOOSE ONE'S OWN PATH IN LIFE

Obviously, when the need to excel academically and financially becomes the paramount goal in life, it may not be possible to follow your heart when it comes to making important choices regarding activities, schools, and career. Having academic and financial success as your most important goal might work out fine it you happen to really want to be an investment banker, a partner in a major law firm, the CEO of a major corporation, or the head of surgery at Columbia Presbyterian Hospital. But what if you really want to be an artist, a chef, or a forest ranger? In many affluent families, children never even consider such options, for it has been made clear to them from birth that there are only a certain number of routes to follow that will lead to acceptable career outcomes, i.e., those representing high achievement in the most competitive and lucrative fields.

These "acceptable" career routes have two primary characteristics: (1) they are paths that involve intense competition in which the indicators of success are generally acknowledged and fairly objective; and (2) they are paths in which success is ultimately reflected in high levels of financial remuneration. Children from affluent families understand from an early age that they are expected to do very well in secondary school, as indicated by a high grade point average, admission to the honor society, participation in advanced placement courses, assumption of leadership positions, and ultimately by admission to a highly prestigious university. For these children, simply going to college means little. Admission to less than one of the most prestigious universities is viewed as a failure.

Once in college, the children of the affluent are expected not only to do very well, but to do very well in a course of study that will lead them to admission to a prestigious business or professional school that will prepare them for a lucrative career. The options that are clearly acceptable are law, business, and medicine. If the child of affluent parents goes to a good college but chooses to major in a field that does not prepare one for one of these clearly acceptable career paths, the decision is likely to be interpreted as a failure in the form of "taking the easy route" and choosing not to engage in the competition that constitutes the essence of life. If Johnny goes to Columbia but then decides to major in secondary education, the chances are you will not find his parents bragging about him at the country club. If Johnny goes to Harvard and turns out to be a mathematics genius who ends up in a doctoral program in geophysics at MIT, his talent will most likely be recognized and his decision tolerated, but he will nevertheless tend to be regarded as a bit of a nut.

Let us get back to the children of the affluent who do follow one of the acceptable career paths. If they go to law school, they are expected to get high grades and take a position with a prestigious law firm. If they go to business school, they are expected to get high grades and take a position with a major bank or brokerage firm. If they go to medical school (which is becoming something of a less prestigious path these days), they are expected to do well in medical school and obtain a residency at a prestigious teaching hospital. In each of these career paths, the indicators of success throughout the course of a lifetime are clear and unambiguous, and in each case, success is tied to and in large measure determined by the financial rewards one receives.

We see many affluent, successful clients who come to us in the midst of the midlife crisis that results when they recognize that they have spent their lives following a path that was laid out for them by others, and that they have been pouring their time and energy into a career that they really do not find fulfilling, and earning money that they do not know how to enjoy.

The message here is clear. If you are at such a midlife crossroads, you need to give yourself permission to change course. If you are a parent, you need to be aware of the expectations placed on your children. You need to give them permission to follow their dreams, even if these dreams deviate from the acceptable paths. If you are a young person who has still to make major decisions about the interests and activities that you might wish to pursue, the peer group with whom you choose to associate, the course of studies you plan to follow, and the vocational goal you set for yourself, you need to learn a lot about yourself and explore the many options that are available to you. Do not follow the path of least resistance. If you think that you might be interested in studying law, fine. But do not go to law school just because it seems like "the thing to do."

The Loss of the Possibility of Any Real Sense of Accomplishment

A second problem with the emphasis on achievement within the culture of affluence is the loss of the possibility of having any real sense of accomplishment in regard to one's career. This paradoxical outcome lies in the fact that when high levels of academic and financial success are expected, taken as a given, then it is almost impossible to exceed these expectations. Therefore, it is almost impossible for individuals who grow up in affluent families to take any real pride in their accomplishments.

Ironically, individuals from less affluent families who achieve substantial financial success are frequently better able to appreciate their accomplishments, because they are free to view these accomplishments as something special, something out of the ordinary. In addition, these individuals are likely to have extensive contact with family and friends who are not so successful, so they tend to look good to themselves by comparison.

In contrast, individuals who grow up in affluent families from affluent neighborhoods come to view high achievement and affluence as the norm. They grow up wearing T-shirts from their parents' alma maters, and they are familiar with hearing stories about kids from the neighborhood getting perfect SAT scores and getting admitted to the best schools. Therefore, when these individuals are themselves admitted to the college of their choice, they are not likely to view this as a very special accomplishment, because most of the kids in the neighborhood and most of their friends were similarly admitted to a prestigious school. Moreover, if these children of affluent parents go on to succeed in college and professional school and ultimately end up working as investment bankers, they will evaluate themselves in comparison to other investment bankers, not in comparison to the population in general or even in relation to friends or relatives with more modest levels of accomplishment and more modest incomes. This makes it very difficult for even the most successful children of affluent parents to view their personal accomplishments as really special.

To illustrate this point, consider that we have worked as therapists with high school students who were devastated because they were not admitted to the particular Ivy League school that was their "first choice," even though they were accepted by one or more other equally prestigious Ivy League colleges. We have also worked with countless affluent men and women at the midpoint of highly successful careers who honestly viewed themselves as failures relative to members of their peer group.

Whether they are youngsters or adults, individuals from affluent families do not compare themselves to people in general when they evaluate their personal accomplishments. Instead, they compare themselves and their accomplishments to those of the other highly educated and highly affluent individuals with whom they associate. In this regard, it is highly desirable for high achieving and affluent individuals to maintain a broad range of social connections that will provide them with the opportunity to compare themselves and their accomplishments to those of less affluent persons as well as those of similarly successful and affluent peers. Participation in community organizations can expose us to individuals of varying degrees of affluence. So can participation in national organizations that have broad membership bases representing diverse communities. Having friends who are not all investment bankers or lawyers is important on many levels. First, these friends will provide you with firsthand evidence that one need not be wealthy in order to be happy. Second, these friends will provide a point of comparison that will allow you to really appreciate just how successful you are relative to the world as a whole. That way, if your year-end bonus of $250,000 is not as large as that of some of your colleagues at the bank, you will still be aware that your yearly income is well up into the 99th percentile of incomes in general.

THE CORRUPTING INFLUENCE OF THE PRESSURE TO SUCCEED

Still another problem with the intense pressure to succeed that is part of the culture of affluence is the corrupting influence of this pressure. Human nature is such that, when only the highest levels of achievement are considered acceptable, there is a tremendous temptation to do whatever it takes to ensure that you do in fact attain these acceptable high levels of achievement. Thus, in the case example presented above, we saw Barbara and Josh knowingly and willingly engaging in behavior that was clearly inappropriate and unethical in order to increase the probability that Heather would be admitted to the preschool program that they considered the "best."

We would certainly expect that in the future, Heather would be the beneficiary of many forms of academic assistance aimed at helping her succeed. Such assistance can represent a broad continuum in terms of ethical appropriateness, ranging from legitimate assistance in the form of intensive professional tutoring when necessary, through more questionable assistance such as obtaining extensive editorial help correcting the spelling and grammar of school papers, all the way through the increasingly common practice of actually hiring professionals to research, organize, and write school papers.

We have heard affluent parents defend some very questionable forms of academic assistance that they have provided for their children. They have argued that school is preparation for life, and life is inherently competitive. They have argued further that in this competition, one must be fully armed and prepared, and that to fail to give their children every possible advantage is at best a sign of weakness, or at worst an indication of a lack of caring. Clearly, such parents have elevated the competition for academic achievement and ultimately for financial success to the level of a life-and-death struggle in which the ends justify the means. In effect, they are saying, "It's a jungle out there, and we need to take whatever steps are required to make certain that we survive." In this argument, survival is defined in terms of academic achievement that is ultimately consistent with earning a high six- or seven-figure income.

THE LOSS OF THE ABILITY TO RELAX AND ENJOY LIFE

Another problem derived from the unrelenting pressure to succeed experienced by individuals from affluent families is the inability to relax and enjoy life. This problem of the culture of affluence also impacts both the children of the affluent and successful high-achieving adults as well. As we saw with Heather, the pressure to achieve may begin very early. Children feel pressure to excel at their academic work as well as their extracurricular activities. They may be "overbooked" in terms of their schedule, and they may spend great amounts of time doing the homework that is required to do well in school.

They may have little free time, little time to decompress, and little time to simply relax and have fun.[1]

Given the academic and career paths that many of these children choose, this maladaptive behavioral pattern of excessive striving may continue throughout the course of a lifetime. Consider the life course of the most successful attorneys. They need to excel in high school to get into a very good college, excel in college to get into one of the best law schools, excel in law school to obtain a position with a prestigious law firm, and excel as an associate in the firm in order to make partner. Because they are so focused on achievement, these individuals tend to tie their self-worth to their accomplishments, and their striving for success often takes on a desperate quality. Fourteen- and 16-hour workdays are the norm rather than the exception. To fail is not simply a matter of simply ending up with a somewhat smaller income, but rather to cease to exist as a person of worth.

By the time such a driven individual has finally made partner in the law firm, the habit of working 14 hours a day may be so ingrained that he or she is no longer even aware that this is abnormal. These folks can become so completely identified with their work that they are unaware that there is another side of life involving leisure and relaxation, which they are missing. In short, the achievement pressures of the culture of affluence may literally destroy the individual's awareness that there are activities that one can pursue "just for fun." Relaxation is essential to maintaining physical and mental health, and to the extent that high-achieving workaholics are unable to unwind and take a deep breath, they render themselves vulnerable to a broad range of ailments, including hypertension, ulcerative colitis, chronic anxiety, and depression.

Such driven individuals are also very likely to experience difficulties in their relationships with their spouses and children, based in large measure on the fact that they have very little time that they can actually spend with the family to develop and nurture close and rewarding relationships. The commitment to work may prevail over commitment to family, and both parents and children may suffer as a result. We will have a great deal more to say about these negative outcomes in later chapters. For now, let us simply note that research has shown clearly that individuals who have a very strong need to achieve and individuals who rely on their accomplishments to bolster their sense of self-worth are at elevated risk for psychosocial adjustment disorders, including depression and anxiety.[2]

Closely associated with the inability to relax and enjoy life is the frequent inability of achievement-driven affluent individuals to derive pleasure from the wealth that they work so hard to achieve. Affluence is most appropriately regarded as a vehicle through which we can satisfy our needs and occasionally pamper our desires for entertainment and pleasure.[3] However, the culture of affluence is such that the financial rewards that high achievers receive as a result of their hard work and success become less a real source of enjoyment than simply a means of keeping score in the never-ending competition. This is why the investment banker whose year-end bonus is only a quarter of a million feels like a failure if his colleagues get more. On the basis of any objective assessment of the needs of these individuals and their families, they are all earning far more than they could ever spend to meet their needs, and probably more than they could ever need to gratify even their most extravagant desires. Yet the man with the smallest bonus feels like a failure. There is clearly a problem when a couple is dissatisfied with their million-dollar home, simply because their colleagues are living in $3 million homes.

In this regard, there is an interesting parallel between the attitudes of the affluent toward their wealth and the tendency of organizational, corporate, and government policy makers to make important policy decisions almost exclusively on the basis of the "bottom line" in terms of economic outcomes. Seligman has argued that what is important in individuals' lives is their sense of well-being, which includes positive emotions, engagement with others, satisfaction derived from one's interests and activities, and a sense that life has meaning.[4] However, Seligman and Diener have argued that most of the important policy decisions that are made in our society are based on economics alone, with the implicit assumption that money increases well-being.[5] These authors suggested that this assumption is not warranted. Wealth is only one predictor of well-being, and perhaps not the best predictor. Accordingly, they suggested that when important policy decisions are made at various levels of society, "well-being needs to be assessed more directly."[6] They argued that individual well-being is related to: (1) the intrinsic satisfaction derived from one's work (as opposed to extrinsic financial rewards); (2) the state of one's physical and mental health; and (3) the rewards derived from close and mutually supportive social relationships, including the quality of one's marriage, one's relationships with children, and one's friendships. Yet these sources of satisfaction are the very aspects of life that are jeopardized by the overemphasis placed on academic and financial success by the culture of affluence.

The Disconnect between Affluent Parents and Their Children

SANDRA'S DOUBLE LIFE

Sandra, an attractive and articulate 16-year-old, was ordered to enter treatment with me (OC) by the court following her arrest outside a suburban Connecticut mall for possession of controlled substances and prostitution. She was arrested by an undercover officer who had been engaged in a police effort to disrupt the drug trafficking that was going on among teenagers at the mall. In the course of attempting to establish a relationship with the teenagers who were the targets of the undercover investigation, the officer talked with Sandra, who was hanging out with the suspected drug dealers at a restaurant in the mall. To his surprise, during this conversation Sandra told the officer that she thought he was "cute," and because she liked the way he looked, she would "make him an offer that he couldn't refuse." She offered to perform oral sex on the officer in his car for $100, or to accompany him to a motel to have genital intercourse if he preferred for $250. Her offer was tape-recorded by the officer, and as she and the officer left the mall, ostensibly to go to his car, she was arrested by the officer and his colleagues. When she was arrested, she was found to be in possession of a small quantity of methamphetamine.

It is always disconcerting and distressing to meet a young woman who has chosen to engage in self-destructive behavior such as premature and promiscuous sex, substance abuse, and especially prostitution. But in this case, I was flabbergasted when I learned that Sandra was the daughter of two extremely successful parents who lived in a $3 million home quite close to my office, and that Sandra was a junior at an exclusive country day school, where she was both an excellent student and a very popular student leader. Sandra had been leading a double life.

When Sandra's parents received the call from the police station to come and pick up their daughter, they were dumbfounded. They had absolutely no idea that Sandra was anything other than a well-behaved, hardworking student. They had no idea that she was sexually active or that she spent time at the mall with the drug-dealing crowd. They did not think it odd that she went out in the evening several nights a week. She told them that she was going to the library or to school sporting events, and they said they had no reason not to believe her. They figured everything must be okay because they knew that she was getting her schoolwork done. They never had anything but the most glowing reports from school.

The idea that Sandra was prostituting herself was devastating to her parents. Over and over, they said that they could not understand it. They gave Sandra all the money she needed. Sandra had a substantial allowance and credit cards to use to buy clothes, school supplies, and personal items. They had bought her a car when she got her driver's license, and she had never gotten a ticket or had an accident. They had considered Sandra far too intelligent to ever get involved in risky behaviors, including promiscuous sexual behavior and going off alone with strangers. They had always believed that Sandra felt good about herself and her accomplishments, and now it seemed that she was engaging in behavior that would indicate a very low self-concept, if not self-hatred.

As I got to know Sandra, I began to understand some of her behavior a bit better. First of all, despite the obvious dangers involved in her behavior, Sandra firmly believed that she was not "out of control." She explained that she hung out with the drug crowd because they added an element of excitement to an otherwise rather humdrum life at home and school. She viewed her becoming sexually active at 16 as completely normative. She said that she did not know any virgins, and she could not imagine why anyone would want to be a virgin.

Furthermore, Sandra made it clear that she was not selling her sexual services to anyone with $100. She only went with men whom she really thought were attractive. She felt that she was an excellent judge of character and that it was highly unlikely that she would ever pick up a man who might harm her or put her in a position where her safety was jeopardized. She always practiced safe sex. She had no intention of becoming pregnant or getting AIDS. She said that she took money from men because the money they gave her made her feel like she was "worth something." She felt like girls who had sex with strangers for nothing were simply "sluts," whereas she viewed herself as a kind of a high-class courtesan in training. She said that many of the men she had been with gave her expensive presents, and that she had saved all the money that she had made.

I asked her why she felt it necessary to save money when her parents were so generous. Sandra replied that she intended to "make it on her own" at some point in her life, and what she had put away up till now would eventually be part of her "seed money." Sandra said that she had come to resent the money that her parents gave her, because that was all they ever gave her. She said that they were both so tied up with their work that they never really had time to spend with her just being together and having a good time. They never went on vacation together, and they seemed annoyed if she wanted to talk to them about problems she might be having or issues with which she might be struggling. Sandra said that it seemed the only time they were really concerned with how she was doing was when report cards were sent home from school. Eventually, Sandra said, she had learned to give them what they wanted. She brought home good grades from school, and she did not bother them with her problems or concerns. Sandra said she got better personal advice from the drug dealers at the mall than she did from her parents.

Sandra also said that she was not seriously into taking drugs, in spite of her fascination with the drug culture. She said that was why she hung out with the drug dealers rather than just drug users. She said that she only did "a bit of speed now and then," and that she sometimes found the speed helpful in doing her schoolwork.

Sandra's primary concern with respect to her being arrested was that it might jeopardize her chances of getting into a really fine college. She knew that I would have some input regarding the final disposition of her case, and she was very clear that she was anxious to have me recommend that her arrest record be expunged. I asked Sandra whether she felt as if she had disappointed her parents. She said that in retrospect, she could see that in fact she had disappointed them, but she had not even considered this aspect of her behavior at the time. She said that she had always done well in school, and that was what they really cared about.

I asked Sandra whether she thought that her parents loved her and wanted to protect her. She found this question difficult to answer, and she became somewhat teary-eyed as she thought it over. She said again that in retrospect, she was beginning to realize that they were concerned for her safety, although she had not considered this concern before she saw how upset they had become following her arrest.

On the most obvious level, Sandra's "double life" consisted on the one hand of hard work, high levels of achievement, and exemplary behavior at school and at home, and on the other hand of recklessness, self-abasement, and even criminal behavior several nights a week in and around the mall. On a more subtle level, Sandra's double life was a manifestation of the emotional estrangement that often occurs between affluent parents and their children. Sandra's parents made it very clear to her that they expected her to do well in school, but they certainly had not made it clear to her that they loved her unconditionally. Sandra did what was expected of her in school and earned her parents' approval for her efforts. However, the most important connection between parents and child was missing. In order to feel loved, Sandra found it necessary to become sexually intimate with men.

Although Sandra was unaware of this motivation for her sexual risk-taking behavior, it seems quite clear that she was seeking to be loved for herself, for who she was, rather than for her accomplishments. The fact that she took money from men in exchange for sex may be viewed as a result of the fact that Sandra had been taught by her parents that love is manifested in tangible rewards and gifts. Whereas her parents gave her money, credit cards, and a new car for being a good girl and for her achievements at school, Sandra's sexual partners gave her money and gifts for herself, for her body, for being allowed to be close to her.

That an intelligent young woman such as Sandra could develop such an unhealthy set of conscious values and unconscious needs is a testament to the insidious tendency of affluent parents to be physically and emotionally unavailable to their children, even as they place heavy demands on the children for high levels of achievement. Further, Sandra's story illustrates the resulting tendency of the children of such parents to seek out love and emotional closeness where they can find these things. Unfortunately, where these children do find love and emotional closeness is often the wrong place, because they do not have the benefit of parental experience and guidance to lead them to the right places. In the absence of parental guidance and direction, children tend to absorb the norms of the popular culture and their peers as their measure of what is and is not appropriate. This is most likely why Sandra considered it perfectly normative to be sexually active at 16. She was setting her moral compass on the basis of what she saw on TV, in the movies, and at the mall, rather than on the basis of the experience and the loving concern of her mother and father.

In the remainder of this chapter, we consider specific elements of the emotional disconnection between parents and children that characterizes the culture of affluence. Specifically, affluent parents tend to: (1) be physically absent from their children's worlds far more than less affluent parents; (2) be emotionally unavailable to their children, even if they are physically present; (3) fail to provide their children with appropriate opportunities to develop and implement moral, ethical, and spiritual values; and (4) model values and behaviors that stress conditional rather than unconditional love, acceptance, and validation. In this chapter also, we consider negative elements of the culture that tend to fill the vacuum left by these parental failures.

PHYSICAL ABSENCE OF AFFLUENT PARENTS

Among affluent couples who have been socialized to place great value on achievement, both spouses typically have careers. Of course, in the majority of all married couples in America, both husband and wife are employed.[1] However, the proportion of couples in which both spouses work increases with level of family income, as does the degree to which both spouses regard their work as a career or profession, rather than "just a job." Women who have worked hard all their lives to get into the best colleges and professional schools seldom put aside their professional interests and commitments simply because they get married. They may well have put off marriage until they completed their education and became established professionally, and for this reason, they may feel the pressure of the "biological clock" telling them that they had better start their families soon after they marry, but they are not at all likely to discontinue their professional roles when the children begin to arrive.

So imagine, if you will, a typical high-achieving couple—let us say a couple in which the husband is a 32-year-old investment banker who works on Wall Street and the wife is a 29-year-old obstetrician who recently completed her residency and accepted a job with a group practice in an affluent suburb of New York. They elect to start a family at this point in time because they want to have children while they are young enough to enjoy them, and because they do not want to wait until the likelihood of fertility issues or the possibility of complications or birth defects begins to increase.

Now let us consider their respective work schedules. Our prospective father gets up each day at 5:30 to take the commuter train to the city. He typically works until 6:00 or 6:30 each day, and then he takes the train home, arriving around 8:00. Once each month, he has a meeting in London that keeps him away from home for the better part of a week, and in a typical month, he might also make one or two additional overnight business trips to meet with clients. Often these trips involve some fun activities as well as work. Golf is frequently on the schedule. However, the trips still keep him away from home. Meanwhile, our prospective mother will be working at least a 40-hour week with very irregular work hours, including both regular office hours and two days each week when she is on call for possible deliveries. Ironically, compared to the hours that she had been working during her residency, this work schedule does not seem to her to be all that daunting.

Assuming that this couple will be able to spend enough time together for our prospective mother to become pregnant, we now add a baby to their schedule. Mom most likely takes a week or two off from work, but probably no more. Of course it goes without saying that they will have help with child care, most likely a full-time nurse at first, followed by a full-time, live-in nanny or mother's helper.[2] Given that both dad and mom are away from home early each morning, the live-in option is essential. Mom will likely go out of her way to breast-feed, because she knows that this is best for the baby's health. She will manage this with the help of a breast pump and her nanny bringing the baby to the office to be fed during mom's breaks. Although mom will spend a good deal more time with the baby than dad, most of the baby's waking hours will be spent with the nanny.

Once the baby has grown up enough to begin preschool programs, the nanny will be responsible for feeding the child breakfast and getting him or her to and from school each day. Later on, when the child begins to participate in various activities outside of school, the nanny will similarly be responsible for coordinating transportation. Dad will not be able to spend very much time at all with the baby during the week, but he will do his best to be present on the weekends when he is at home. Because of the demands of their respective professions, it will be difficult for either mom or dad to spend much time just hanging out with their child. Although dad and mom will likely struggle mightily to attend soccer games and ballet recitals, the chances are that their heavy work obligations will make these parental observations far less frequent than they would like. The child will likely grow up most often hearing his or her nanny cheering or applauding.

Numerous studies have suggested that children from affluent families "tend to spend much more time with hired help than they do with their parents."[3] Several child and adolescent development experts have suggested that the reliance on paid surrogates can result in the failure of children of affluent parents to develop authentic relationships with appropriate role models.[4] We are not saying that it is impossible to get a nanny who genuinely cares for one's child and has a good relationship with him or her. However, we *are* saying that a nanny cannot take the place of parents who cannot be present in the lives of their children. No matter how good the time is that overworked professionals manage to spend with their children, this time may simply not be sufficient. It is not possible to control the times that our children need us to be there for them. If your child is troubled by something that happened during the day, you cannot be of much help if you do not get home until after he or she is asleep. If your level of commitment to your profession is such that there is no alternative to such absences, so be it. But you should be aware that you must make special efforts to provide your child with support, guidance, and the sense that he or she is loved unconditionally. Even with such efforts, your absence may impact negatively on your relationship with your child, and on his or her development.

In regard to the struggle to be present in the life of one's child, research has shown that affluent parents are more likely to be "over-employed" than less affluent parents.[5] Over-employment simply means working more hours each week than one would like to work. Over-employment is much more typical of highly educated individuals in professional and managerial positions than it is of individuals engaged in nonprofessional occupations. This may be due to the dedication of professionals to their careers, and to the pressures faced by managers to make important decisions in a timely manner.

It is worth noting, however, that over-employment is typically measured by self-report. Therefore, an individual who claims to be working more hours than he or she might prefer will probably not be taking into consideration the unconscious motivations of the workaholic. The intense pressure to succeed experienced by the affluent as they mature, along with the work ethic developed over the course of a lifetime, may result in a situation in which overworking is both comforting and security-inducing. When asked if they are working more than they would like, workaholics are likely to consider their situation objectively and respond affirmatively. But at the same time, however, workaholic parents may be secretly quite satisfied with their overworked status. Therefore, they are not about to take serious steps to cut back on work, even if this is the only way they can carve out more time to spend with their children. In fact, they often take pride in their overworked status and/ or the fact that their efforts are indispensable to their clients or to society in general. For the affluent workaholic professional, being overworked can be an unconscious way of "having your cake and eating it too." They are saying, in effect, "Because my work is so important, I am morally obligated to give it priority in my life, and my children will come to understand this as they mature." They may even express the feeling that their long work hours set a good example for their children. For now, however, the nanny will simply have to suffice at bedtime.

Furthermore, as the children of these driven affluent parents mature, the children are likely to find that they lose even their nannies. The teenage children of affluent parents are particularly likely to find themselves alone and without supervision of any kind during the hours between the time that school lets out and the time one or both parents comes home at night. A recent Frontline report on PBS Online focused on the teenagers in a prosperous town in Georgia.[6] This report concluded that many of the affluent adolescents in this town were left completely unsupervised during the hours from 3:00 PM to 7:00 PM each day. Other reports suggest that this phenomenon is quite characteristic of affluent neighborhoods across the nation.[7] This lack of supervision is obviously not a matter of financial necessity.

Some authors have argued that affluent parents are more comfortable than less affluent parents leaving their adolescent children unsupervised after school, because they know that the neighborhoods in which they live are relatively safe.[8] However, other investigators have argued that many affluent parents leave their children home alone after school because they believe that after a certain age, their children should be responsible enough to look after themselves.[9] We have observed that affluent parents, parents who feel that they themselves have been highly responsible over the course of their lifetimes, tend to expect similar levels of responsibility on the part of their children. Therefore, they may well believe that allowing their children to be at home alone after school will help the children to develop self-sufficiency.

Unfortunately, as we will see in greater detail in later chapters of this volume, lack of supervision can also lead to difficulties for the children of the affluent. Studies have shown that teenagers in affluent suburbs are actually more likely than inner-city teenagers to engage in the use of alcohol and illicit substances, and that affluent young people are more likely than less affluent children to manifest internalizing symptoms such as anxiety and depression.[10] These disturbances have been linked to the tendency of affluent young people to be disconnected from adults, both physically and emotionally.[11]

Therefore, if you are an affluent, hardworking parent, we urge you to ask yourself whether you are really spending enough time with your children. If the answer is no, or if you are not sure what the answer is, we urge you to ask your children. You will very likely find that they feel they do not get enough of your time. You may need to reassess your priorities. You may need to rethink your schedule. You may need to rethink the importance of the year-end bonus.

EMOTIONAL UNAVAILABILITY OF AFFLUENT PARENTS

In addition to the difficulties that affluent parents may experience in simply finding enough time to be physically present in the lives of their children, there is evidence that affluent parents tend to manifest an impaired ability to be emotionally available, even when they are physically present.[12] There are many reasons why this is the case. It goes without saying that if mom and dad come home from work physically exhausted and mentally drained, their ability to attend to their children's accounts of the events of the day will likely suffer. Mom and dad may have spent the entire day up to their ears in professional alligators. Dad the investment banker may have been making decisions that could impact the financial security of many individuals; and mom the obstetrician may have been making decisions that could literally involve life vs. death. Coupling the gravity of their professional activities with long and often irregular work hours, it is hardly surprising that these parents might be too wiped out at the end of the day to really focus on their children.

Furthermore, it may be difficult for these high-powered professional parents to leave their work at the office. They may be preoccupied with the issues with which they have been wrestling. They may be second-guessing the decisions of the day or preparing for tomorrow's decisions, even as they attempt to listen to their children. If you are a professional or a top-level manager within an important industry, you may very well be justified in considering your work to be both unique and important to society. You may even be justified in thinking that you are performing an occupational role that you are uniquely qualified to perform. However, if you also a parent, you must recognize that this role is the one role that *you alone* are qualified to perform. It may be very difficult to put aside your weighty, challenging professional concerns to focus your attention exclusively on the more mundane issues that impact the daily lives of your children. But you must discipline yourself to do just that. If you can successfully direct your full attention to the concerns of your children for a period of time each day, you will find yourself rewarded in a way that does not show up in annual income or achievement awards, but rather in a profound personal experience of comfort and satisfaction.

Affluent professionals may also be subject to a more subtle obstacle to developing emotionally close relationships with their children. Psychologists Ed Diener and Martin Seligman have commented that within our society, policy decisions made at the organizational, corporate, and governmental levels tend to be based primarily on the economic outcomes of these decisions.[13] Such decisions tend to ignore or give relatively little weight to non-economic indicators of subjective well-being, including people's subjective evaluations of their living situations and their satisfaction with their lives. These authors pointed out that there is a disconnect between the nation's prosperity and the perceived well-being of its citizens. Although economic output and inflation-adjusted personal income have risen steadily in America over the past several decades, there has been no concomitant increase in our happiness, satisfaction, or peace of mind.

Based on our experience working with affluent clients, we would argue that the same relationship between economic and noneconomic indicators of success manifests itself on the individual level. Our clients are extremely focused on economic indicators and success, and on concrete indications of achievement such as academic honors, publications, and public service achievement awards. They tend to exhibit a concomitant lack of awareness of the more subjective elements of life that bring happiness and satisfaction. On the simplest perceptual level, we can describe this as failing to "stop and smell the roses." On a deeper emotional level, we note that many of our dissatisfied affluent adult clients fail to recognize the importance of working hard to develop deep emotional relationships with others, including their spouses and their children.

These individuals work very hard on their professional pursuits, but they sometimes fail to even recognize that emotional relationships constitute an area that one can actually work on and nurture. Because the indications of success in developing deep emotional relationships with others are not objective and socially agreed upon, these affluent adults seem to assume that relationships do not constitute an area on which they need to work hard. They understand quite well the connection between hard work and the size of their year-end bonus, or the honor of becoming a full professor. However, they do not have the slightest clue that there is a connection between how hard you work to become emotionally close to your child and the satisfaction that you and your child derive from this relationship.

We note as well that many of the troubled children of these dissatisfied affluent parents readily express the view that mom and dad do not love them, or that mom and dad do not care how they really feel, or simply that mom and dad only care about how well they are doing in school. This is certainly how Sandra felt, as described in the case study at the beginning of this chapter. She clearly felt that all her mom and dad really cared about was how well she did in school, so she made sure that she did do well in school. But she did not feel that they loved her for herself. They had never developed the type of close emotional relationship with her that would be needed to communicate this love. Sandy had closer emotional relationships with her friends at the mall, and greater personal validation in the sexual relationships that she sought out.

The moral here is that parental responsibility consists of more than making sure that your children are healthy, well fed, attending school, and doing well in their studies and their extracurricular activities. You need to spend time with your children, *and* you need to make the effort to ensure that the time you spend with them is quality time. You need to work on finding out who they are and how they feel. This work is the essence of a deep emotional relationship. This work is what lets your children know that you love them.

One of the traditions that help to promote both contact and communication between parents and children is having family meals together.

Unfortunately, this appears to be a tradition in danger of extinction. In this case of our hypothetical investment banker father and obstetrician mother, both parents are out of the home before the children have breakfast, dad is never home in time for dinner with the kids, and mom may or may not be home on a given night. If mom is home, there is little chance that she has actually cooked food for the children. She has neither the time nor the energy to cook, at least not during the week. This is really too bad, because family meals not only provide an opportunity for parents and children to communicate with each other, but the act of preparing and serving food for children is an unmistakably nurturing behavior that communicates the parent's love.

In this regard, I (JT) recall a weekend when my stepson, who was 16 years old at the time, invited two of his friends from school to sleep over at the house on a Saturday night. When they all came down on Sunday morning, I was making omelets for breakfast. I asked the two boys if they would like breakfast. They both looked at me with shock, and then one of them asked, "Do you really *cook*?" When I said yes of course, one of them said that his parents never cooked. He said that his family literally either went out to dinner or had takeout food *every* night. Unfortunately, in many of the affluent professional families in our town, I suspect that this is the case. Dinner comes from the housekeeper or is delivered from the Chinese restaurant. Furthermore, dinner is frequently eaten individually by each family member, depending on his or her individual schedule. There is no opportunity for communication, no shared period of relaxation. Often, there is no opportunity to even sit down for a moment between activities. We have become skilled at eating on the run.

LACK OF OPPORTUNITIES FOR MORAL, ETHICAL, AND SPIRITUAL GUIDANCE OUTSIDE THE FAMILY

The hectic pace of life and the materialistic values that characterize the culture of affluence also tend to keep the children of the affluent from being exposed to sources of moral, ethical, and spiritual guidance that exist outside the family. Children are overbooked with schoolwork and extracurricular activities such as the soccer team, music lessons, dance lessons, personal training, and riding lessons. Weekends are precious, and going to church or synagogue tends to be viewed as just another time-consuming obligation. Parental focus on achievement and success, along with the materialism associated with the culture of affluence, tend to militate against serious involvement in religious or spiritual practice.

The emphasis of the secular progressive educational establishment further alienates young people from religion and discourages participation in religious activities. Prayer has been eliminated from school, and students who are involved in religious education and observances are likely to experience social stereotyping as "Jesus freaks" or "beanie boys." Organizations like the Boy Scouts and Girl Scouts that espouse traditional values are also under attack by the intellectual establishment, to which affluent intellectual parents tend to turn for information and guidance with respect to acceptable behavior. At the same time that overbooking and scheduling conflicts make participation in large organizations much more difficult for the children of the affluent than participation in individually scheduled activities, the social milieu of political correctness and cultural relativism suggests that being a member of a church or synagogue is old-fashioned and not cool, and that being a Boy Scout or a Girl Scout is for "rednecks" and "nerds."

As a high school student in the 1960s, I (JT) can remember being selected to attend Boys State, a weeklong conference for high school students that was sponsored by the American Legion. The purpose of this conference was to give students a firsthand experience with the American political system, but a healthy dose of religious and patriotic values was included in the curriculum. At that time, I viewed being chosen from my high school class to attend this conference as an honor and an opportunity to learn important lessons. Today, youngsters raised within the culture of affluence tend to have a much more cynical view of experiences of this nature. Religious observance and religious training in Judeo-Christian values stressing self-sacrifice and community service are given little emphasis in the popular culture and the media.

Among the affluent, self-interest and narcissism tend to follow from materialism. Affluent youth are told by the culture that it is acceptable and even desirable for them to expect to be pampered, to wear only the finest and most trendy clothes, to drive the fanciest cars, and to own the latest electronic gadgets. The culture conveys the message that success gives you the wherewithal to have things done for you, rather than to do things for yourself.

Given this attitude toward success and its rewards, affluent adolescents also tend to accept the premise that one does what is necessary to succeed, even if that means cutting a few corners with respect to moral and ethical behavior. In this regard, the reader may recall from Chapter 2 how willing Barbara was to engage in unethical behavior in order to further the academic career of her daughter Heather. One can imagine how the values modeled by her mother may ultimately impact the moral and ethical development of that young lady. Speaking of modeling, we now turn to the manner in which the values and behaviors of affluent parents tend to affect the values and behaviors of their children.

ATTITUDES AND BEHAVIORS MODELED BY AFFLUENT PARENTS

We have seen that affluent parents tend to spend too little time with their children. We have also seen that affluent parents tend to experience great difficulty developing the type of close emotional relationships with their children that convey love and a sense of unconditional positive regard. Nevertheless, these parents do influence their children's development. Every day, whether the parents are at home or away at a professional conference or on a business trip, they model attitudes and behaviors that their children readily learn and adopt as their own. This modeling works on many levels.

On the broadest level, almost everything that mom and dad say and do conveys the value that they place on education and on occupational success. The $3 million home in the fancy suburb makes it clear to the children where it is appropriate to live. The fact that mom and dad are too busy or simply not inclined to go to church on Sunday tells the children that religion is not a priority. The fact that mom and dad do not cook themselves eliminates the possibility that they can teach their children to cook. The fact that mom and dad have a housekeeper to make the beds and clean the house is likely to result in children who grow up not knowing how to perform these simple tasks, and not even thinking that one really ought to know how to do these things. The same goes for other household chores such as mowing grass, trimming hedges, shoveling snow, and painting doors.

I (JT) recall an incident that a patient related to me about trying to get his teenage son to help him with shoveling snow. This patient was a successful chiropractor with a home office, and one snowy winter morning he got up early to go outside to shovel the walkway from his driveway to his office entrance, so that his first patients of the day would be able to get in easily. The family had a lawn care company that did the plowing and snow shoveling routinely, but you could never tell how early in the morning they would come after a snowfall, so he figured he had better do that part of the job himself. When he got up, my patient's wife told him to knock on their son's door and get him to help. When he did this, the 16-year-old first yelled at his dad for waking him up. Then he told his father, "I have a test today and I need my sleep. Besides, I don't do manual labor. That's why we have Mexicans." My patient was so upset by his son's comment that he made it the major focus of the session. He was disgusted by his son's laziness, his sense of entitlement, and his classist and racist attitudes. What is more, my patient could not understand where these attitudes came from.

I asked my patient whether this incident had come as a complete surprise to him. He said yes. He was completely taken aback. I asked him whether his son had ever given his father any indications that he was unwilling to help out with chores. My patient said no. His son was always well behaved at home and at school, and he was a good student who always got his schoolwork done on time. But then my patient observed that he had never really asked his son to help out around the house, because quite honestly, they had "people" to take care of pretty much everything that needed to be done. Clearly, by virtue of his actual lifestyle rather than his own beliefs and values, my patient had inadvertently conveyed the message to his son that manual labor was somehow beneath him, that it was something that was done by "other people" whom we hire for that purpose. No doubt this message was reinforced by the attitudes of peers at school and by messages communicated in the media.

I pointed out to my patient that the kids of the successful people who lived in this area quite often developed such attitudes, even though their parents were not at all averse to hard work of any kind, including manual labor when necessary. I noted that when a professional can earn several hundred dollars an hour working at his profession, the decision to hire someone else to do chores at a much lower hourly rate is simply a logical economic decision. I knew that my patient did not have any problem with shoveling snow when shoveling was necessary. He was not lazy. He did not mind a bit of physical labor, and he did not consider the work beneath him. He simply hired someone at a cheaper rate to do as much of this work as he could, to free up his valuable time for other work. However, my patient's son saw only what was actually happening, without understanding the economic rationale behind the decision to hire people to perform various types of labor around the house. He viewed the situation and concluded logically that, "We study and do professional work, and Mexicans shovel snow."

Then I pointed out to my patient that the most fundamental problem here seemed to me to be his failure to know his son well enough to have anticipated his response to the request to help with the shoveling. I asked him how much time he spent actually talking to his son about topics that would give him an indication of how the boy felt about life, the things that he considered important, and his aspirations for the future. It became clear that my patient really had only a very superficial relationship with the boy. Time after time, he mentioned that his son was doing well in school. That was all that he seemed to know about the boy. My patient said that his practice kept him occupied about 70 hours each week, and even though his office was in his house he rarely saw his son except in passing. They did not typically have dinner together as a family, and they had no regularly scheduled forum for sharing the events of their respective lives.

My patient did not know what his son had in mind regarding possible careers. He did not have a very clear idea of who his son's friends were, or what sort of relationships his son might have with members of the opposite sex. He was not sure of the type of music that his son liked or the types of movies he went to. He did not know whether his son had any hobbies that occupied his time, or whether his son was active in any extracurricular activities.

So my patient provides another example of an affluent professional parent who has failed to establish and nurture a close emotional relationship with his child. Yet my patient's lifestyle and behavior still had a profound impact on his son's values and behaviors. When people say that "the apple doesn't fall very far from the tree," they are not talking so much about genetics as they are about what we teach our children. If you are a workaholic, your child may very well become a workaholic as well. If you value material success over spiritual growth and moral development, the chances are very good that your child will as well. If your behavior indicates that you place great value on expensive clothes and a fancy car, you can hardly expect your son or daughter to think differently. If you have a housekeeper to clean the house and make dinner, you can hardly expect your children to learn how to clean and cook. They will grow up thinking that these things are done for them by people we hire. And God forbid your children should somehow turn out less successful than you and be unable to afford the housekeeper. What will they do then? Will they learn to fend for themselves, or will they expect you to pay for their housekeeper? Will they even have the courage to move out of your house? These are questions that we will consider in detail in chapters that follow.

The Negative Aspects of Having Wealth

In the last two chapters, we have considered two of the most important negative aspects of the culture of affluence: the intense pressure to achieve experienced by the wealthy and their children, and the difficulties experienced by highly pressured, achievement-oriented parents in developing emotionally close and nurturing relationships with their children. In this chapter we consider several aspects of affluence that pertain less to the struggle to achieve wealth than to the state of having wealth. These include: (1) becoming the victim of negative stereotypes toward the wealthy that are widely held in American society; (2) experiencing difficulties when socializing with less affluent individuals; (3) succumbing to the false belief that one is, or should be, in complete control of one's life; (4) falling prey to the addictive potential of affluence; and (5) becoming isolated as a result of one's affluent lifestyle.

NEGATIVE STEREOTYPES REGARDING THE WEALTHY

The wealthy have long been viewed by society in highly negative terms. On the one hand, the wealthy are seen as self-interested, avaricious, ruthless, and uncharitable. On the other hand, they are frequently assumed to be pampered, self-indulgent, incompetent with regard to the practical skills of daily living, and completely unable to perform even the simplest tasks without paid helpers who are capable of doing "real work." These stereotypes are evident in literature and popular culture. Stereotypical portrayals of the selfishness of the wealthy are found in classic fairy tales and novels, as well as modern television shows and movies.

NEGATIVE STEREOTYPES OF THE AFFLUENT IN LITERATURE AND THE POPULAR CULTURE

In the fairy tale *Cinderella*, the poor heroine is kind and good-natured, while her rich stepmother and half-sisters are depicted as selfish, spoiled, and unnecessarily cruel. They are also portrayed as snobbish, entitled, ugly, and stupid. In her novel *Silas Marner,* George Eliot depicts the protagonist as wealthy, but also as a pathetic and lonely misanthrope who spends his evenings alone counting his hoard of gold coins. In the Charles Dickens story *A Christmas Carol,* Ebenezer Scrooge is a wealthy businessman who is depicted as totally lacking in humanity and incapable of experiencing any real joy. He refuses to make a charitable donation at Christmas, and only with the greatest reluctance does he give his employee Bob Cratchit a day off for the holiday. In both *Silas Marner* and *A Christmas Carol,* the crucial aspect of the plot is a transformation of the protagonist from the inhumanity that is associated with wealth to an appreciation of the joys derived from close human relationships.

In popular culture, consider the *Rocky and Bullwinkle* cartoon show. In each episode of the Dudley Do-Right segment of this show, the rich evil villain Snidely Whiplash attempts to foreclose on pretty Nell Fenwick's mortgage. When she cannot pay, he seeks to exploit her impoverished state by forcing his romantic attentions upon her. When she modestly and courageously resists his advances, he tries to murder her by tying her to a train track to be run over. Clearly, the children who watched this cartoon show were being socialized in negative stereotypes regarding the wealthy. More recently, in a cartoon show clearly intended for both children and adults, we have the character of Charles Montgomery Burns from *The Simpsons.* Burns is a wealthy industrialist who seeks to control the world and seems to take great delight in the exploitation of workers and the pollution of the environment.

The other stereotype of the rich is that of helplessness born of always having everything done for you. In J. M. Barrie's play, *The Admirable Crichton,* the obsequious butler and the wealthy family he serves in England are marooned on an island. In this new environment, the rich members of the family of Lord Loam are shown to be completely inept and unprepared to fend for themselves, but the butler Crichton has practical skills that enable the group to survive. Inevitably, the tables turn and the class hierarchy is reversed. The competent butler becomes the leader of the group, because he is the only one capable of feeding the family. Just before their rescue, Crichton is about to marry the wealthy daughter of Lord Loam, who has conveniently forgotten her engagement to a wealthy lord back in England. However, the social upheaval ends when they are rescued and returned to England. In the final act of the play, Crichton has resumed his servant status, and the Loam family has resumed its presumptuous attitude of superiority.

A similar theme is presented in the movie *Swept Away*. In this movie Amber is the rich, spoiled, arrogant wife of a pharmaceutical manufacturer who books a sailboat for a Mediterranean cruise. Amber has a massive sense of entitlement and demands all sorts of special treatment from Giuseppe, the first mate of the sailboat. He tries to please her, but he is embarrassed and clumsy in his efforts to satisfy her demands. But then a storm comes up and the two of them are marooned alone on an island. Before the storm, she was the queen, and she treated him like dirt. He was just a poor servant. But when they wake up alone on an island, he is the key to her survival. Suddenly he becomes the alpha male, and he becomes assertive. At first she resists his efforts to take over, but ultimately she develops an uncontrollable sexual attraction toward him.

How the Affluent Are Viewed in Our Popular Culture

Pernicious negative stereotypes of the affluent include: (1) the idea that affluent individuals are driven by self-interest; (2) the belief that the wealthy are avaricious, ruthless, and untrustworthy; (3) the expectation that affluent individuals are entitled and overly demanding; (4) the idea that wealthy people are helpless to the point that they need to hire people to perform the normal chores associated with daily living. In the sections that follow, we consider each of these stereotypes and how each stereotype can make life difficult:

The Affluent Are Driven by Self-interest. People tend to assume that affluent people got that way by consistently looking out for their own self-interest. They reason that people become wealthy and remain wealthy because they focus their energy on acquiring and preserving personal wealth, power, and influence. For this reason, if it is clear that you have wealth, you may well find that people suspect your motives. Consider Brian, a wealthy client of mine (JT) who offered to make a substantial contribution to his town's Little League program:

> Brian found out from his son that the field used by the town Little League had a serious problem with drainage and really needed to be regraded to make it fit to play on. Brian was not a baseball fan, but he knew that the Little League was important to his son and his son's friends, so he generously offered to foot the bill for the repairs, including repainting the bleachers and fences, repairing the backstop, and adding to the inadequate lighting. He called the league council, asked one of the council members to get an estimate for the repairs, and told the council member that he would pay the bill.
>
> Much to Brian's surprise, his offer was initially rejected by the league council. When he called the same council member to find out why his help was not wanted, he was told that

several members of the council were afraid that he would expect special treatment for his son, who was now playing in the Little League, as well as for his two younger sons when they were old enough to play.

By making some discreet inquires, Brian found that the politics actually went a bit deeper. One of the council members had a son who was the same age as Brian's son, and the two were engaged in a personal competition as to which one was the best pitcher in the league. The rival's father was one of those highly competitive dads who feared any threat to his son's success. He did not know exactly how Brian's offer might benefit Brian's son and hurt his own son, but the man did not want to take any chances. This member convinced the other council members that it might be unwise to accept a donation for the field from any single benefactor. At one point in a meeting, he said that Brian would "probably want the field to be named after him or his company."

Brian's wealth became a factor in the politics not only because he could not have made the offer if he did not have the financial wherewithal to follow through, but also because the members of the council had a clear preconception that wealthy people never did anything that was not designed to benefit themselves in the long run. This perception was probably exacerbated by the fact that Brian's business was extremely demanding of his time, so he had never been able to volunteer as a coach or an official, and had never really gotten to know the people who ran the league. When he did go to a league council meeting to discuss his offer, he found that several of the council members expressed surprise that he actually seemed to be a "nice guy." They had assumed that he was standoffish and snobby, and that he had no interest in interacting with them, except insofar as it was necessary to get what he wanted for his son.

Brian was able to win over the council. He pointed out that his son had been selected to be on a team and had succeeded as a pitcher before Brian ever made the offer, and he assured the members that he would not expect any favors or special treatment for either this son or his younger sons. He even became friendly with the competitive dad who had raised the objections in the first place. However, it is clear that Brian had to go out of his way to overcome the stereotyped views of the wealthy that the council members held initially.

Brian handled this situation very well. However, it is easy to imagine another individual in the same situation running into substantial difficulties that might even have impacted negatively on his son. When informed that the council did not think it was a good idea to accept his donation, Brian could have become angry, further alienating the members and confirming their negative stereotypes regarding the wealthy. He could have simply accepted the idea that they did not want his money. This would have been bad for the Little League players, including his own son.

The lesson here is simple. If you have money, it is important to be aware that many people will assume that you are driven primarily by self-interest. If you do not keep this in mind, you may experience negative reactions to your well-intended actions, and you might misinterpret these responses as signifying that there is something wrong with you. Paradoxically, the success that you thought would elicit the respect of others may in fact engender their animosity. You must be careful not to take such responses to heart and begin to think of yourself in negative terms.

The Affluent Are Avaricious, Ruthless, and Untrustworthy. This stereotype can affect both your personal relationships and your business dealings. When I (JT) was a student in high school and college, I worked for my grandfather, who was a housepainter. I also worked for a general contractor and for a salvage-diving company. In the course of this work, I often heard tradesmen make negative references to their wealthy clients. My grandfather often said that he never had a problem getting paid by middle-class customers, but he often had problems with the really wealthy ones. He said rich customers were very demanding. They often assumed that tasks would be performed that had never been discussed and had not been included in the contract. Then they refused to pay for the work until these extra tasks were completed. He also said that they frequently changed their minds about what they wanted during the middle of a job, and they expected him to incorporate these changes at no additional cost to them, despite the fact that he had to do double work, and despite the fact that he frequently had to purchase additional materials. Finally, God forbid there was some aspect of his work that a wealthy client perceived as suboptimal. Even if a job came out looking less than perfect due to some preexisting condition in the house, my grandfather complained that the wealthy customers never hesitated to make him come back to do work over and over, until they were satisfied. He also complained that even when his affluent clients were perfectly satisfied with the work he had done, they frequently still failed to pay their bills promptly. My grandfather also said that for all these reasons, he frequently built into the estimates that he gave the wealthy clients a profit margin that was sufficient to cover the anticipated difficulties. He regarded this practice as a form of insurance.

I heard the same type of remarks from my boss, Fred, when I worked as a salvage diver. He told me that if I recovered a mooring for a wealthy boat owner when the boat broke off following a storm, I had to be sure to get paid *in cash* and *before* the job. This was because we used to charge the owner $500 to find and reattach a mooring, and often the job took only a few minutes. My boss said that the fee was worth it for the owner, because it would cost much more to buy a new mooring and have it set. However, sometimes the owner would see that it took us virtually no time to do the work, and he would object to the high fee.

In retrospect, it seems clear to me that Fred was also charging a very high fee at least in part because he assumed that the boat owners were wealthy and they could afford it. I called it, "progressive taxation as per Fred." It was also totally clear to me at the time that Fred's policy of requiring payment in advance was based on his belief that rich people have no compunctions whatsoever about refusing to pay. He told me that they didn't get rich by being nice guys, and they have lawyers to fight you so you can't get paid if they decide to tell you to "Go to Hell." Therefore, Fred would only do work for someone he perceived as wealthy if he was paid in advance. Furthermore, Fred would only take cash, because he felt that rich people would not hesitate to stop payment on a check.

These experiences suggest that if you are wealthy, you need to be particularly careful in selecting the people who work for you. Paradoxically, it may be even more important for a wealthy person than for a person of more modest means to get several estimates for work and to have the prospective supplier listen carefully to what you want and explain clearly what he thinks needs to be done to accomplish your goals. Even if a prospective tradesperson does not suspect your motives and does not feel compelled to protect himself against your presumably avaricious nature, your perfectionism, and your willingness to behave ruthlessly when it comes to payment, you may still find that the tradesperson makes unwarranted assumptions about the prospective job. He or she may automatically assume that because you are wealthy, you "want the very best," regardless of the price. This may simply not be the case. You may want only what you need to get the job done, without spending a lot more money than is necessary simply to buy "the best." You may not even find the most expensive alternative to be the most attractive one. We will have a good deal more to say about how to avoid the negative impact of these stereotypes in Chapter 7.

The Affluent Are Entitled and Unreasonably Demanding. The perception that the affluent are self-centered and ruthless is frequently accompanied by the negative stereotype that the affluent are pampered, entitled, and demanding. One affluent young woman with whom I (OC) worked told me the following story of a blind date that she had with a friend of her college roommate:

> At first I thought my date was cute and smart and it might be a fun evening. But then I let it slip that my dad was the CEO of the Megatel [name made up] Company, and suddenly my date seemed to get an attitude. He started asking me a lot of questions like, "Are you really rich?" and "Do you live in Shaker Heights?" and "Where did you go to prep school?" He asked how big my house was, whether I had a horse, whether we had a summer house in the Hamptons, and where we went on vacations. He asked if we had servants and if we flew on private jets. Then he had the nerve to ask me if I was one of those "overindulged stuck-up rich girls" who would expect to have a maid and to never work. He asked me if I would be expecting to marry an investment banker and if I expected to get a 10-carat engagement ring.
>
> Needless to say, this was the one and only date I had with this guy. In fact, the one date didn't last very long. I excused myself right after dinner. He was such an asshole. I mean, even if you're thinking those things, you should have enough sense not to ask your date all those offensive questions.
>
> But then I thought to myself, what about all the other guys I've dated who did not ask these questions? Did they have some of the same apprehensions about dating a rich girl,

and just have enough sense not to be offensive by asking her so directly. I wondered whether I had dated men who were afraid that I would be one of those spoiled and entitled rich girls who would make all kinds of unreasonable demands. I wondered whether I had dated men who wrote me off their list of potential dates simply because they assumed that they could never measure up to my demands, or because they could not possibly meet the expectations of my father and mother. Finally, I came to the conclusion that I really shouldn't tell a guy anything about my family or being wealthy, at least not on a first date, because that would only make it difficult for the man to get to know me as a person.

This young lady was so afraid of being stereotyped as overindulged and stuck up simply because she was wealthy that she resolved to avoid discussing her family financial situation with her dates, at least until she got to know them a bit. We both have had other wealthy female and male clients who have also told us that they avoid revealing or acknowledging their financial status in social situations, because they are afraid that this knowledge will alienate people.

The Affluent Are Helpless. Still another negative stereotype that affects the affluent is the notion that wealthy people have been taken care of to such an extent by paid help that they are unable to care for themselves. This belief provides the basis for grossly overcharging wealthy persons for minor home and auto repairs. I (JT) have an uncle who was an auto mechanic for most of his life. Although he has always been scrupulously honest in his repair work with all his customers, he used to tell me stories about some of his friends who made jokes about how they made up the names of nonexistent parts that needed to be replaced whenever they dealt with rich guys who had fancy cars and no idea about how the cars ran. My uncle told me that it is important for all car owners to take the time to identify and patronize trustworthy mechanics, and it never hurts to get several opinions and several estimates for all repairs. But my uncle also told me that these precautions are particularly important for those who have expensive cars or are perceived as being wealthy.

The stereotypical view that the affluent are necessarily incompetent can also have significant implications for those individuals who enjoy participating in sports and activities that have an element of challenge or danger. The rich kid who joins the Boy Scouts may well have a more difficult time proving his outdoor survival skills than a poor boy of the same age. A wealthy "white-collar guy" who wants to take up skydiving, rock climbing, or scuba diving is similarly likely to encounter somewhat greater difficulty than a less affluent "blue-collar guy" in gaining the trust of his instructors and his fellow students.

I (JT) am very fond of wilderness canoeing, camping, fishing, and hunting. I have done these things my whole life, and I feel perfectly safe and comfortable in the wilderness. I particularly enjoy vacations that involve hiring a seaplane to drop me off with a canoe on a remote lake in the woods that has no access by road or trail. In that way, I can be pretty certain that I will not be disturbed by anyone coming in while I am there camping. It is like having the world to yourself for a week or so, until the seaplane comes back to pick you up. From time to time, however, I find that I have a hard time convincing the people at the seaplane companies to fly me in and drop me off in the woods unaccompanied by a guide, especially if they get wind of the fact that I am a psychologist, or if they see the New Jersey license plates on the car.

To deal with this possibility, I have taken to carrying some pictures of previous wilderness trips with me when I plan such a fly-in vacation, just to let the seaplane people know that I have done this before and most likely will not kill myself out there. I make sure these include pictures of me cleaning fish and cooking over an open fire. The photos constitute a sort of wilderness camping equivalent to a SCUBA certification card. They do not really prove anything, but they give the individual supplying the required service the idea that at least you have some experience, and you are aware that some level of knowledge is required to engage in the activity safely. On the other hand, I am always careful to acknowledge the sensible nature of the safety concerns that the seaplane company personnel may have, and if they suggest it (which they often do), I am always willing to pay extra for a midweek checkup flight to reassure the people at the air service that I am okay.

DEALING WITH PROFESSIONALS

Still another area in which negative stereotypes impact the affluent is in their dealings with professionals. Although affluent persons are undoubtedly fortunate because their wealth gives them access to the best physicians, surgeons, psychotherapists, personal trainers, and massage therapists, the affluent often find that these professionals adhere to the same negative attitudes toward them that characterize the population in general. The affluent may find that providers are overly patronizing, or they may find that providers assume that their affluent patients/clients are overly indulged and entitled, operating on the assumption that everything in life should be perfect, and "making mountains out of mole hills" when it comes to assessing the magnitude and seriousness of their physical complaints and psychological stresses.

Needless to say, the possibility of receiving treatment from professionals that is based on such stereotypically negative views of the affluent has the same implications for those requiring professional services as potential stereotyping on the part of tradesmen and other service providers. If you are affluent, you must be very careful in selecting the professionals who treat you. Furthermore, in working with professionals you must be very clear regarding how you expect to be treated: You expect to be listened to, and you expect to be taken seriously. This topic is sufficiently important that we have dedicated an entire chapter to working with professionals (Chapter 6).

THE STIGMA OF WEALTH

Apparently, the experience of being perceived negatively because one is wealthy is sufficiently widespread that significant numbers of individuals avoid telling their friends and colleagues that they have money. A recent newspaper article on the children of the wealthy in Los Angeles indicated that many young adults who "come from money" choose to hide rather than flaunt their affluence.[1] Instead, these young people choose to go to school, work regular jobs, and live modest lifestyles. Some of the individuals interviewed for this chapter indicated that their parents had instilled a sense of values and a strong work ethic in them by limiting their allowances and encouraging them to have part-time jobs as they grew up. These individuals said that they simply expected to work, and that they felt more comfortable living on what they earned and keeping their trust funds for a rainy day. But others indicated that they did not want new friends to know that they had grown up in a wealthy family, for fear that this knowledge would have an unfavorable impact on how others might view them.

Not only do many wealthy young adults hide their wealth, but some may even feel compelled to lie about the fact that they are wealthy, or about the reality that they like being wealthy and have an interest in maintaining and even increasing their wealth. I (OC) recently worked with a male business school student from a very wealthy family. This young man planned to become an investment banker like his father, and his goal was to make even more money than his father had already accumulated. But he did not always share this goal with the new friends that he met. He told me that whenever he met a new woman, he always tried to figure out "where she was coming from" before deciding whether to tell her that he was planning to become an investment banker.

He said that being in business school was a plus with some women, but a major negative factor with many others. He said that some of the more liberal women that he had met assumed that anyone who was going to business school was "part of the establishment." This meant that they assumed he was avaricious, materialistic, politically and ideologically conservative, insensitive, insufficiently concerned with women's issues, boring, and probably a potentially poor husband and father. He said that whenever he met a new woman, he tried to figure out quickly whether she would be likely to fall into this group who were "likely to hate you because of your money." If he thought that his date did fall into this group, he would play down his interest in investment banking and suggest that even though he was enrolled in business school now, he was considering applying to a doctoral program in industrial relations. In that way, he could talk about how he could use his education to promote employee job satisfaction, which was a career objective that seemed more socially acceptable to liberal women than his true goal, which was to carry on the family tradition of making lots of money in finance.

He said that in the long run, it did not make any real difference what he said about his career goals, because there was very little chance that he would have a second date with a woman whom he felt could not get on board with his actual career plans. But he also said that the slight "massaging" of his career goals and ambitions generally helped to make the evening a lot more pleasant.

Difficulties in Socializing with Less Affluent Individuals

Another area in which affluence can be problematic is socializing with individuals who are less affluent. Of course, it is true that affluent individuals are somewhat more likely to associate with other affluent individuals than with less affluent individuals. This is the natural result of the fact that we tend to socialize with individuals who are in the same profession and with individuals who belong to the same organizations. Obviously, if you are an investment banker and you socialize primarily with other investment bankers and with the CEOs of large companies, then most of the time, you will participate in activities along with individuals who are similar to yourself in terms of financial status. However, many relatively affluent individuals also socialize with individuals who are less affluent.

You may be a professional, such as a physician, psychologist, architect, or attorney. You may be very successful and therefore affluent, or you may be affluent through a combination of inherited family wealth and your own professional earnings. Yet you may have colleagues who are not as affluent as yourself. They may be very interesting, and they may share some of your own professional interests. They may belong to the same professional societies, and they may attend the same professional conferences. But they are not wealthy. Perhaps they selected a different specialty area that is less lucrative than yours. Maybe they have no family money to supplement their earnings. Maybe they have simply chosen to work fewer hours and get along on a more modest income. For whatever reason, it is quite likely that most affluent professionals will find themselves at one time or another engaged in social activities with less affluent individuals.

Regardless of your profession, and regardless of any additional sources of income that you may have, you will have to live somewhere. Although there are communities in which the residents are all very wealthy and a community resident is not likely to meet and socialize with anyone who is not wealthy, most affluent people do not live in such communities. Many affluent individuals live in affluent suburban communities like Greenwich, Connecticut, Scarsdale, New York, or Tenafly, New Jersey. These communities are characterized by diversity with respect to the income levels of the residents. While many residents are quite wealthy or even fabulously wealthy, there are also residents who have more modest incomes. These less affluent residents may be from families who have lived in the town for some time, and often they have very strong ties to the community. They may be the owners of small local businesses, and they are often represented heavily in local government and community organizations, such as the town board, the police and fire departments, the chamber of commerce, the board of education, religious institutions, the Boy Scouts, and various children's sports and recreation councils. Therefore, in the course of normal living, the affluent residents of these towns will naturally come into contact with less affluent residents. They may share common interests, and they may find themselves working together in community organizations and special projects sponsored by such organizations. Opportunities for socializing will arise. We are pointing out here that social contacts among individuals of very different income levels can be difficult.

DIFFERENCES IN WHAT YOU AND YOUR FRIENDS CAN AFFORD

If you plan to go out to dinner with folks you have met who are on a serious budget, you had better give some thought to the restaurant to which you suggest going. The place where you have dinner every Friday may well be out of their price range, even for special occasions. You might be able to pick up the check without thinking twice, but you might want to think twice before doing so. They might be uncomfortable or even offended if you do. It may be better to have them over for dinner at your house first. This will avoid the immediate issues of how expensive the restaurant is and who will pick up the check.

However, if you do invite them over to your house for dinner, you will have other decisions to make. Will you serve a $200 bottle of wine? If you do, will you discuss the cost of the wine and whether you consider it a bargain, as you might if you were in the company of other affluent wine lovers like yourself? This might well make your guests uncomfortable. Speaking of others, you will need to give some thought to whether or not to invite other people. If you do invite other friends, you will certainly want to give some thought to who these other guests might be. Certainly, you would avoid having any wealthy friends whom you already know to be stuck up or obnoxious about being wealthy, or anyone who is insensitive who might make your less affluent guests feel uncomfortable. On the other hand, you will not want to avoid asking other friends to attend your dinner party simply because they are affluent. In short, you need to exercise good judgment. These are certainly not impossible problems, but they do require you to consider an additional factor in deciding what to do with whom and when.

Keep in mind also that this issue pertains not only when a wealthy individual socializes with a person of modest means, but also when persons of great wealth socialize with people who are affluent, but less affluent. Everything is relative. My wife and I (JT) recently had the experience of spending some extended periods of time with a good friend who was recently widowed. We did this because we love her and we knew that she needed emotional support for a good long while following the sudden death of her beloved husband. A problem arose, however, because she is extremely wealthy, and because she and her husband had made a habit of dining out *every day* at the finest and most expensive restaurants. For a while, we simply joined her in her dining habits, but we quickly realized that this was costing us several thousand dollars a week, and we were gaining weight to boot. We were somewhat reluctant to introduce still another change into her routine, which had changed so drastically when her husband died. But we had no choice. So we had a talk with her. We explained that we were neither as wealthy as she nor as metabolically blessed, and we simply could not afford to do this every day. Of course she understood, and we worked out a dining schedule that worked for all of us. But it required a real act of will on our part to bring up the subject and to work it through.

A related problem that can prove quite difficult is what to do when your children want to bring their friends along when you engage in family activities and vacations. Suppose that you take your children out to Aspen for a week every winter to ski. But now your son has a best friend who also skis, and your son wants him to come along on the trip. The only problem is that your son's friend does not come from a wealthy family, and they could not begin to afford to pay for his airfare, let alone his lift tickets and meals. You might not think twice about inviting him and picking up the cost for his trip, but again, the boy might feel awkward if you did this, and so might his parents.

Once again, I would stress that these problems are not insurmountable, but they do require sensitivity and flexibility in planning. Perhaps this year you might consider changing the usual plans, and maybe renting a condo in a ski area in Vermont. That way you could drive, eliminating the airfare issue. You could probably also arrange a family rate for the lift tickets, to eliminate that expense for your son's friend. Alternatively, if you know the young man and his family really well, you could simply say that you normally go to Aspen and that is what will make you happy, and it will also make you happy if you can take him as well. You can acknowledge the difference between your family and his in terms of the types of vacations that each can afford, and you can tell him that you want to include him in this trip. It all depends on the type of relationship that he has with your son and with you, as well as on how his parents feel about it and how freely you can discuss these issues with them.

SHE ONLY WANTS ME FOR MY MONEY

A closely related problem that arises when more and less affluent individuals socialize concerns the motivations of the less affluent party. We often hear of the guy who married his wife "for her money." We also hear of young women who go off to college looking more for a wealthy husband than for an education. So it is only natural for an affluent individual to wonder about the extent to which money is a factor when a member of the opposite sex appears to show an interest. This is a thorny problem, because if you are paranoid regarding people's intentions, your suspicions will probably keep you from ever making any new friends; but if you blithely assume that everyone's motivations are perfectly honest and transparent, you will probably ultimately end up being used and getting hurt.

When you find yourself in a position in which commitments are likely to be made, whether to a friend or to a prospective mate, you must feel free to discuss financial issues. If they are genuine in their concern and care for you, they will understand your position, and they will not resent your apprehensions. If they become indignant at the thought that you should raise such questions, you should consider this response a warning indicator and back off a bit. Obviously, affluent individuals may wish to consider a prenuptial agreement when contemplating marriage to someone who is much less affluent. Your prospective partner's response to your initiating this discussion will also serve as an indicator of where he or she is coming from. The topic of prenuptial agreements is also sufficiently important that we have devoted substantial attention to the issue in Chapter 9.

THE FALSE PERCEPTION OF CONTROL

Wealth has an insidious complication that affects most affluent people to one degree or another, although most are not aware of how they are being affected. Being wealthy provides an individual with a high degree of control over many aspects of life. Material wealth enables one to purchase an endless variety of goods and services. It enables the affluent to live where they want in the type of house that they want, to drive the kind of car that they want, and to enjoy whatever forms of entertainment they desire. The affluent are free to travel anywhere in the world they would like to go, and to participate in an endless variety of possible activities. In short, it seems as if the affluent can do pretty much anything they want. Unfortunately, however, as argued perceptively by Barry Schwartz,

> increases in experienced control over the years have been accompanied, stride-for-stride, by increases in expectations about control. The more we are allowed to be the masters of our fates in one domain of life after another, the more we expect to be. Education is expected to be stimulating *and* useful. Work is supposed to be exciting, socially valuable, *and* remunerative. Spouses are supposed to be sexually, emotionally, and intellectually stimulating *and* also be loyal and comforting. Friends are supposed to be fun to be with *and* devoted. Children are supposed to be beautiful, smart, affectionate, obedient, *and* independent. Everything we buy is supposed to be the best of its kind. With all the choice

available, people should never have to settle for things that are just good enough. In short, life is supposed to be perfect.[2]

Researchers Luthar and Sexton pointed out that the problem with this type of thinking is that despite one's wealth, no one has control over all aspects of life, and as a result, life is *not* likely to be perfect.[3] The result of heightened expectations for perfection juxtaposed with the impossibility of realizing these expectations is the likelihood of disappointment. This risk is exacerbated by the prevailing emphasis on individualism and autonomy that characterizes our culture in general and, to a heightened degree, the culture of affluence. The bottom line is that our wealth conditions us to expect perfection in all things, and when this expectation is unmet, we tend to blame ourselves.

Worse still, as Seligman has pointed out, the tendency to attribute the blame for negative outcomes to the internal causes is a significant predictor of depression.[4] The affluent come to expect that their considerable efforts will result in the perfect life. They are very hard on themselves when this perfect life does not materialize. They have no one to blame but themselves. Furthermore, the emphasis that the culture of affluence places on competition and on individual autonomy and self-determination tends to attenuate the individual's connections to social institutions, including their own families, community organizations, and religious congregations. But these social connections are known to be the best antidote to depression. Thus, it would seem that the goal of achieving wealth is sometimes not what it is cracked up to be. When we achieve wealth, it does not necessarily make us happier. It may simply raise the bar over which we must jump to impossible levels, leaving us more frustrated than ever. This explains why, in the face of increasing levels of wealth in the United States over the past century, the incidence of depression in the population has actually increased, possibly by as much as a factor of 10.[5]

Recall the highly paid pitcher we talked about in Chapter 1, who cautioned us to remember that money solves only one set of problems, out of the myriad of problems that each of us face over the course of our lives. If you have worked hard and achieved some financial success, do not allow yourself to fall victim to the illusion that you are in control, and that everything should be exactly the way you want it to be. You do not have that degree of power. If you think that you do, you are setting yourself up for disillusionment, self-blame, and depression.

THE ADDICTIVE POTENTIAL OF AFFLUENCE

It is very easy to get used to being affluent. We get used to living in our large beautiful homes with the landscaped grounds, the swimming pool, and the home gym. We get used to our electronic devices and our new cars.

We get used to fine food and wine, nice clothes, beautiful furniture, fresh flowers, and fine artwork. We get used to having the masseuse come to our home, and we get used to spending long weekends at fancy spas. We get used to multiple vacations each year at luxurious resorts. We get used to having a housekeeper to keep the house spotless, and landscapers to keep the grounds beautiful. We get used to having everything work the way that it should. If something does not work, we get used to having someone in immediately to get it taken care of and get things restored to proper working order.

THE TREADMILL OF RISING EXPECTATIONS

There are many problems with getting used to all this. One obvious problem is what to do if we fall on hard times and can no longer afford to maintain the privileged lifestyle to which we have become accustomed. A more troublesome problem is that when we become "used to" one level of affluence, we are likely to raise our expectations still higher and aspire to the next-higher level of affluence.[6] Life becomes a treadmill, which always has settings for faster speeds and greater elevations. As we pointed out in Chapter 1, affluent people generally do not compare themselves to the population as a whole in evaluating their success. Rather, they compare themselves to other affluent people. Therefore, in the midst of lives that are clearly comfortable or even luxurious, the affluent may suffer from "relative deprivation."[7]

We hasten to point out that the phenomenon of relative deprivation is not unique to the affluent, but ubiquitous across cultures and income levels. Goff and Fleisher have suggested that

> A primitive villager desires a hut that is a little more comfortable than the current one. The family in a comfortable three-bedroom home imagines the same home or a different one with a little more room, a swimming pool, a game room, a home theater, and improved décor. The estate owner yearns for more luxurious appointments, a second home by the sea, a summer house in the mountains.[8]

The broad applicability of the phenomenon of social comparison has been documented by recent empirical research. Economists have demonstrated that across socioeconomic status levels, satisfaction with one's income level depends not so much on the actual amount of current income, but rather on the comparison of one's current income to one's past income and the comparison of one's current income to the incomes of social and professional associates.[9]

Despite the ubiquitous nature of materialism and the desire we all have to acquire a little more, no matter how much we have now, the affluent are more likely than the less affluent to experience disappointment and depression arising from the continuing drive to accumulate more and more wealth.

This is partly because the affluent are more heavily conditioned to compete than the less affluent, and more likely to regard income as a means of keeping score in this competition. However, it is also partly because the affluent are, in fact, able to control so many aspects of their lives that they are more likely to buy into the idea that life should be perfect. Individuals who are poor or middle class know quite well that they cannot have everything they want or control every aspect of their lives. It is the affluent who can sustain this illusion for a time, and it is the affluent who are most likely to regard themselves as failures when they ultimately find that they cannot maintain the perfect lives that they feel compelled to achieve.

GROWING UP AFFLUENT

Another area in which the addictive potential of affluence manifests itself is in the incredibly high expectations of the children of the affluent regarding what constitutes an appropriate lifestyle. In the affluent towns in which we both live and work, these expectations have resulted in an *epidemic* of children who have graduated from college but return home to live with their parents, rather than getting out on their own.

This phenomenon is in part simply the "failure to launch" scenario, which has been a problem for some families for as long as anyone can remember. But what we are talking about here is not that phenomenon alone. When we think of the "failure to launch" scenario, we typically envision a young adult who is somewhat immature for his age and educational level. He is shy, insecure, anxious, and apprehensive about beginning a career or taking on adult responsibilities. Often, the child who fails to launch has been a poor student in college, and he lacks confidence in his ability to obtain respectable employment. Therefore, he comes home for shelter from the cold, cruel, threatening world, and while he is taking shelter, he takes a menial job somewhere for pocket money. With time, he begins to adapt to the greater world and adjust to his place in this world. He begins to develop a network of friends who are in similar positions. Eventually, he finds a niche for himself where he can feel comfortable. He adjusts his expectations for the future to his qualifications and to the job market. When he has had a chance to reassess who he is and what he can expect, he comes to accept his situation, and he moves away from home into an appropriate living situation.

In contrast, what we are seeing more and more of among the children of the affluent is not so much a "failure to launch" based on immaturity and insecurity regarding one's ability to function in the world, but rather a conscious economic decision to continue to live at home, based on the rationale that it is expensive to live on one's own, and moving out would require a dramatic reduction in one's lifestyle. We see kids coming home from college who have done very well in school and have obtained entry-level positions with companies where they make relatively good salaries and have tremendous potential for advancement.

These kids come home simply because they know that if they were to establish a residence of their own, their salaries would not enable them to maintain the lifestyle they had while they were growing up. Consider Steve, a 26-year-old systems analyst from Alpine, New Jersey, who earns $80,000 a year, yet still lives at home. He explains his decision to remain at home as follows:

> If I were to move out now, it would cost me at least $2,000 a month to have a decent apartment, and I would just be pissing that money away. I wouldn't be building any equity. I wouldn't have enough money left over after paying the rent to have any kind of life at all. I wouldn't be able to go out to eat very much, and I certainly wouldn't be able to go on vacation every spring, like I did all through college. My car is getting a lot of miles on it now. It's almost four years old, and I'm going to have to get a new one. Dad's not paying for my car or my car insurance anymore. That's another $1,500 to $2,000 every month. There's no way I could afford to move out on my own and meet all these necessary expenses.
>
> Besides, it's nicer living at home than in some apartment building. I have a separate entrance, and the family playroom is never used, so that's my living room. There's a pool here and a barbecue and a gourmet kitchen. I wouldn't have any of that if I had my own apartment. Then there's the housekeeper. She keeps the place clean and she does my laundry. I don't even know how to do those things, and I'm not really interested in learning. My folks are always going off on weekends and on vacations, and I often have the whole house to myself. I'd be nuts to give this up.
>
> I'm doing really well at work and I have already gotten several raises since I came. It won't be too long before I get a more substantial promotion and a really significant pay raise. Then I can think about moving out. Also, when I'm 30 I get access to my trust fund, and then I'll have enough money for a down payment on a really nice home of my own. In the meantime, I'm living well. I can devote all my energy to work, and I'm even saving a bit.

This new form of prolonged dependence on one's parents is understandable among the children of the affluent. The children have grown up seeing mom and dad always having pretty much anything they wanted, and throughout their childhood and their college years, the children shared in their parents' luxurious lifestyle. They are used to being taken care of, and they are used to being able to do pretty much anything they want. Thus, it is perfectly understandable if they are not enthusiastic about the prospect of giving this up and supporting themselves.

In the culture of affluence, the only really acceptable outcomes for children involve doing very well in college and then going to a graduate or professional school that will lead immediately to a high-paying job such as a lawyer or an investment banker. Only a career trajectory of this nature will allow affluent young adults to begin work with high enough salaries to allow them to set up their own household immediately after the completion of their educations.

Sometimes, even these successful academic outcomes are not sufficient to allow the children of the affluent to become independent. I (JT) recently worked with a family whose son came home to live with mom and dad, along with his new wife and baby, following his graduation from medical school. This enabled the son and his wife to save money for a down payment on a home of their own while he was completing his residency. It also enabled the couple to take advantage of the free child care provided by the family housekeeper. We are not saying that there is anything necessarily wrong with such arrangements, as long as everyone understands the logic for the decision, and as long as everyone is okay with it and everyone gets along. However, these extended periods of partial or complete dependence are certainly a new and unique phenomenon that requires planning and discussion. Also, such arrangements can be problematic when the parents are ready to have some time to themselves, but the children expect to be taken care of well beyond the age at which children have traditionally become independent.

THE ISOLATION OF THE AFFLUENT LIFESTYLE

Several aspects of the culture of affluence contribute to the tendency for affluent individuals to be more isolated and less socially connected than less affluent persons. These include increased job mobility with concomitant reduction in the formation of strong personal bonds with one's coworkers, as well as the isolated character of the lifestyle of hardworking high achievers.

PROFESSIONAL CREDENTIALING AND INCREASED JOB MOBILITY

The ground rules of the competition for academic and career success require a high level of individual academic achievement leading first to entry into one of a number of prestigious colleges, followed by entry into one of a number of prestigious graduate or professional schools. At each point in the course of a long academic career, the individual receives a certificate or some other credential signifying his success in the competition, and together these credentials form a resume that effectively summarizes the worth of the individual as an employable commodity. There is an impersonal quality to this competition. At each point in the process where the individual must choose the next school or the next professional position, considerations of the prestige of the university or the firm are likely to take precedence over considerations such as proximity to one's home or to the part of the country in which one wishes to live.

It is not like the nineteenth century, when the son of an affluent businessman could be expected to go off to college, but then return home to take his place in the family business. Of course, there are still some sons and daughters who go into their families' businesses, but there is a great deal more mobility with respect to careers than there once was. A half century ago, the norm was for individuals to work in one firm for a career, or at least the better part of a career. Now frequent job changes are typical among highly trained managers and professionals. This mobility reduces the strength of the bonds that a given individual is likely to develop toward his associates at work. Often, professionals come and go from one firm to another, capably performing their technical function for a limited period of time, but barely connecting with other employees on a personal level.

THE ISOLATED NATURE OF THE HOMES OF THE AFFLUENT

Most of the affluent individuals with whom we work live in one of two types of dwellings: apartments in Manhattan, or suburban homes situated on reasonably large pieces of property in one of the counties surrounding Manhattan. In either case, the residents are isolated. They do not live in neighborhoods where they see familiar faces each day and get to know their neighbors. Residents of New York City apartments are famous for living in an apartment for several or even many years, and never even knowing who their neighbors on either side are, let alone becoming friendly with them. Residents in affluent suburbs buy homes with long driveways, surrounded by trees and hedges, so that they can have privacy. These affluent residents may similarly never get to know their neighbors, unless the neighbors happen to be in the same business or profession, or unless the neighbors have children the same age as their own. This type of isolation is quite different from the situation in lower- and middle-class neighborhoods in either urban or suburban areas, where the more limited financial resources of the residents imply fewer square feet of breathing room or privacy space per resident.

Luthar and Sexton argued that neighbors in affluent suburbs are "unlikely to casually 'bump into each other' as they come and go in their communities."[10] This reality is exacerbated by the fact that most residents of affluent suburbs get up each day and go to work in some other place. Their most important affiliations are likely to be professional in nature, and these affiliations are likely to be nurtured at work or at professional conferences that take place far away from their residences. The residents of an affluent suburb may be only vaguely aware of what is going on just down the street, unless it impacts upon them directly.

But this means that the residents of these affluent communities are vulnerable to the effects of low levels of social cohesiveness. The affluent do not generally have neighbors in whom they can confide or to whom they can complain. If the kids are doing something that they should not be doing after school, chances are the neighbors will not know and will not care. Certainly, the neighbors will not be likely to come around in the evening and warn the parents that there may be trouble brewing.

Promoting Class Envy and Class Warfare

TOM JUNIOR'S GRADUATION ADDRESS

Tom Clancy is an executive in the treasurer's department of a large energy company. His 28-year career began as a financial analyst. His years of hard work won him promotion after promotion, and he is now the assistant treasurer of the corporation, a position of great responsibility that commands a high six-figure salary and regularly puts him in the company of the political and financial leaders of the nation.

This month (May 2008) Tom's son, Tom Jr., graduated from the prestigious prep school he attended. Tom Jr. was a star in school, both a hardworking student and a respected leader among his peers. He was class valedictorian, a two-sport varsity athlete, and the vice president of his class. Tom Jr. will be attending Princeton in the fall, where he plans to major in economics and political science. Tom Sr. is justifiably proud of his son.

However, the relationship between Tom Sr. and his son was rocked rather substantially by the remarks Tom Jr. made in his valedictory address at his commencement. With all the passion of youth, Tom Jr. hopes for a career in politics that will enable him to help improve the lives of his fellow citizens. He has already been active in local politics in his hometown, helping to conduct voter registration drives and involving himself in issues affecting the many undocumented foreign workers who are employed by local businesspeople.

In his commencement address, Tom was exhorting his classmates to engage in noble causes and "ask what they could do for their country." At one point in his speech Tom Jr. noted that he and most of his classmates had come from extremely affluent families, and that they all would have ample opportunities to continue the family tradition of achieving financial success. Although he did not mean any offense to his dad or to anyone else's parents, Tom Jr. called upon his classmates "to be better than that [and to] rise above the self-interest and petty materialism that had placed them in their position of great advantage in comparison to other young people their age."

On one level, Tom Sr. understood his son's youthful passion and even admired his idealistic goals for the future. But on another level, Tom Sr. felt that his son lacked appreciation for how hard he had worked to make a good life for his family. When he gave voice to his reservations about the speech later that day at dinner, Tom Jr. apologized for offending his dad, but in his efforts to defend his position, he actually made matters worse by making reference to the fact that his father worked for "big oil," which was directly or indirectly responsible for high gas prices, the war in Iraq, and the danger of global warming. Tom Jr. suggested that his dad's preoccupation with his highly successful corporate career placed him in a position where he could not possibly feel any sympathy for the struggles of working-class Americans or poor people in other lands. He hoped he could rise above such concerns.

Although Tom Sr. could remember the idealism of youth and could not really become angry with his son, he could not help but remark that Tom Jr. would probably find it somewhat easier to "rise above self-interest and petty materialism" because he did not have to worry about where the money would come from for his tuition at Princeton.

This incident did not precipitate a great war within the Clancy family. Tom and his son loved each other too much for this to happen, and they were both sufficiently bright and well educated to understand Churchill's admonition that if you are not a liberal at 20, you have no heart, and if you are not a conservative at 40, you have no brain. Nevertheless, the fact that Tom Jr. felt that his father's position in corporate America rendered him unable to appreciate the struggles of the poor and incapable of understanding the negative impact of "big oil" on the world illustrates one of the pernicious outcomes of the exploitation of class envy for political ends.

POLITICAL EXPLOITATION OF CLASS ENVY

From the point of view of the affluent, one of the most damaging aspects of contemporary American culture is the predilection of politicians with a populist bent to exploit class envy and promote class warfare. The most publicized recent example of this phenomenon is the failed 2008 presidential candidacy of John Edwards, the multimillionaire personal injury lawyer and U.S. senator who based his populist campaign on the evils of the "Two Americas." In a political stump speech, Edwards opined:

Today, under George W. Bush, there are two Americas, not one: One America that does the work, another that reaps the reward. One America that pays the taxes, another American that gets the tax breaks. One America— middle-class America—whose needs Washington has long forgotten, another

America—narrow-interest America—whose every wish is Washington's command. One America that is struggling to get by, another America that can buy anything it wants, even a Congress and a president.[1]

Edwards's comments are not simply aimed at encouraging his listeners to want to do more for those members of society who are not wealthy. They are aimed at securing political support by vilifying those who are wealthy. The passage quoted above contributes to the stereotypical picture of the affluent as the unworthy beneficiaries of privilege. According to Edwards, the poor do all the work, while the rich simply reap the rewards of this work. He gives no credit to the affluent for the efforts that they and/or their parents put forth to achieve their wealth.

Edwards also suggests that the poor and middle class pay all the taxes, and that the wealthy pay none. This is a demonstrably false assertion. In fact, according to the Internal Revenue Service, the top 10 percent of earners pay nearly two-thirds of all the federal income tax that is paid in the United States, and the top 25 percent of earners pay approximately 83 percent of all federal income taxes.[2] In contrast, the lowest 50 percent of earners pay just 4 percent of income taxes. Nevertheless, populist politicians do not hesitate to ignore the facts and to use rhetoric that will exacerbate naturally occurring class envy by demonizing the affluent. The effect of such political exploitation is to reinforce negative stereotypes of the wealthy as selfish, ruthless, and unable to do any real work themselves.

OBAMA, CLINTON, AND MCCAIN

Of course, one could argue that the American electorate did not buy into Edwards's message of the "Two Americas," as evidenced by the fact that they repudiated his candidacy at the polls, and he dropped out of the presidential race fairly early in the process. Nevertheless, the class warfare message put forth by Edwards still had a life of its own that has extended beyond his candidacy. The presidential candidates who persisted in the race longer clearly recognized this reality. Certainly the idea of redistribution of wealth was an important element of President Barack Obama's message, and implicit in the idea of redistribution of wealth is that there is something unseemly or immoral about having a great deal more wealth than the average person.

Obama is a populist. His message of class warfare is clear in his frequent references to the salaries earned by the CEOs of American companies as unreasonable or even exploitative. In a speech made on Martin Luther King Day in 2008, Obama stated that, "We have a [moral] deficit when CEOs are making more in ten minutes than some workers make in ten months."[3] On other occasions, he has argued that "[s]ome CEOs make more in 10 minutes than some workers make in a year,"[4] or that "[s]ome CEOs make more in one day than their workers make in one year."[5]

In an article on the American Thinker Web site, Lee Cary pointed out that the "sliding comparative equations" that Obama has used to describe the earnings of CEOs are generally pretty far out of line with reality, but they nevertheless represent a strong appeal to class envy that appears to fuel his popularity among supporters.[6] We would argue that such assertions also exacerbate the disdain with which the general public tends to regard the wealthy, and that this disdain is ultimately reflected in poor treatment received by the affluent.

Obama's democratic primary opponent, Hillary Clinton, also adopted the rhetoric of class warfare. In stump speeches, she routinely targeted hedge fund managers, oil company profits, drug company subsidies, and trade agreements that she says encourage companies to export jobs.[7] She told a Wisconsin audience that the Democratic primary election in that state was "a chance for all of you here to help take our country back."[8] She also told her supporters that, "We need tax breaks for the middle class, not for the wealthy and the well-connected," and she vowed that "We're going to rein in the special interests and get the $55 billion in giveaways and subsidies they've gotten under Republicans back into your pockets."[9]

Senator Clinton did much of her campaigning from a bus named "The Middle Class Express."[10] She spoke out against the evils of inherited wealth and pledged to increase the estate tax to bring in an additional $400 billion in revenue to the federal government over the next 10 years. Mrs. Clinton consistently decried the fact that there were two "oilmen" in the White House, and she frequently emphasized the problem of income inequality in the nation, arguing that "We have the greatest income inequality that we've had since the Great Depression [and] if we stay the way we're going we're going to have a huge jump in inequality."[11]

Although neither Obama nor Clinton presented income inequality as inherently wrong and the wealthy as inherently evil to the extent that Edwards had done, they nevertheless both recognized the populist appeal of his message. During the primary campaign, both Obama and Clinton courted Edwards's endorsement. On February 18, 2008, Obama stated that Edwards "has a lot of credibility ... and we would love to have his support."[12]

The Republican presidential nominee, John McCain, has also criticized the compensation packages that have been negotiated by the CEOs of major U.S. corporations. He characterized the compensation of the CEOs as unseemly at best, and obscenely excessive at worst. Throughout much of the campaign, McCain also opposed the Bush tax cuts that were enacted in 2001 and 2003. He stated in 2001 that, "I cannot in good conscience support a tax cut in which so many of the benefits go to the most fortunate among us at the expense of middle-class Americans who need tax relief."[13]

We note that implicit in McCain's statement are the populist ideas that: (1) the affluent are wealthy because they are fortunate, rather than because they have worked hard and achieved success; and (2) the idea that tax relief accorded to the wealthiest Americans come at the expense of the less affluent. These views are in marked contrast to the more traditional conservative economic viewpoint that tax relief accorded to wealthy taxpayers has the effect of stimulating the economy to the benefit of all citizens. In 2003, McCain stated that the Bush tax cuts benefited primarily the wealthiest Americans, and that "I would like to see some of that redistributed more heavily to middle-income and low-income Americans."[14]

Later in the campaign, under pressure to address the concerns of his conservative Republican base, McCain modified his position to support legislation that would make the Bush tax cuts permanent. However, the fact McCain could so easily adopt class warfare rhetoric endorsing redistribution of wealth indicates that class envy is sufficiently entrenched in the American culture that many politicians feel compelled morally or politically to pander to this envy in their political positions.

THE INTENSITY OF CLASS ENVY IN THE AMERICAN CULTURE

Of course, the politicians would not be so quick to employ the rhetoric of class warfare were it not the case that class envy is deeply ingrained in the American culture. People who are not so affluent have a choice when it comes to explaining their financial status. It would appear that at least three possible explanations are available to those who are attempting to understand why they are not wealthy. These are as follows: (1) I never really cared that much about becoming wealthy. I chose my job because I think my work is important and/or enjoyable, and the fact that I am not wealthy is of little concern to me. (2) I would like to be wealthy, but quite honestly it was not worth putting in 60 hours a week of hard work for the length of time that it would take to become a lawyer (or doctor, investment banker, successful real estate developer, or whatever). So I just did the minimum that was necessary to get by, and now my income is about what I would expect, given my relatively modest effort. (3) Of course, I would like to be wealthy, but people like me never have a chance. I was not born with a silver spoon in my mouth, and I did not have some kind of rare talent that would get me a big scholarship. I have done just about all that I could, given the class structure of our society, and the fact that the government does nothing to give guys like me a fighting chance.

The first two of these explanations for achieving only modest personal financial success involve internal attributions of causality. Individuals who adhere to either of these explanations for their financial status are accepting primary responsibility for where they are in life financially. In the first explanation, individuals are simply saying that their choices were not based primarily on the goal of achieving wealth, but on some other important personal value. Into this category would fall individuals who chose to become artists or skilled craftsmen, not because they anticipated that these activities would make them rich, but because they simply love the activities so much that they cannot imagine doing anything else just to make more money. Also in this group, we might find teachers and professors, some clergymen, forest rangers, farmers, and fishing guides. Of course, a small proportion of individuals who choose a career on this basis do end up making a lot of money. Their artwork may become trendy, or they might write a best-selling book. But generally, these folks are simply contented doing what they love, and they are really not concerned with not being wealthy. Therefore, they have no reason to resent the wealthy. They are not driven by envy, and they do not need to find a scapegoat on whom they can blame their relatively modest financial status.

The second explanation also involves recognizing and accepting one's personal motivational limitations. There are people who would just rather relax and have a good time than work hard, whether the work they chose was potentially wealth-producing or not. These folks tend to have jobs rather than careers. They do what they need to do to get by, but they are primarily interested in relaxing and enjoying life. They put in their time at work and earn what they need to in order to pay the bills, but they do not make Herculean efforts at work. They would rather be wealthy than not wealthy, but they do not want to be wealthy badly enough to make a concerted effort to make it happen. They do not consider their work to be intrinsically important or rewarding, and they are not driven to achieve financial success to a degree sufficient for them to work really hard at something that they do not find entertaining or absorbing. These folks might envy the rich, wishing that they were as lucky as those who inherited wealth or were blessed with great talents. However, these individuals are not likely to hate rich people simply because they are rich. These folks are aware that they had an opportunity to become wealthy within the American economic system by working really hard, and they simply chose an easier path.

Therefore, the people in these first two groups are not particularly prone to class hatred. They recognize that their failure to become wealthy was the result of their own choices, whether these choices involved the nature of the work they chose to pursue or the intensity of the effort they put into their work. However, there are many people who would love to be wealthy and are not wealthy who would much rather attribute their lack of financial success to the influence of pernicious social forces that have stacked the deck against them and made it impossible for them to achieve the outcomes they desire. This is the group that is most vulnerable to class envy. This is the group to whom Edwards and other populist politicians appeal, and in whom the seeds of class hatred find fertile ground. Furthermore, if you happen to be wealthy, these are the individuals who resent your financial position and consider you a fair target for policies aimed at redistributing your wealth.

PROMOTING CLASS WARFARE IN THE POPULAR MEDIA

The politics of class hatred are also highly visible in the mainstream media. On May 6, 2006, an article by Erik Eckholm appeared in the *New York Times* entitled "America's 'New Poor' Are Increasingly at Economic Risk, Experts Say."[15] In this article, Eckholm argued that "Americans on the lower rungs of the economic ladder have always been exposed to sudden ruin. But in recent years, with the soaring costs of housing and medical care and a decline in low-end wages and benefits, tens of millions are living on even shakier ground than before, according to studies of what some scholars call the 'near poor.' "[16] The article consists primarily of detailed and extremely sympathetic descriptions of several families who had fallen upon hard times. The stories paint a bleak picture of the life these folks have led, a picture that would lead the reader to become angry that such travails could befall good, hardworking Americans. The stories could also lead the reader to become much more apprehensive regarding his own financial security. Consider these examples:

One family, the Abbotts, consisted of a near-retirement age couple and their teenaged son. They had fallen on hard times. They attributed their economic difficulties to a precipitous drop in the demand for aviation-related electronic parts. The husband, Stephen, used to make about $40,000 a year selling these parts, but in 2001, he lost his job when the demand for these parts fell off. Stephen was on unemployment until it ran out. At this point, the couple was evicted from their apartment with their son. They lived for a year in a borrowed motor home, then for eight months in a motel room with a kitchenette. Eventually, Stephen was able to get a lower-paying sales job, and they were able to move into a one-bedroom apartment. The article describes in graphic detail how bad conditions were in the motel, with "people screaming and fighting and the cops being called."[17] The article also describes how both Mr. and Mrs. Abbott became sick. Stephen went on state disability, which pays him $1,436 a month and gives him health coverage. Mrs. Abbott was described as being without health insurance. She indicated that if she got sick, she would have to go to a medical van that serves the homeless.

In the story of the Sauer family, the husband in the family was described as a licensed electrician, and the wife, Machele, was described as a waitress. The family lived in a large mobile home. They had three children with a fourth on the way. The husband planned to start his own electrical business, and Machele planned to stop working when the new baby arrived. But then everything fell apart. The husband was arrested for theft, linked to a drug addiction that the wife did not know about. Because he had a prior criminal record, he received a long jail term. This led Machele to go on welfare. At first, she received $600 per month along with paid child care and counseling for herself and her children. She went back to waitressing—four night shifts and two day shifts each week—and earns about $1,300 a month. This led her welfare payments to be cut to $300 per month, although she still gets $200 in food stamps.

Eckholm noted that these families sought aid from food banks and other charities. He wrote:

> In Orange County, about 220,000 people received food from 400 local charities last year, according to the Second Harvest Food Bank, which distributes donations. Recipients include many families, often Hispanic, with several children and both parents working minimum-wage jobs. Over all, half the families seeking food had at least one working adult, according to a recent study by the food bank.
>
> In the center of Orange County, a world away from its polished coastal towns, borderline poverty is common but seldom visible. On small streets behind strip malls and fast food restaurants, families, sometimes two of them, cram into small, aging bungalows.
>
> What look like tourist motels along Beach Boulevard are mostly filled by working families or single people who stay for months or years, paying high weekly fees but unable to muster up-front money for an apartment rental.[18]

The article stated that "about 37 million Americans lived below the federal poverty line in 2004, set at $19,157 a year for a family of four. But far more people, another 54 million, were in households earning between the poverty line and double the poverty line." Eckholm cited a sociological study on "the vulnerability to poverty," which concluded that "the risk of a plummet of at least one year below the official poverty line rose sharply in the 1990s, compared to previous decades ... By all signs, such insecurity has continued to worsen."

In a critique of the *New York Times* article, Eric Arr suggested that Eckholm was in effect arguing that "vulnerability to poverty is now the new poverty."[19] Arr suggested that Eckholm used the cases studies he presented to elicit sympathy for the lower-paid workers, but pointed out that the case studies related by Eckholm were in reality examples of temporary financial difficulties due to market forces or to personal failings, rather than the result of the existence of a permanent economic underclass created by a conspiracy of the wealthy.

Arr noted that Stephen Abbott had his job selling aircraft parts dry up due to a decreasing demand for these products, and that in time he found a similar but somewhat lower-paying job, which enabled him to get his family back into an apartment. Then Stephen became ill (also not the result of the pernicious activities of the wealthy). When this happened, Stephen went on disability, which was sufficient to keep the family housed and fed.

Arr also pointed out that the difficulties encountered by the Sauers were the direct result of the husband's drug addiction and criminal behavior, rather than the result of class inequities created by the wealthy. Furthermore, in spite of the criminal nature of the circumstances through which the family's economic difficulties arose, Machele and her children benefited from public assistance payments to the extent that they were actually never in danger of being homeless or undernourished. In fact, Arr presented some calculations indicating that Machele's income from her work and her public assistance placed her above the poverty line for a family of four, even without factoring in the cost of health care they received or the counseling that was provided to them at no cost. Arr concluded that "the bottom line is that things may be tight for a while [but] the kids aren't starving or dying from lack of care or from strange diseases, and the mother is employed."[20]

Arr also criticized Eckholm's misleading use of the statistics to create the impression that there is widespread poverty in Orange County. Arr noted that the 220,000 people in the county that Eckholm reported as receiving food from local charities had to be considered in relation to the county's total population of over three million. He also pointed out that the median per capita income in the country had risen by almost $17,000 per year since 2000, from $64,611 in 2000 to $78,606 in 2005. Based on these observations, Arr concluded that Eckholm's article "seems to do little more than fuel class envy and to attempt to elicit pity for people who are not being 'victimized' by anybody."

Another example of the media exploiting and exacerbating class envy is found in a *Washington Post* article from July 10, 2006, written by Neil Irwin and Cecilia Kang and titled "Well-Paid Benefit Most as Economy Flourishes." The lead sentence in this article is "Wages are rising more than twice as fast for highly paid workers in the Washington area as they are for low-paid workers, an analysis of federal data by the *Washington Post* shows."[21] In the next sentence of the story the authors explain to the readers the class-envy implications of this trend (in case we missed it):

> That means the spoils of the region's economic expansion are going disproportionately to workers who are already well-paid, widening a gap between rich and poor in a place where it is already wider than in most of the country.[22]

The language in this sentence is clearly loaded. The income pie that is being symbolically divided up is referred to as "spoils," as if it had been taken by pirates or marauding barbarians. And of course, these spoils are described as going "disproportionately" to the already well-off, and widening a "gap between rich and poor."

The article continues with a brief explanation of some of the economics underlying the allocation of income, specifically the fact that the world economy gives educated workers leverage to negotiate for higher wages but makes "low-paid workers replaceable." Note the authors described these workers as "low-paid" rather than "unskilled." The authors continue by citing the statistic that:

from 2003 to 2005, the average wage for people in the lowest pay bracket, with salaries around $20,000, rose only 5.4 percent in the Washington region—not enough to keep up with rising prices. For the jobs that pay around $60,000 salaries rose 12.4 percent, well ahead of the 6.8 percent inflation for that period ... In the highest wage bracket, where chief executives, lawyers, and other professionals earn six figures, average wages rose 8.5 percent from 2003 to 2005. The increase in their incomes is probably even higher, because employees at that level also often get better benefits, partnership income, stock options or other compensation.[23]

The implication of this article is clearly that income inequality is a problem that needs to be fixed, rather than a result of the same naturally occurring market forces that have resulted in the prosperity from which the region is benefiting. And of course, the most well-off are depicted as the chief culprits, since they not only have the greatest power to negotiate their compensation, but also have "extra" benefits and methods of being compensated that are not available to lower-paid workers.

Since the advent of the mortgage crisis in the last year or so, the choice of stories covered by the major media sources has become more blatantly anti-affluent, and the language of class warfare that has been employed in these stories has become increasingly strident. On February 25, 2008, the CBS *Early Show* with news anchor Harry Smith aired a story entitled "Snow Job."[24] This story concerned Countrywide Financial, the nation's largest mortgage company, and the story indicated that the same executives "who foreclosed on 90,000 homes and laid off 12,000 people" were off to vacation at the lavish Ritz-Carlton Bachelor Gulch ski resort in Avon, Colorado. In this segment, CBS correspondent Jeff Glor reported that "while the economy in general and many homeowners remain in serious trouble, Countrywide has picked a place where troubles will go away, for a price. It's a winter retreat for the rich ... Rooms start at $725 a night." Presenting footage of the resort fit for the Travel Channel, Glor went on to report,

> The mountains are snow-capped, the skiing top-notch. And then there's the food. At the famed Spago restaurant, goat cheese layer cakes, tuna tartare, and sliced Kobe steak dish for $91. For the budget conscious, only 36 bucks for chicken. This is where the troubled home lender Countrywide scheduled a lavish wine-and-dine getaway for mortgage bankers from around the country, for three days, all expenses paid.[25]

The only problem with this report was that the event never occurred. The company had planned the event, but it had cancelled all gatherings with business partners and clients in light of the mortgage crisis. In addition, the founder and CEO of Countrywide had given up his salary for the year, and Countrywide had agreed to sell itself to Bank of America. Only later did CBS report that the event had been cancelled. In the event that you might be wondering what CBS would have to gain in going ahead with its report despite the cancellation of the event, we can only speculate that the popular media, like the populist politicians, is aware of the attraction of class envy for the audience and the appeal of stories catering to class envy. In short, class envy sells.

The exploitation of class envy is even more blatant among those with a clear political agenda. For example, the liberal blogger Tomcat describes himself as "just a retreaded activist from the 1960s trying to defeat the Bush regime one day at a time and remove the GOP stranglehold from our nation."[26] In April 2008, Tomcat argued that

> A major reason why we're feeling so down now is that for working Americans the boom [of the 1990s] never did come back. Job creation in the post-2001 recovery was pathetic by Clinton-era standards; wages barely kept up with inflation. Instead, corporate profits and the incomes of a tiny elite surged— sucking up so much of the economy's growth that only crumbs were left for everyone else.[27]

This view of the economy makes clear Tomcat's liberal political agenda. Now let us look at how he exploited class envy. Tomcat argued that Bush and GOP economics "succeed only at shifting wealth from the pockets of the poor and middle classes into those of the super rich and huge greedy corporations."[28] He went on:

> Here's how the super rich are enjoying those gains: Who said anything about a recession? Sometime between the government bailout of Bear Stearns and the Bureau of Labor Statistics report that America lost 80,000 jobs in March, Lee Tachman spent roughly $50,000 last month on a four-day jaunt to Miami for himself and three close friends . . .
>
> The trip was an exercise in luxuriant male bonding. Mr. Tachman, who is 38, and his friends got around by private jet, helicopter, Hummer limousine, Ferraris and Lamborghinis; stayed in V.I.P. rooms at Casa Casuarine, the South Beach hotel that was formerly Gianni Versace's mansion; and played "extreme adventure paintball" with former agents of the federal drug enforcement administration.
>
> Mr. Tachman, a manager for a company that executes trades for hedge funds and the owner of a "handful" of buildings in New York, said he has felt no need to cut back.[29]

Tomcat explained that Tachman is "hardly alone" in his eagerness to keep spending. Tomcat reported that some businesses that cater to the superrich report that clients—many of them traders and private equity investors whose work is tied to Wall Street—are still splurging on multimillion-dollar Manhattan apartments, custom-built yachts, contemporary art, and lavish parties.

Tomcat also indicated that "buyers this year closed on 71 Manhattan apartments that each cost more than $10 million, compared with 17 during all of 2007." He noted that "last week a New York art dealer paid a record $1.6 million for an Edward Weston photograph at Southeby's [*sic*]." And he added that The GoldBar, a downtown lounge, reports that bankers continue to order $3,000 bottles of Remy Martin Louis XIII cognac.

Just in case Tomcat's opinion of these affluent individuals and their lifestyles was not clear from his descriptions of the affluent, in his blog he came right out and told us his views:

> Personally, I feel angry to see such obscene conspicuous consumption at a time when so many have to do without so much. These are people who received over 90% of the benefit from the Bush/GOP tax cuts.
>
>   Seven years of GOP tyranny have transformed the US into two societies. There is free enterprise for the poor. They may help themselves in any way they can, on their own, as long as they can find a way to circumvent a system designed to transfer what little they have to the rich. There is socialism for the rich, as they often pay far less in taxes than middle class taxpayers. The GOP had aided the super rich in class warfare against the rest of us. They have created an economic pyramid that is so top heavy that the capstone is crushing the base.[30]

At least Tomcat is clear about where he is coming from, which is apparently more than can be said of CBS News or the *New York Times*. However, regardless of how clearly one's use of class envy rhetoric may be tied to one's political leanings, the fact remains that these constant negative portrayals of affluent individuals breed resentment and are ultimately hurtful.

Because of the widespread use of such rhetoric, many people in our society assume that all people who are affluent are greedy, selfish, and entitled. Many people also assume that those who have inherited wealth are spoiled and incompetent; and many people assume that those who have made a lot of money themselves must have employed illegal or unethical methods to do so. These assumptions frequently result in affluent individuals being treated with contempt and derision. These assumptions also provide a convenient rationale to those who seek to take advantage of the affluent. In the following section of this chapter, we consider some of the ways in which the affluent can be impacted negatively by those who foster class envy.

How Class Warfare Harms the Affluent

Those who promote class envy and class warfare harm the affluent on both the macro level, by using class warfare to promote public policies that are contrary to the interests of the affluent, and on the micro level, by promoting disdain for the wealthy on the part of those who are less wealthy, as well as feelings of guilt on the part of affluent individuals due to nothing more than the fact that they are affluent.

Class Warfare and Public Policy: The Flat Tax Proposal. Many public policies that impact successful individuals adversely are justified on the basis of class envy and the accompanying philosophical position that any inequality in income that may arise from differences in the personal achievements of individuals is inherently wrong. It is not our purpose here to consider all these issues in great detail, nor is it our purpose to engage in the debate surrounding the morality of differences in individual income levels. However, we would like to consider one such issue just to give you a feeling for how class envy is used.

Let us take the ongoing discussion of problems with current federal tax policy, and the specific issue of the flat tax. Many have argued that the Internal Revenue Service is inefficient, and that the complex tax codes are subject to abuse on the part of clever CPAs who can manipulate the system to help their clients avoid paying taxes. For example, economist Daniel Mitchell has argued that:

> the current tax system is a complicated failure that hinders the nation's growth while allowing the politically well-connected to manipulate the system to get special breaks that are not available to average workers and businesses. This is stimulating a great deal of interest in shifting to a simple and fair flat tax.[31]

Mitchell described the flat tax as follows:

> Unlike the current system, a flat tax is simple, fair, and good for growth. Instead of the 893 forms required by the current system, a flat tax would use only two postcard-sized forms; one for labor income and the other for business and capital income. Unlike the present system, which discriminates based on the source, use, and level of income, a flat tax treats all taxpayers equally, fulfilling the "equal justice under the law" principle etched above the main entrance to the U.S. Supreme Court building. And unlike the current system, which punishes people for contributing to the nation's wealth, a flat tax would lower marginal tax rates and eliminate the tax bias against saving and investment, thus ensuring better economic performance in a competitive global economy.[32]

The considerations noted by Mitchell have led legislators to propose legislation that would replace the current federal tax system with a flat tax.

However, the political opponents of the flat tax have used the rhetoric of class envy and class warfare to argue against the flat tax. For example, in a 1994 op-ed piece in the *New York Times,* Molly Ivins argued that, "Common sense shows a progressive income tax is just plain fair," based on the logic that an individual who earns $40,000 a year "feels" the burden of taxation more than an individual who earns $200,000 a year.[33] Of course, the key words here are "fair" and "feels." The use of the word "fair" is aimed at making the reader see the affluent as unfair in the way they would treat the less affluent, and the use of the word "feels" in reference to the less affluent taxpayer is aimed at eliciting sympathy on the part of the reader for the pain that the less affluent taxpayer feels when he is forced to pay his taxes.

Of course, what Ivins did not include in her editorial is the fact that under the flat tax, the higher-income taxpayer *does* pay more in taxes than the lower-income taxpayer. This point was made by Mitchell, who noted that "A wealthy taxpayer with 100 times more taxable income than his neighbor *will pay 100 times more in taxes*" (emphasis added).[34] Since the flat tax will be a fixed proportion of the taxpayer's income, the higher-income taxpayer will pay proportionately more in taxes. Eddie Hamm pointed out that with a flat tax of 15 percent, an individual who earns $40,000 would pay $6,000 in taxes, whereas an individual who earns $200,000 would pay $30,000 in taxes.[35] Furthermore, Mitchell pointed out that in fact, the amount of taxes that a family earning $40,000 would actually be less than $6,000, because the flat tax proposals typically have an exemption based on family size.[36] For example, under HR 1040, sponsored by Representative Michael Burgess (R-TX), a family of four would not begin to pay annual income tax until income reached more than $30,000.[37] Under this bill, the family of four earning $40,000 would pay $1,500 in taxes.

Mitchell noted that although higher-income taxpayers would certainly pay more in federal taxes than lower-income taxpayers, "a flat tax does not impose special penalties on those who contribute the most to the nation's prosperity by subjecting them to punitive and discriminatory tax rates."[38] Hamm criticized Ivins's editorial use of class warfare rhetoric on the ground that such rhetoric "has created a whole society who believe: 'They have too much and ought to give me some' or 'They've got more than they need.' "[39] Hamm also linked the exploitation of class envy to the glut of slip-and-fall lawsuits that has plagued the U.S. court system, on the grounds that people are socialized to believe that one little lawsuit will not hurt the rich guy. This observation brings us full-circle back to where this chapter began, with John Edwards.

Obviously, the flat tax proposal is just one area of public policy in which affluent individuals are demonized in order to further the political agendas of specific groups. Other areas in which the same type of class envy rhetoric is used and the same type of vilification of the affluent occurs are the death tax levied on inheritances and the double taxation that currently takes place on dividends. There are several reasons why you should be aware of the persistent use of the class warfare strategy. First, if you should find yourself in the position of having to advocate for your own interests or defend an economic policy that you feel is fair in favor of a policy that you feel discriminates against you, you should be aware that this type of emotional argument will likely be used against you. Second, you need to avoid falling into the trap of buying into such arguments, consciously or unconsciously assuming the "guilt" for your good fortune and/or hard work, and therefore accepting the truth of the class envy argument without even attempting to defend your own best interests. One of the important points we are anxious to make here is that if you happen to be an affluent individual, you have no need to feel guilty simply because you are affluent, and you should feel free to make this clear to anyone who would attempt to make you feel this way. If you have any doubt that there is a danger of simply accepting the premise that you have something to feel guilty about just because you have some money, consider the furor that erupted in a liberal university when some students attempted to develop a business cleaning students' dormitory rooms.

The Impact of Class Warfare on the Individual: The Harvard DormAid Boycott. In 2005, Harvard students Michael Kopko and Dave Eisenberg got the idea to develop "DormAid," a business that would hire students to provide cleaning services to other students for their dormitory rooms. They charged a minimum fee of $17.99 per roommate, and if some roommates wanted the service while others did not, then DormAid would clean only the rooms of those who did want the service. Although it might be difficult for some of us to imagine the difference between this service and such traditional campus services as the campus "clean and fold" laundry service, the idea resulted in a storm of protest at the liberal institution, followed by a rather substantial backlash. The Harvard *Crimson* attempted to organize a boycott of the service, based purely on considerations of class envy. The *Crimson* argued as follows:

> Hiring someone to clean dorm rooms is a convenience, but it is also an obvious display of wealth that would establish a perceived, if unspoken, barrier between students of different economic means ... It's up to each one of us to ensure that our peers feel comfortable on campus, and if that means plugging in a vacuum every two weeks, then so be it.[40]

When this editorial was posted on *Talkleft: The Online Magazine with Liberal Coverage of Crime-Related Political and Injustice News,* students responded by posting a broad range of comments, ranging from individuals who equated using the cleaning service with either total moral bankruptcy or some form of major underlying psychological issue, to individuals who defended the business as just another service.

As an example of the former type of response, a student visitor to the site commented:

> Personally, if you can't maintain your own laundry and clean up your own room, you have much bigger issues at stake than one of possibly instigating class warfare. I almost feel bad for people who may use this service ... The only people who will use this service are the momma's boys and daddy's little princesses who have the wealth to do it.[41]

Another student carried the class warfare view further. He not only saw the potential users of a dorm room cleaning service as morally lacking, but recommended that sanctions be imposed on the "rich lazy snobs" who might use the service in order to benefit the students who would do the cleaning, since the latter were obviously "hurting for cash":

> There is something shameful about an able-bodied college kid who can't be bothered to keep a minimum standard of decency in a dorm room. And, beyond differences in cars or clothing, there could well be a level of discomfort in sitting in a classroom next to someone whose hairs you just wiped out of the shower stall for a few bucks, just because they were too lazy to be bothered. Or someone sitting next to you who just scrubbed your toilet because they were hurting for cash and you are a rich lazy snob. The differences are bad enough with the cars and the clothes. Why take them to the next level? The college should fine all dorm students who can't maintain a decent standard of cleanliness $50.00 per day. Let the money go into a scholarship fund for those in need.[42]

A third student could not see what all the fuss was about:

> I have to say this seems pretty dumb to me. American has never been and will never be a classless society. Should you tell the rich kids not to buy better computers [and] stereo systems and display them in their room because someone's feelings might get hurt? Give me a break. The real issue from my perspective is that money is associated by almost everyone as an indicator of self-worth. The real problem is that belief, because it turns the rich kids into snobs and the poorer kids into victims. If your sense of self-worth is so tied to money that spending $17.99 on cleaning makes you feel superior or not being able to spend it makes you feel inferior, then you need a better value system. In some small way, the banning of this cleaning service would be reinforcing the concept that such differences in income do make a difference.[43]

Finally, several of the individuals who commented on the issue turned the table on the editorial staff of the *Crimson*. For example, an alumnus argued that,

> the *Crimson's* distaste for "student" dorm cleaners arises from their own issues with class ... They see the work these cleaners do as so degrading, so outside the scope of their lives that they are projecting their own loathing and elitism onto what they perceive as the embarrassment and humiliation of showing up at their friend's dorm room with a vacuum and some Pledge ... I was lucky enough to bartend my way through college. There is an awkwardness to a group of your better off friends coming in and ordering from you. So what? That's college. I know a lot of doctors, lawyers, and businesspersons who have been waiters, waitresses, movie attendants, etc. [and] I would bet most of these folks are better people for having seen and put up with what the "lumpenproletariat" spends its life doing.[44]

Granted, colleges tend to be left-leaning these days, but the fact that a dormitory cleaning service could elicit such virulent anti-affluent class envy is a testament to the forces with which affluent individuals must deal in our society.

The issues that flow from the demonizing of the affluent will be discussed at length in subsequent chapters of this book. For now, we will consider our work done if our readers are more sensitive to the forces in the world who seek to make the affluent into villains. We have found that the chance of being a really bad person is pretty much independent of how much money one has. You need not be ashamed because you have been successful, and you need not be ashamed if your parents or grandparents were successful. This is still a free country, and you have the right to stick up for your own interests, and the right to spend your money as you like. If you free up some time by hiring people to do some of the chores associated with everyday living, you are not necessarily a lazy slob. You may be using the time you have freed up to engage in any number of productive activities that will benefit your nation, your community, your family, or even (Heaven forbid!) yourself.

Professionals' Attitudes toward the Affluent

Professionals tend to share many of the unflattering stereotypical views of the affluent that characterize the public at large. These stereotypical attitudes can be particularly damaging when held by professionals, due to the fact that we depend upon professionals to perform very important roles in our lives. If professionals consciously or unconsciously view affluent clients negatively, it can impair their ability to perform these roles competently. In this chapter, we consider the impact of negative attitudes toward the wealthy among various groups of professionals, including psychotherapists, physicians, and attorneys.

PSYCHOTHERAPISTS

Should the reader doubt that psychotherapists may hold negative stereotypical views of the affluent, please consider this abstract to an article entitled "Psychoanalytic Understanding and Treatment of the Very Rich," written by psychiatrist/psychoanalyst Silas Warner:

> Because personal affluence and an alloplastic adjustment tend to go together, psychiatric treatment encounters special problems in trying to help the very rich. These patients frequently show a strong sense of entitlement and a denial of any psychological problem. This creates special treatment problems. They feel entitled to the "very best," which includes the "best doctor." If their psychological problems cannot be magically erased they will switch psychiatrists

until they find the "right one." Part of this problem is a tendency to externalize their emotional problems. Problems are thought to be caused by the environment and not by intrapsychic conflicts. This encourages the therapist to make environmental changes to improve the psychological state. Other special problems that the very rich present are the V.I.P. syndrome, excessive concern with litigation, their excessive narcissism, and their emotional neglect by their own parents. Many were raised by parent surrogates and have problems with self-esteem. All of these special problems make the rich very difficult to treat with psychodynamically oriented psychotherapy or psychoanalysis.[1]

The extent to which Warner has stereotyped the affluent in this description is remarkable. He sees them as entitled, expecting a magical cure, likely to sue their therapist if the expected results are not forthcoming, and narcissistic. He assumes that because they are affluent, they were raised by nannies and lack self-esteem. In the article, Warner argues that their sense of reality is distorted because "if they get in trouble they know they will always be bailed out," and "they expect special favors."[2] Warner acknowledges a positive aspect of working with affluent clients, which is that they can "afford to pay your top fee and always pay promptly without quibbling."[3] However, this positive aspect of treating affluent clients is offset by the following negative:

> Among the very rich who seek psychoanalysis there are individuals with warped values who have been corrupted by the power of money and show a destructive mindset that undermines the analyst's efforts. Their cynical, skeptical attitude helped them to succeed in the world's marketplace and prevented others from exploiting them. However, it also prevents them from entering into a therapeutic alliance in psychoanalysis because of their lack of trust.[4]

If I were an affluent individual contemplating beginning a course of psychoanalysis, I do not think I would want someone with Warner's attitudes being my analyst. The clear message here is that if you are affluent and you are contemplating psychotherapy, you had better find out at the outset whether your prospective therapist has any problems with your financial status, and whether he or she will be likely to make any assumptions about your adjustment or your personality based solely on the knowledge that you have money.

Nor is it only among psychoanalysts that we find such negative stereotyping of the wealthy. Even more egregious in their stereotyping of the wealth are the rational-emotive therapists Wolfe and Fodor, whose biases are ironically displayed in an article that was ostensibly written to demonstrate to other therapists that wealthy women as well as poor women may require professional treatment:

> Why, the feminist therapist might inquire of us, are we taking our time to write about the woman who comes into our office in a $2000 Armani suit, en route

from her cosmetic surgeon to a charity ball planning luncheon (or a Right-to-Life meeting)? How fair is it for us to devote our time to a woman complaining about her maid's "unreliability" when it is the women of the class to which the maid belongs—the single mothers struggling to keep their families above the poverty level—who seem to need our help far more?[5]

These authors clearly disdain the lifestyle of affluent women. They assume that wealthy women will have an antifeminist orientation, as indicated by the sneering reference to a "Right-to-Life meeting." They also assume that the type of problem that an affluent woman would bring up in therapy would involve the unreliability of a maid. It is as if these authors cannot imagine an affluent woman having a more weighty personal problem or psychological disorder.

Furthermore, Wolfe and Fodor freely disclosed their biased opinion that affluent women cannot possibly be competent and effective individuals. They see such women as hyper-indulged emotional and psychological cripples:

> Peel away the packaging and accessories—the personally-trained bodies, the houses in Palm Beach, the Mercedes and the nannies of those women who seem to represent the fulfillment of the American dream—and we find only too often a vast well of pain and loneliness, depression and fear, and remarkable skill deficits, including not having the foggiest notion of how to earn a living or even read a brokerage statement.[6]

Their lack of respect for the capabilities of affluent women is almost equally matched by their assumptions regarding the social/political role of the affluent woman in a male-dominated, classist society. They argued that "upper class women are members of the ruling class, the maintenance of which organizes much of their lives."[7] They also suggested that "Like the men of the ruling class, they often display ignorance and disregard for the rights of the oppressed."[8] In short, Wolfe and Fodor clearly view affluent women as *the enemy*. If I were an affluent woman seeking help with a personal problem, I believe that winding up in the office of one of these therapists would probably be the prologue to my worst nightmare.

We hasten to point out that the type of negative stereotyping that we find so problematic in the writings of these psychotherapists is by no means confined to professionals with a radical political agenda. On the contrary, negative assumptions regarding the wealthy and the suboptimal treatment that can flow from such assumptions are characteristic of many mainstream psychotherapists, who may be unaware of the prejudiced nature of their views and the impact of these views on their patients. In this vein, please consider the two case vignettes presented below.

I (JT) was working on a research project with a colleague who was a social worker in private practice in one of the "Five Towns," an extremely affluent area on the North Shore of Long Island. One Monday, my friend arrived at my office to do some work on the project, and she began by telling me that, "Before we start working you just have to hear this one." She went on to tell me the following incident that had transpired over the weekend with one of her clients:

BRIANA'S GRAND CHEROKEE

This Saturday at 9:00 PM I got a call at my home from Briana, a client of mine who just turned 16. She had never called me at home before. She was extremely upset. She was crying and had difficulty even telling me what the problem was. But she was able to tell me that she had to see me, and she asked if I could I do it "right now." Although I do not make a habit of seeing people without notice on Saturday night, I made an exception this time. She was so upset that I was actually frightened. It was not like her to be this upset, and she said she was so furious with her dad that she could not even tell me what he had done.

I told Briana to come to my office right away and I would meet her there. On the way down, I was wondering what had happened. Given how upset she was, I was thinking that perhaps I would be dealing with a case of physical or sexual abuse. I was quite apprehensive.

We arrived at my office at the same time, and after we went in and sat down, I asked her to tell me what had happened that had been so upsetting. Briana proceeded to tell me that this was the night of her "sweet sixteen" party, and that there were still around 30 of her friends hanging around the pool at her house, along with a bunch of her parents' friends. She said that she could not stay there because she was "just too embarrassed." She went on to say that she had just gotten her junior driver's license and she expected that her dad would be buying her a car for her birthday present. She had been thinking very hard about what kind of car she wanted, and she had been talking to her friends about their cars. She had finally decided that she wanted either a Porsche or a BMW, which were the cars that most of her friends were driving. She had dropped any number of hints to her dad about her preferences. She had even talked about what colors she liked and what options she thought she should have.

But she did not get a Porsche or a BMW. Her dad had the nerve to buy her a Jeep Grand Cherokee. When he took her out to the driveway to show her the car, she was devastated. She could not understand why he had been so insensitive to her needs and wishes. She felt completely embarrassed and humiliated to get a Jeep, when all her friends had received "really nice" cars. She broke into tears and ran off.

She said that her dad came to find her and asked what was wrong. When she said that she was disappointed with the gift, he explained that he was thinking primarily about Briana's safety when he bought the Jeep. He did not want her in a sports car that was very fast and very low to the road. He wanted her to be in a sturdy car that could enable her to survive a possible accident. He also said that he did not want to spend as much money as he would have had to spend on one of the other cars.

Briana responded that his excuse about safety only showed that he did not trust her, and his unwillingness to spend any money just showed that he was "cheap" and that he "didn't care."

At about this point in the conversation, Briana's dad was hit with an "Ah-hah!" moment. He suddenly realized that he was apologizing to his daughter for buying her a

> beautiful and not inexpensive new car for her 16th birthday. He suddenly saw his daughter as a thoroughly spoiled young brat, and himself as a foolish enabler. He told her that she should be grateful for what she had been given. He said that very few girls her age got new cars on their birthday, and she should understand how privileged she really was. He said that when he got his license, he had to work for a year to buy an eight-year-old Buick. He also said that if she persisted in being so ungrateful, he would be just as happy to return the Jeep and let her figure out what to do for a car on her own. He even suggested that it would not hurt her to get a part-time job. He said it might give her "a much-needed dose of reality."

So this was what had driven Briana to the point of near hysteria: She had gotten a Jeep Grand Cherokee instead of a Porsche; she had embarrassed her father by making her disappointment perfectly clear to everyone at the party; and her father had called her on her ungrateful behavior and hinted that she might actually benefit by being forced to earn some of her own money. My colleague laughed after telling the story. I asked her how she responded to Briana. She laughed again and she told me that:

> I really let her have it. I told her that her father was absolutely right, and that she had behaved badly. Instead of showing her gratitude for an extremely generous present, she had in fact behaved like a spoiled brat. I told her that even if she felt disappointed, she should have had the sense to smile and thank her dad and bring up her complaints at a later point in time. She certainly should not have run off crying during the party. I also told her that I was really sorry that I had taken time out of my Saturday night to come in to listen to her. I said that I had been frightened that something really bad had happened, and that she owed me an apology, just as she owed her father an apology.
>
> My response to Briana's story must have had a favorable impact. At first, Briana was surprised that I was critical of her behavior. She was angry at me, and she broke down and cried for a while. But eventually Briana did indeed apologize to me for calling me on Saturday night, and she also said that she would go back and apologize to her father as well. I gave her a few minutes to pull herself together, and then I asked her to go home and think about what had happened. We would talk about it more when I saw her at her regular session.

I had an interesting reaction to my colleague's story. My first response to Briana's behavior was much like that of my colleague. I thought that she was acting like a spoiled brat who felt entitled to anything that she thought that she needed to make her happy. I thought that she was rude to her dad, and I completely understood his feeling angry with her and calling her on her selfishness. I also shared my colleague's anger at Briana for demanding to be seen on a Saturday night. But as I thought about the situation more, I began to have second thoughts.

I remembered that Briana had never called her therapist at home before and had never demanded to be seen on short notice; and I remembered that my colleague's first reaction to Briana's phone call was focused on how very upset Briana seemed. I thought about her friends who had received fancier cars when they got their licenses, and I recalled that one of Briana's major problems with the gift was the comparison she made between what her friends had received and what she had received. She had described herself as embarrassed and humiliated. She had clearly felt that her father did not consider her feelings. I also recalled that she had taken her father's explanation of the relative safety of the larger Jeep as an indication of his lack of confidence in her safe driving ability. For an adolescent in the midst of developing self-confidence and assurance in regard to life's challenges, this is not a small consideration.

In short, however out of touch Briana may have been with the realities of the world, and however unaware she may have been of how lucky she was in comparison to the typical 16-year-old in this country, the feelings that she had at that moment during her party were nonetheless real. Her disappointment arose from the comparison of her gift to the gifts received by her friends, who comprised her primary frame of reference and point of comparison. Briana had probably not been disappointed very many times in the past. She had no reason to expect that she would be disappointed on this important birthday. And her father had not shared his decision regarding the car with Briana prior to the party. Had he done so, they could have discussed their respective ideas and perhaps have come to some agreement. At least it would have avoided Briana's sudden disappointment and "humiliation," as well as the resulting hasty and ungraceful exit. It would also have avoided the embarrassment her father felt, because everyone realized that he had disappointed his daughter, as well as his angry reaction when he realized that she really was a spoiled brat, and he was acting like a fool.

In short, just because Briana was a spoiled brat who behaved badly does not mean that she was not hurting. Viewed in this context, I came to believe that my colleague's reaction to the incident, while certainly understandable, may have been somewhat insensitive. I think my colleague would have done better to allow Briana to vent her feelings of disappointment and anger with her father first, and then move on gradually to making her more aware of just how lucky she is and why her father may have reacted so negatively to her display of disappointment. Although my colleague believed that her critical response to Briana's behavior was helpful, I cannot help but think that Briana would have been much better able to take in the message that she was really very privileged if my colleague had first validated Briana's feelings and explained to her that they were understandable, given her rarified frame of reference.

Of course, in this example, the modest insensitivity of my colleague did not appear to do any real damage. She and Briana had a good relationship of long standing, and Briana was able to process the criticism and learn from it. They continued to work together, and Briana has matured and gained insight. However, not all instances of professionals' negative responses to affluent clients are so innocuous. Consider the following:

AN AFFLUENT VICTIM OF DOMESTIC ABUSE

Sandra is a 36-year-old stay-at-home mother of three children ranging in age from 3 to 8. She is married to John, 42, who is an extremely successful criminal lawyer. They live in a $3 million home set on six acres in Westchester County, New York. They have had a rocky marriage. John is attractive and exciting, but he has a drinking problem, and he is sometimes verbally and physically abusive. On four occasions over the past five years, John has slapped or struck Sandra with sufficient force to cause significant bruising, and twice Sandra went to the local emergency room. Each time, Sandra sought to avoid embarrassment by saying that she had fallen and bumped her head. On neither occasion did any nurse or physician in the emergency room question this explanation or attempt to open up a discussion of the topic of possible physical abuse.

Sandra has given some thought to ending her marriage, but she has refrained from doing so, in part because she is fearful regarding her ability to support herself and her children satisfactorily, and partly because she is genuinely afraid that John might really hurt her seriously if she were to tell him that she wants a divorce.

After the last violent incident, however, Sandra was sufficiently fearful that she called a local domestic violence hotline and made an appointment to see a counselor. When Sandra told her story, she explained her reluctance to leave the home and seek a divorce from John, due to her apprehension regarding the financial security of herself and her children. To Sandra's surprise, once Sandra's counselor had a good idea of the family finances, she recommended that Sandra seek private marital therapy. She said that her assessment of the situation was that Sandra was not in imminent danger. If Sandra wanted to leave the house and bring the children to a shelter, she could, but the counselor really did not feel that Sandra would want to do that, since the shelter would be a very modest place to stay, and there would be women there with whom Sandra would have little or nothing in common.

Sandra left her meeting with the counselor feeling that she had gotten very little support from either the counselor personally or the agency she represented. Sandra felt put off. She felt as if she would have received more active assistance if she had been poor. She was not sure whether the counselor tended to minimize the severity of the abuse she had reported because John was a professional, or whether the counselor assumed that the situation could not be all that bad, since Sandra had not chosen to leave the house. Sandra also felt that the counselor was telling her that she would not be able to "fit in" at a battered women's shelter.

Sandra followed the counselor's advice and sought private therapy, but she was not able to get her husband to agree to accompany her. Her decision to enter treatment was something of a wakeup call to John, who has limited his drinking around the house and has not been verbally or physically abusive since Sandra began treatment. Sandra is not convinced that this change will be permanent. She and her therapist are in the process of clarifying her options.

Sandra appears to have experienced several different forms of less-than-exemplary professional care based on her affluence. When she went to the emergency room, none of the professionals there questioned her account regarding how her injuries were sustained; and when she contacted the domestic violence program, she was left feeling that there was little to be done.

Unfortunately, the literature indicates that affluent women who are the victims of domestic violence frequently fail to receive adequate professional support, for a number of different reasons. First of all, affluent women may be more reluctant to disclose abuse than less affluent women, due to the perception that "marital abuse doesn't happen . . . to people like us . . . with education . . . in this neighborhood."[9] This reluctance to disclose the abuse on the part of the victim works in conjunction with the tendency on the part of professionals to make the same assumption that marital violence is rare within upscale families. Based on conversations with physicians, Weitzman concluded that:

> Some initially said that they tended to drop the matter once a woman explained a scar or bruise, so as not to offend or pressure her; they believed that within the doctor-patient relationship, patients would confide as needed.[10]

The physicians appear to be less willing to challenge denial among affluent women than among less affluent women, perhaps in part because they share the assumption that domestic violence is rare among the wealthy, in part because they believe domestic violence in affluent families is less severe than in poor families, and in part because they are aware of how very embarrassing it is to an affluent, well-educated women to become the victim of such violence.

With regard to the embarrassment factor, the myth that domestic violence does not occur among the affluent and well educated makes the affluent wife feel that her situation is a terrible deviation from the norm. Furthermore, if she has typically been a high achiever, she may regard her choice of a husband as a significant failure, an indication of poor judgment that is not compatible with her self-concept as a competent individual. The cognitive dissonance created by the recognition that she is being abused may very well lead her to minimize the problem. Even if she is clear that her relationship is abusive, she may be extremely reluctant to "go public," either by revealing the situation to friends or family, or by disclosing to a helping professional. Given the tendency of most therapists not to make direct inquiries regarding possible abuse, the reluctance of affluent victims to bring up the issue constitutes a significant impediment to identifying the problem and taking steps to address it.

In addition, it appears that some professionals regard affluent victims of domestic violence as somehow less worthy of assistance than victims of more modest means. This may be due to the perception of some therapists, like Wolfe and Fodor described above, that the affluent are members of an oppressor class who are enemies of those who would seek to achieve social justice. One can hardly expect a professional with such a view of the wealthy to go very far out of his or her way to help such an "enemy." But even among therapists whose views are not so heavily colored by their political orientation, there is still a tendency to assume that upscale women are entitled, demanding, and unreasonable.

This broad stereotype of affluent women as overly demanding opens the door to viewing the physically abusive husband as motivated at least in part by the frustration involved in trying to satisfy his wife's unreasonable expectations. The therapist may conceptualize the abuse as occurring when the abuser finally "loses it" because of the pressure that his wife has been putting on him to satisfy her wants. Even though the professional may believe that the abuser's frustrations in no way justify his abusive behavior, the perspective tends to foster a sense that the spouses share responsibility for the problem. This is particularly problematic for an abused woman who may already be rationalizing the abuse and blaming herself. It gives rise to justifications on the part of the victim for the abusive behavior such as, "He has really been under a great deal of pressure at work," or "I should not have pushed him so hard on this issue." This type of thinking can lead an abused woman to remain in an abusive marriage, even though realistic considerations regarding her personal safety suggest that she should leave.

THE PROFESSIONAL SOCIALIZATION OF NEGATIVE ATTITUDES TOWARD THE AFFLUENT

Among counselors and therapists who have been trained as social workers, the tendency to view the affluent as enemies is particularly pronounced, due to the historical foundations of the profession. The social work profession began in settlement houses created to house the poor, and the primary goal of the profession was the promotion of social justice. Social workers are therefore inclined to focus their attention on the poor and to focus their professional efforts on obtaining justice for those who are without resources. Social workers are, in fact, trained to advocate for the weak and the disenfranchised, and where possible to help the least privileged members of society to obtain relief from their poverty by affording these citizens access to the material goods that sustain life. These goods include food, clothing, and shelter, which are presumed to take precedence over such intangibles as mental health and subjective well-being.[11]

The primacy accorded to the goal of obtaining social justice within the social work profession tends to be associated with the view that our society is characterized by a powerful and relatively unchanging class structure, and by the idea that the members of the upper classes exploit the members of the lower classes. The wealthy are viewed as oppressors who work actively to maintain their favored place in society and to continue to take advantage of the less fortunate members of society. Perhaps individuals who view society in such terms are drawn to the social work profession, or perhaps the professional training that social workers receive tends to consolidate and amplify the perception that the rich are oppressing the poor. Perhaps both tendencies pertain. In any event, it is quite clear that many social workers view the wealthy with disdain and are not particularly predisposed to help the wealthy become any happier or better adjusted than they already are.

To illustrate the bias within the social work profession against affluent individuals, consider the following anecdote: I (JT) recently served as the statistical consultant on a social work graduate student's doctoral dissertation, which concerned the impact on postpartum depression of professionally led self-help groups for new first-time mothers. Due to circumstances beyond the control of the investigator, the sample employed in this study consisted of women participating in such groups conducted at a community center in an affluent suburb of New York. Thus, the women participants were predominantly affluent. Although the investigator tried very hard to find new mother groups in diverse areas representing a broad range of socioeconomic strata, this ultimately proved impossible.

Therefore, when the investigator submitted her proposal for the study to her doctoral committee, she noted that the external validity of the study would be limited by the restricted socioeconomic range of the women represented in the sample. That is, she acknowledged that any results she might obtain indicating that the women she studied were helped by the group experience would be applicable only to similarly affluent women participating in similar groups, and that further research would be required to demonstrate the possible impact of such groups on less affluent women. Of course, this limitation in no way threatened the internal validity of the study. Significant decrements in postpartum depression among the participants still indicated that these specific self-help groups were effective with these particular participants.

You cannot imagine how hard it was to get the committee even to give approval to conduct the study. Their problem was not that they believed that the study would not indicate that the groups were effective with the women who were participating in the study. Rather, the problem was that no one on the committee really cared about these affluent new mothers or any problems that they might be experiencing with postpartum depression. Some of the committee members even went so far as to suggest that the study would not work, because the women at this community center could not possibly experience postpartum depression. "After all," one committee member said, "don't these women all have nurses and housekeepers and mother's helpers to do all the work for them? Why should they be depressed?"

Eventually, the student convinced her committee that the study she was proposing would be valid and worth doing. She did so by showing the committee members a substantial amount of empirical data indicating that affluent as well as less affluent women can and do experience postpartum depression. Therefore, the committee ultimately allowed her to do the study as she had proposed, using the affluent population from the community center. However, the committee members insisted that the student include in the discussion a lengthy disclaimer pertaining to the relevance of the findings to the social work profession, since the participants were not poor or otherwise disadvantaged. They required her to reaffirm that the focus of the profession was on achieving social justice, and they required her to state that it was essential that the study be replicated as soon as possible on samples of less affluent women, who constituted a far more appropriate client group for the social work profession. They even asked her to obtain a statement from the social worker who facilitated the groups indicating that of course the worker would prefer to work with a broader range of women representing greater diversity. It appeared that the committee members felt that is was necessary to apologize to potential readers for taking the time and energy to do research pertinent to the psychosocial well-being of a group of women who happened to be affluent.

The paramount importance of social justice within the social work profession has actually generated a debate regarding whether it is even appropriate for social workers to engage in the practice of psychotherapy, as opposed to dedicating 100 percent of their professional efforts toward direct action aimed at the goal of redressing social and economic injustice in society. In this ongoing debate, Wakefield felt compelled to defend the provision of mental health care by social workers on the basis of Rawls's Theory of Distributive Justice,[12] arguing that psychosocial well-being constitutes a scarce social and psychological good to which all members of society are entitled on an equal basis. Based on this argument, it is possible for social workers to provide clinical interventions aimed at promoting self-respect and self-esteem, developing social skills, and promoting assertiveness, all of which are relevant to the overriding goal of achieving social justice.[13]

Thus we have seen that professional therapists and counselors representing various professional disciplines tend to adhere to stereotypical views of the affluent as demanding and entitled; and we have seen that some professionals have been socialized to view the affluent as members of an oppressor class who may very well be unworthy of assistance. The message should be clear at this point. If you are an affluent individual who has a problem requiring psychotherapeutic intervention, you want to be very careful in your choice of a therapist. You should look for someone who has had experience working with affluent clients, and you should obtain recommendations from former patients who can reassure you that the individual you are considering will not view your economic status in a negative light.

PHYSICIANS

Psychotherapists are not the only group of professionals who may have difficulty dealing with affluent clients. A very good friend of mine (OC) is an obstetrician who frequently complains to me that his most difficult patients are "the rich ones." He is firmly convinced that his wealthiest patients are more demanding than the typical patient, less easily pleased than the typical patient, and even more difficult to obtain payment from than the typical patient. He has often commented that the patients he likes best are the ones who are willing to make appointments that fit his office hours, ready to follow his advice without question, and anxious to pay his bill. He complains that his wealthiest patients demand to be seen at odd hours, expect him to answer telephone calls at pretty much any hour of the day, challenge his recommendations without hesitation, and insist that he answer all their questions until they are completely satisfied that they understand exactly why he has recommended what he has. He also complains that the "rich ones" simply do not understand that their bills need to be paid in a timely manner. He attributes this attitude to the fact that they have never had to worry about money. They have no idea that he has salaries to pay and other expenses to meet in conjunction with his practice. Why should they? Someone has always taken care of these mundane chores for them.

While these attitudes are disturbing in and of themselves from the point of view of an affluent woman who might be considering becoming one of his patients, one other opinion that my friend holds is even more problematic. He is firmly convinced that wealthy women have zero tolerance for pain in comparison to the typical patient. He believes that wealthy women are very likely to demand pain medication for even the slightest discomfort, and that they are quite likely to complain if they feel that they have experienced any distress. He believes that the affluent women in his practice simply assume that he should be able to deliver their babies easily, without pain, and with a minimum of effort on their part. At the same time, they expect him to avoid Caesarian deliveries, which may result in a potentially unflattering scar. In fact, my friend has suggested that his wealthiest patients feel free to complain to him if they find so much as a stretch mark after giving birth.

In spite of his fine reputation, his general dedication to his practice, and his substantial professional success, one has to wonder what the impact of such beliefs may be on the nature of the care that my friend provides for his affluent patients. If a woman has been a bit of a complainer throughout the course of her pregnancy, will he assume that she is being histrionic if she requests pain medication at a point in the birthing process that he might consider premature? Will his response to her request be colored by his preconceptions regarding affluent women? Will he assume that he is dealing with a "princess and pea" situation, and therefore under-medicate her?

I do not know the answer to these questions, but I do know that even though I refer many women to my friend, I sometimes hesitate to refer some of my more affluent acquaintances and clients to this particular friend for obstetrical care, particularly if I feel that the potential patient being referred may be perceived as (or may actually be) somewhat more demanding than the typical patient. I have generally attributed this hesitation to a simple concern with achieving a good match of personalities between the doctor and the potential patient. In the back of my mind, however, I believe that I must suspect on some level that my obstetrician friend might actually fail to provide appropriate and/or completely compassionate care to an affluent woman whom he considered too demanding.

Here again, we stress that the affluent individual is well advised to choose his or her physicians carefully, on the basis of referrals from trusted friends or colleagues who have had experience with the professionals in question. An adequate assessment of a physician must be based on information regarding both the doctor's medical qualifications *and* his or her attitudes toward affluent clients. It is not enough to find a doctor who will not assume that you are a hypochondriac or malingerer simply because you are wealthy. You must also find a doctor who is competent to deal with the medical issues at hand.

With respect to the question of locating a physician who is not likely to resent your affluence or assume that because you are wealthy, you will expect an inordinate level of pampering, we note that there are practices that specifically target and cater to more affluent patient groups. Recently, a good deal of attention has been paid to the so-called "boutique practice physicians" who accept limited numbers of patients and offer increased levels of service in exchange for higher fees.[14] These boutique medical practices typically provide unlimited access to a physician at any time of the day, immediate-access appointments, research on rare or complex diseases, coordination of care with specialists, guidance through hospitalizations, and particularly thorough routine physical examinations aimed at early detection of medical conditions in need of attention. In exchange for these special services, the boutique practices charge steep fees, often as much as $20,000 per year.

Of course, one would expect that physicians in such boutique practices, having made the decision to focus on a patient group who can afford to pay higher fees in exchange for greater access and more personalized care, would most likely pass the test of not harboring negative attitudes toward the affluent. Therefore, it might be reasonable for an affluent individual to consider using the services of a physician in such a practice.

However, even if this logic pertains and the boutique physician does not hold your affluence against you, this does not guarantee that the physician will be necessarily well qualified or particularly talented. He or she may be a very affable individual who is reliably available, polite, and attentive, yet not all that knowledgeable. Therefore, regardless of the fees charged by a physician or the type of clientele that he or she typically treats, you must be certain of his or her qualifications. In short, you should know that it is very important to obtain as much information as you possibly can about *any* physician with whom you are considering a consultation. Preferably, such information should come from multiple sources, including both current or former patients and medical colleagues who would have a sound basis on which to evaluate the physician's credentials and expertise.

ATTORNEYS, ACCOUNTANTS, AND INVESTMENT ADVISORS

Most of the same considerations apply with respect to the selection of other professionals, including those on whom we rely to handle our financial affairs. The major difference, of course, is the money. If someone who handles your money thinks that you have more than you really need because he harbors a deep-seated resentment toward the affluent, he may be tempted to redistribute your wealth, possibly to himself. If he thinks that you are utterly unaware of financial matters, he may feel that it would be relatively easy to take advantage of you. I am not talking primarily about actual embezzlement or stealing (although this may actually be a possibility in some cases). Rather, I am talking about such matters as the choice of investment options. For example, a financial advisor may well earn a very large commission by selling you an annuity. The annuity may be a good thing, in the sense that it represents steady income upon which you can depend. But the investment may not represent the best possible use of your resources or the wisest course of action directed toward maximizing your wealth. For this reason, it is important to have financial advisors whom you feel you can trust, and it is always important to know how they are being compensated for their services. It is not rude in any way to ask an advisor who proposes a certain investment how much he will be making if you follow the course of action that he has proposed.

The same is true for brokers who make money on commissions when they execute stock transactions for you. It is axiomatic among savvy investors that one should make investments cautiously and stick with them for the long term, particularly if the investments in question are regarded as part of one's long-term retirement planning. The commissions you may pay on trades may easily offset any gains that the stocks you have purchased may make. In this case, your broker may get wealthy, while your net worth does not increase the way that it should. Once again, the lesson to be learned here is that you must feel comfortable enough with your financial advisors and brokers to ask them what they have to gain if you follow their advice, and whether the advice really represents the best course of action for *you*.

Lawyers are similarly in a position to guide your actions in ways that will benefit them more than you. For example, when they draw up wills, they may make themselves executors or your estate, and in so doing they may draw hefty fees that might otherwise go to your children or other heirs. In addition, just as physicians may practice defensive medicine, spending lots of your money on marginally relevant tests only to avoid the possibility of a lawsuit later on, so lawyers may engage in large amounts of questionable work that may protect you from possible threats that are really quite unlikely ever to materialize.

For all these reasons, you need to be very careful choosing these professionals. Ideally, they should be considered based on referrals from people you trust; and you should be ready and willing to grill them regarding how they feel about the wealthy and what steps they take routinely to avoid taking advantage of affluent clients. When you hire someone to look after your financial interests, you must be willing to be assertive. You must refuse to worry about being stereotyped as just another rich person who is used to special treatment. On the contrary, you should make certain that you hire people who will gladly explain their recommendations to you and indicate how they are proposing to serve your best interests.

7

How to Cope with Negative Stereotypes

In Chapter 4, we considered some of the negative consequences of having wealth. One of these consequences is that affluent individuals are likely to be the victims of negative stereotypes regarding the wealthy. These stereotypes include the idea that the affluent are driven by self-interest, the belief that the affluent are avaricious, ruthless, and untrustworthy, the idea that affluent people tend to be entitled and overly demanding, and the idea that the affluent are helpless, unable to perform even the most mundane tasks of daily living without paid assistance of some form.

In this chapter, we would like to provide you with some strategies, tools, and techniques that you can employ to help you cope with these negative stereotypes. Our goal is to help you to avoid being hurt by these stereotypes. These coping strategies begin with refusing to fall into the trap of believing that these stereotypes are true and that they apply to you. It is easy to buy into widely held prejudices, even when these prejudices concern yourself. But if you allow yourself to accept these stereotypes, you will unconsciously provide justification to those who would use the stereotypes to justify taking advantage of you.

Assuming that you can successfully avoid buying into the negative stereotypes yourself, you still need to take proactive steps to defend yourself against those who would use these stereotypes to hurt you. You must be willing to set the record straight when people misread your motives, and you must be appropriately assertive to protect yourself if people try to take advantage of you. The sections that follow describe situations in which affluent individuals refused to buy into stereotypes of the affluent, and instead acted proactively in their own best interests.

"Who Says I'm Self-centered?"

If you accept the popular notion that affluent people are driven by self-interest, you may find yourself bending over backward to avoid being labeled as selfish. You may even do things that are foolhardy or allow yourself to be taken advantage of, just so that you can support a self-image as an individual who cares for others and is capable of rising above your natural tendency to be selfish. For example:

> Lois was born into a very wealthy family. She attended the finest schools and traveled extensively during her childhood. She was a debutante and a member of the most exclusive social circles. She was an attractive and sociable young lady, but she was not an intellectual and had no particular interest in going to school beyond college. Instead, she married well and settled down to a life of affluence and privilege. She concentrated on raising three children and doing a good deal of volunteer work.
>
> Lois had always felt vaguely guilty for being wealthy. She had read all the literature in which the wealthy were depicted as selfish and unsympathetic toward the plight of the poor. She had seen poverty in the course of her travels, and she had felt very guilty when she looked out the window of her four-star hotel to view the poor people in the streets struggling to make enough money to feed themselves. In college, she took a number of courses in political science, sociology, and women's studies that led her to believe that the wealthiest members of society were part of an institutionalized system of class exploitation that was perpetuated to maintain the privileged status of the rich through the exploitation of the poor. Lois also felt guilty because her lack of academic talent and interest made it seem to her that it would be difficult or impossible for her to pursue what she thought might be a socially relevant career, such as that of an activist social worker or a legal aid attorney who could take up the cause of the underprivileged and downtrodden members of our society.
>
> Lois's husband died young, when their children were still in college. His death left an immense void in her life. Her loneliness was exacerbated by the fact that the children had all gone away to college, so that most of the time she lived alone. There were times when she felt that she was being punished for having been born wealthy and never having done anything to redress the social inequities that she saw all around her.
>
> In the midst of her despair and self-deprecation, Lois heard an advertisement for a charity that helped children in underdeveloped countries by recruiting sponsors in wealthier nations who could provide donations that enabled the poor children to obtain good food and medical care, and to attend school. At first she participated in this charity by simply becoming a sponsor herself, which involved only a relatively small monthly donation. However, it was not long before she was solicited to make more substantial contributions, which she did. Eventually, she was approached by the executive director of the

organization to become a board member. This involved further, even more substantial monetary contributions, and it also involved attending meetings and participating to a limited degree in some of the organization's policy-making activities.

Lois's affiliation with this organization quickly became the most important part of her life. Her ever-increasing donations helped to alleviate the pervasive feelings of guilt that she had always had regarding her privileged position in society, and social contacts with other individuals who were on the board or otherwise active in the charity came to be her most important source of social contact. Lois also became infatuated with the director of the organization, an elegant-looking gentleman who had spent much of his career working for the United Nations Children's Fund. He was a dozen years her senior, and a widower. While he never made any romantic overtures toward Lois, he was always charming and flattering. He made her feel important and useful, and he saw to it that she was honored regularly in one way or another for her contributions of money and time.

The problem with all this is that Lois's role in this charity came to consume almost her entire life. She ended up giving so much money to the charity that her children became concerned about her future ability to support herself, as well as her ability to fund the rest of their college and graduate school expenses. They also became concerned about the possibility that Lois was giving away money that should rightly one day be included in their own inheritances.

In addition, Lois ended up spending so much time on the charity work and making such a large emotional investment in this organization that she closed off other possible avenues for social contact. Her children regarded her as relatively young, and they felt that she should be looking for a new relationship, and eventually even a new husband.

When they questioned her decisions and priorities, Lois first reacted somewhat angrily, suggesting that they were acting like "spoiled rich kids" and suggesting that they should adopt a more Christian attitude toward their fellow men. The kids were smart enough not to push too hard on this point. They loved her very much, and they did not wish to alienate her.

Eventually, the issue was satisfactorily resolved when the children appealed to the director of the charity to intervene with Lois. Fortunately, he was a good person who realized that not all the funding or all the volunteer work for the organization could or should come from one individual, no matter how generous (or how guilty) that individual felt. With his help, the kids were able to keep Lois's involvement at a very substantial but less than completely insane level, and eventually she did develop some additional outside interests and social contacts.

This example is not particularly dramatic, but it is very representative of the behavior of many affluent individuals who go to relatively less or more extreme lengths to prove to themselves and to the world that they are not interested only in themselves, but in their fellow man as well. The question is one of balance. Regardless of what our religious background might be, or even in the absence of any religious teaching, regarding the importance of caring for others and the desirability of engaging in acts of charity, we know that it is appropriate and uplifting to consider the needs of those who are less fortunate and to act to improve their situations. But we must also consider our own needs and the needs of our family members. We cannot allow our-selves to become so consumed with guilt because we are wealthy that we harm ourselves and our loved ones in our efforts to achieve retribution.

Whether you are a member of the "lucky sperm club" or you earned your money through hard work and personal creativity, you must avoid being led to believe that having wealth in and of itself makes you some kind of evil oppressor. You are allowed to enjoy your wealth, and you are not obliged to do any more than a less affluent person in the way of redressing social inequities. You did not personally cause the world to be unfair in the allocation of wealth, and it is not your personal responsibility to give up everything that you have been given or have earned in order to make the world right.

Do not get us wrong. We are not opposed to individuals engaging in chari-table works or making charitable gifts. Of course you may choose to contrib-ute some of your time and some of your money for the good of others. To do so is good for you and good for those whom you help. But these choices do not require that you give up doing things that you find personally satisfying or that you get rid of everything that you own.

Most religious faiths call upon their followers to redress social wrongs, and most religious faiths suggest that we give a certain percentage of our income to charitable works. But none of our religious and moral institutions ask us to assume that we are tainted by whatever wealth we may have accumulated, nor do any of the major religious faiths demand that we give away everything we have and become poor in order to satisfy a divine higher power or win the favor of our fellow men. Only we as individuals are likely to make such exces-sive demands on ourselves. Moreover, we are likely to make these demands only if we have accepted the ideas that wealth is inherently evil and that those who have wealth are, by virtue of that wealth alone, guilty of exploiting of all those who are less affluent.

"How Dare You Judge Me as Avaricious, Ruthless, or Untrustworthy?"

There is a widespread belief that anyone who has money must be avari-cious, ruthless, and untrustworthy. In Chapter 4, we considered examples of how the wealthy tend to be portrayed in literature and in the popular cul-ture as evil individuals who not only will stop at nothing to accumulate more wealth, but who also seem to enjoy hurting those from whom the wealth is seized. We mentioned Silas Marner and Ebenezer Scrooge, Snidely Whiplash from *Rocky and Bullwinkle,* and Charles Montgomery Burns from *The Simpsons.* These images make it very difficult for anyone who lives in this culture not to assume that wealthy people are avaricious, ruthless, and untrustworthy.

In Chapter 4 as well, I (JT) mentioned my grandfather's firm belief that contractors who worked for the wealthy had to "insure" themselves against the ruthlessness of their wealthy clients by overcharging them up front, and I also mentioned my former boss, Fred the salvage diver, who would work for the wealthy only if they paid him *in advance* and *in cash*. These examples are typical of how negative stereotypes regarding the wealthy lead some members of society to treat wealthy individuals in an unfair manner. Moreover, the wealthy themselves frequently internalize these negative stereotypes and accept the resulting mistreatment as "understandable." But of course, this leaves the affluent open to victimization. It leads at least some wealthy individuals to simply accept the fact that they will be treated poorly and get ripped off by the people whom they hire.

What we are saying here is that if you are a wealthy individual, you should not understand and accept the fact that people assume you are avaricious, ruthless, and untrustworthy. Rather, you should be justifiably outraged that people make the unwarranted assumption that you will not treat them fairly, simply because you have money. Obviously there are unethical people and ethical people in every income bracket, and no one who comes to your home to discuss work that needs to be done has any business charging you any more because you are affluent than he or she would charge someone with less money. Nor does any one who provides a service have any business requesting payment from you under terms that differ in any way from the terms he or she might require from any other client.

No one likes to be stereotyped because of his or her ethnicity or religion, and we have gotten to a point in societal evolution where few of us have any problem telling people who manifest such stereotypes where to get off. If I am Irish, I may very well take offense when someone says that Irishmen are drunkards. If I am a Jew, I do not want to be called a Shylock. If I am an African American, I am quite willing to show my displeasure if someone implies that my people are lazy. But the same sense of outrage does not seem to apply to manifestations of stereotypes regarding the affluent. If someone says that Mr. Smith is a rich old bastard who has the first dime he ever earned and has never been known to pay a bill on time or without complaining, we tend to let that comment slide.

The affluent have not acquired the status of a minority group, and they certainly have not acquired the status of a group that has been treated unfairly. On the contrary, the affluent are most often viewed as the group who hands out the unfair treatment. That is why the points that we have been making in this book are sometimes difficult to get across, even to the affluent themselves. However, think of it this way. If someone were to come right up to your face and tell you that you are avaricious, ruthless, and untrustworthy, you would probably have no difficulty telling them to go to hell. The problem is that when someone gives you an inflated price for work or demands payment in advance, he does not have to come right out and tell you what he is thinking about you personally because you happen to be wealthy. Even if you challenge a contractor on the price he is asking or the terms of payment he is demanding from you, he can say that there is nothing personal involved. It is simply that the cost of labor is driving up his price, and it is simply company policy to obtain payment in advance. Therefore, it requires a pretty firm conviction that you are being made the victim of stereotypical attitudes toward the affluent to even question the reasonableness of the price or the payment policy.

Obviously, if you have consciously or unconsciously accepted the stereotype as actually being true, the chances are pretty good that you will never challenge the contractor's price or payment policy. You will likely never say something to the effect that you are being overcharged simply because the contractor thinks that affluent people will be difficult to work with or difficult to obtain payment from. You will not say it because deep down inside, you believe that he may be correct in his stereotypical attitudes toward the affluent, and his pricing and payment policies may be justified.

"I Am Not Overly Demanding!"

If we accept the stereotypical attitude that the affluent tend to be overly demanding, we may bend over backwards to avoid appearing this way, and we may very well wind up behaving in a most unassertive manner. Consider this couple and their relationship with their building contractor:

John and Ali bought a 20-acre piece of property in the mountains and contracted with a local builder to construct their new weekend home there. The property was about a mile from the nearest hard road, and the existing electric utility lines went only about halfway down the gravel road that led to their lot. The site that they chose for the construction of their home was another quarter mile from the existing gravel road. Therefore they knew in advance that they would need to have the electric utility company extend the existing power line, and they knew that they would need to construct a rather long gravel driveway to allow them to get from the existing gravel road to their homesite. To complicate matters further, a pipeline company had a right of way that crossed their property, and they needed to put in their driveway across this right of way. This would require following the pipeline company's rules and specifications governing the proper manner in which to lay a road across a pipeline. In addition, of course, the builder would have to obtain all the necessary local building permits and arrange for all the required inspections of the new home over the course of the construction.

All of this was explained to the builder, who indicated that he knew the area very well and that he had very good working relationships with all the concerned parties. A plan for the home was agreed upon, and a price was negotiated. John and Ali signed a contract with the builder that called for work to begin within a month and specified that the home would be completed within four months from the start of construction. They paid the contractor one-third of the $375,000 price of the home at the time they signed the contract.

Another third was to be paid when the home was framed and sided. The final third was to be paid when the home was complete, the buyers were satisfied, and a certificate of occupancy had been obtained from the local building inspectors.

The contract was signed in mid-January 2006. John and Ali planned to put their present weekend home on the market that spring, so that they would be able to move directly from their old home into the new home as soon as it was completed. They also planned to use the proceeds from the sale of their old home to make the final payment on the new home.

The way things actually worked out, the spring was extremely wet, and the builder could not build the driveway to the new homesite because his heavy equipment would get stuck. The pipeline company would not approve the construction of the driveway across their pipeline until the land dried out and provisions could be made to shore up the ground around the pipeline to ensure that it would not be damaged when construction vehicles and cement trucks crossed over to get to the building site. For the same reason, the electric utility company could not get in when planned to put up the additional electric poles that were required, or to run the power to the homesite. By the time things had dried out sufficiently for these things to be done, the contractor was heavily into his busiest part of the year, and his crews were spread too thin to get the home built as quickly as he had planned. There were also some unexplained delays in obtaining the necessary building permits, and once construction began, there were some very serious errors in the timing of the purchase and delivery of necessary building supplies and equipment.

To cut to the chase, the work of putting in the roads, the power, and the home foundation carried over to the end of the summer, and the actual building of the house carried over through the fall. John and Ali regularly complained to their contractor that he was not meeting the completion dates specified in the contract, and that the delays were causing them much inconvenience and likely costing them money, since the housing market was slowing and they could not sell their old home until they could be sure that they would be able to get into the new one. The contractor kept reassuring them that he was going as fast as he could, yet they often found when they visited the building site that no one was there and that no one had been there for some time. The home was not actually completed until late in the following January, over one year after the contract had been signed. Even then, there were some things that needed to be fixed, and a certificate of occupancy had to be obtained. John and Ali were not able to actually move into their new home until the end of March 2007.

Unfortunately, the delay proved to be an expensive one, since the housing market in that part of the country had slowed down substantially. Whereas John and Ali had been told in the spring of 2006 that they would likely get about $260,000 for their existing home, when they were actually able to put it on the market the following year, they found they could get only $210,000. They considered renting the old home out until the housing market recovered some, but they really needed the money they would get from selling the old house to finish paying for the new one.

John's attitude toward the whole situation was one of resignation. He looked on the bright side, pointing out that the work on the home appeared to be of the highest quality, even though it was not completed in a timely manner. He rationalized that the builder could not have anticipated the wet spring or the difficulties he encountered trying to coordinate his efforts with the electric utility company and the pipeline company. John knew the builder pretty well, and he really did not want to be perceived as lacking in understanding or as overly demanding. He was inclined to simply allow that "shit happens." When he and Ali got the bill for the third and final payment on the house, it never occurred to him to do anything other than write a check and pay the bill.

Ali looked at the situation differently. She felt that the builder should have anticipated the possibility of a wet spring, and she felt that he had not done everything possible to expedite the efforts of the utility company, to obtain the required permissions from the pipeline company, and to make sure that all the required inspections took place in a timely manner. She also felt that he had been remiss in taking on more work than he could handle, given the size of his company and the number of crews he had working for him. She felt further that he had on several occasions waited too long to place orders for needed building materials and fixtures, and that time had been lost unnecessarily waiting for needed items to be delivered.

Ali felt that the delays had not only screwed up their lives for a substantial period of time, but had also cost them real money. She told John that she did not want to simply make the final payment as specified in the contract, but rather wanted to negotiate some form of settlement that recognized their losses. John was very apprehensive about her idea. He did not want to cause problems or to alienate the goodwill of the builder, who was, after all, a friend. He did not want to be perceived as one of those "rich weekend people" who came up to the mountains and expected to be treated like royalty, regardless of the curve balls that Mother Nature could throw one's way. But John trusted Ali, and he certainly valued her goodwill and affection more than the friendship of the builder.

So Ali called up the builder and politely and calmly explained her feelings to him. Much to John's surprise, the builder did not respond angrily, but rather acknowledged the difficulties and simply asked how much they wanted taken off the bill. A brief negotiation ensued, and Ali ended up getting the price reduced by $15,000. This did not fully cover the loss they had suffered due to the delay in the sale of the old home, but it certainly made both Ali and John feel better. They have remained on very good terms with the builder, who has already done additional work for them on the new property.

So here we see how accepting the stereotype that affluent people are overly demanding could have harmed John and Ali. John's desire to be accommodating would have cost them some serious money, and paradoxically it would not have made the builder like them any more or respect them any more. In contrast to the angry negative response to Ali's complaints that John had anticipated from the builder, he found that the builder felt her complaints were reasonable; and he respected them *more*, not less, because they had the nerve to express their feelings.

The moral here is that you cannot allow your behavior to be determined by your own hangups regarding your status as an affluent individual. Sticking up for yourself in matters of business is *not* the same thing as being unreasonably or inappropriately demanding. You cannot run your life effectively if all you do is run around trying to convince everyone that you are not like one of the "other" wealthy people who expect and demand that everything that is done for them will be done perfectly, regardless of the obstacles encountered, and who simply refuse to pay for anything until they are 100 percent satisfied. You must remember that you do not have to go out of your way to provide evidence that the stereotype of the affluent as overly demanding is false. What you have to do is to consider each business arrangement on its own merit, giving reasonable weight to the terms of the deal, the difficulties encountered, and the resulting satisfaction or distress that you experienced in connection with the service or product provided. Then you need to be appropriately assertive with the service provider, explaining your view of the situation, listening to his point of view, and working out an arrangement that is satisfactory to both of you.

"I May Be Helpless, but I Know Enough to See that What You're Asking for This Job Is Excessive"

One of the stereotypes that affluent people tend to buy into is the idea that they are pretty much incapable of performing a range of chores that other, less affluent people can perform. This idea stems from the fact that less affluent people have no choice but to do much of the work around the house for themselves, simply because they cannot afford to hire people to come in and do all that needs to be done. On the other hand, affluent people can afford to hire others to do these tasks. Furthermore, it is often cost effective for the affluent homeowner to hire others to perform certain tasks around the house, simply because the affluent individual can earn a good deal of money doing whatever it is that he does best in the time that it would take him to do the chores that he typically hires others to do for him. Unfortunately, such specialization tends to leave the affluent individual with no knowledge whatsoever of the tasks that he hires others to do for him, and this can place him in a position where he is rather easy to make fun of or take advantage of. Remember in Chapter 4 that I (JT) mentioned my uncle the mechanic and his warning to those who owned fancy cars to be very careful when they took the cars in to be worked on, since many mechanics rely on the lack of knowledge of car owners to charge them excessive fees to change imaginary parts.

Now, our advice to anyone who hires people with some special expertise to do work for them is to acknowledge that these specialists certainly know things that you do not know and that they can do things that you cannot do, but to always remember that their special skills are in fact not so special that you could not learn them, and they are not so special that there are not a number of other persons out there that you could hire to do the same job.

When I (JT) was younger, I had a house built for me in the Catskill Mountains. To save money, I did a good deal of the interior work myself. Part of what I did was to finish off the basement of the house, which had been left unfinished when the house was first constructed. In the course of this work, I had occasion to install windows, hang doors, run electrical wiring, do all the plumbing for a bathroom and for a utility/laundry room, put up paneling, install registers for heat from the downstairs woodstove to circulate to the upstairs of the house, and install a hung ceiling. I had friends who knew more than I did help me with many of these chores. In the course of this work, I learned a good deal. I am not sure that I learned enough that I could go out now and build a home, but I learned enough to know that most of the tasks involved in building a home are not all that complicated. With a little reading and a willingness to ask questions, most of us could learn to do most of the things that we typically hire people to do for us. We might not be able to do these things as efficiently or as neatly as the professionals, but we could learn to do them.

Therefore, when I am talking with a contractor today about some repair that needs to be done in the house or about an addition or some new construction, I feel as if I can have a reasonably intelligent conversation. I am not intimidated, and I do not feel that I am completely at the mercy of the contractor to charge me an excessive amount for a job, because I have at least an idea of how much time might be involved in doing the work. I also know that if I feel that a contractor is asking a rather large amount to do a particular job, I can always get an estimate from another contractor. Very few services are so specialized that a single provider has a monopoly and can charge whatever he likes.

Here again, the key element in determining the likelihood that you will get ripped off is the extent to which you have bought into the notion that affluent people are helpless. If you believe that you are helpless, you will tend to allow yourself to be taken advantage of by anyone whom you perceive as having some expertise in the job in question. You should always remember that even if you personally do not know how to do the job in question, the chances are that there are many people who do, and you are never so helpless that you cannot pick up the phone and get another estimate.

The importance of being cautious and being willing to shop around is illustrated by the story of Bob and Sarah:

HOW MUCH COULD THIS REALLY BE WORTH?

Bob and Sarah Parker are both attorneys. They each work for a major law firm in New York City. They are very highly paid, and they live in a beautiful loft in lower Manhattan. About five years ago, they inherited a weekend house in Southampton from Sarah's father. It is a beautiful home on three acres located just two blocks from the beach. Sarah's father was a widower who had come from a wealthy family and had made even more money through a successful career as a stockbroker. He had long ago retired from his career. Since the death of his wife, he had lived at the house in Southampton most of the time, although he had also kept a small apartment in the city. Before he died, Sarah's father had spent most of his free time gardening and meticulously caring for the Southampton house and its extensive grounds.

At the time of her father's death, Sarah had not been out to the house for nearly 10 years. Although the house was just a few hours from their loft in the city, she and John had been too busy with their careers to spend weekends out of town, and they saw Sarah's dad frequently when he came into the city. After the funeral and the reading of the will, it was several months before Bob and Sarah decided that they wanted to keep the house and start using it themselves, rather than just sell the property and take the money. Being city dwellers, Bob and Sarah did not give much thought to taking care of their new property. Before they actually went out to Southampton to spend a weekend at the house, the grass had grown very high, the garden had gotten full of weeds, and the place was clearly in need of care. When they saw the place, they knew that they would have to hire someone to come in to do some work.

They looked in the yellow pages, and they called a local landscaping company. They made an appointment for someone to come over to the house when they were there and give them a price for cutting the grass and tending the garden on a regular basis. The landscaper spent about an hour walking the grounds with them. He explained that his business philosophy was to provide a service that allowed the homeowner to never again have to worry about the grounds of his home. His landscape company would monitor the property, see what needed to be done, and do it all. The landscaper sent them a contract for maintenance that included the care of the lawns and the gardens, including routine fertilizing and replacement of shrubs and other plantings when necessary. The price that he quoted for this service was $1,700 per month.

This figure seemed very high to the city-dwelling couple, who really had in mind just getting the grass cut. So they sought estimates from two other local landscapers. In each case, the services that the landscaper thought should be performed were similar, and the other estimates ranged from $1,500 per month to $2,000 per month. Although they could certainly afford to pay this much for the landscaping service, it bothered Bob and Sarah that the price was so high. They had figured out that the bulk of the work to be done each month was cutting the grass, and they learned that fertilizing was done twice a year. They just could not see how these services should run into so much money. Bob kept asking, "But how much could it really cost to run a lawn mover for an hour or two and hire a couple of guys for minimum wage to rake and clean up after the lawn mower?" They realized that landscaping companies in Southampton were likely to charge top dollar for their services, but these prices seemed so high that they felt as if they would be getting ripped off. Being adversarial by nature and profession, they did not like the feeling of being ripped off, and they sought to avoid it.

Bob and Sarah did an experiment. They called a landscaping company that was two towns to the north, between Southampton and Sag Harbor. They got the owner on the phone and they said that they needed an estimate for getting their grass cut once a week. They explained that they had a three-acre piece of property that was flat. Sight unseen, this new landscaper gave them a figure of $600 per month to cut the grass and clean up. He also said that when the grass needed to be fertilized twice a year, he could do this for $300 each time. When they heard this, they had him come over to look at the place. He said that from time to time, they should also have the garden weeded. He suggested that this should be done about three times each year, and he said that he would charge them $200 each time to have his guys do that job. So the total cost for his services for a year would be $8,400. This compared to what would have been a total annual cost of $24,000 if they had hired the first landscaper who gave them a figure. They hired the "out of town" guy to do the job, and they have been completely satisfied with the service he provides.

Bob and Sarah have a strong suspicion that the local landscaping companies they contacted initially have some form of informal price-fixing arrangement, but of course, there is no way that they can prove this. Nor is there really any reason to, since their intelligent approach to the problem avoided the possibility that they would get ripped off. Since they have been occupying the house in Southampton, however, they have come to the conclusion that local service providers routinely assume that the wealthy homeowners in the town really do not care about how much they are charged for the chores that they need to get done. As a result, the fees that are typically charged for landscaping, plumbing, electrical work, paving, painting, and similar homeowner services are simply outrageous. It is therefore particularly important for homeowners in the town to be very careful in shopping for these services.

The tendency of landscapers to overcharge Southampton home owners is just one example of the type of consumer issue that faces affluent people all the time. Service providers tend to assume that people who can afford to pay unreasonably high fees for various services either cannot be bothered to look around to find better deals, or that they have some kind of perverse psychological need to pay exorbitant prices just to prove that they can. There is a tendency among service providers to view the affluent as "fair game." It is as if they believe that it is okay to charge affluent individuals outrageous fees, because they can afford to pay these fees. It is almost a public service, a form of redistribution of wealth.

"DON'T ASSUME I NEED TO PAY MORE"

There is also a widespread stereotypical belief among service providers and retailers that affluent individuals are simply not comfortable purchasing any goods or services that are not extremely expensive, because the affluent assume that the best service providers will naturally charge the highest fees, and the best products will naturally be the most expensive. This is the type of thinking that gives birth to the $500 haircut, $750 prix-fixe tasting menu, $800 shoes, $200,000 sports cars, and $6 million homes. All one needs to know on this subject can be learned by looking at the advertisements for insanely priced, impractical-looking clothing and jewelry that appear in the *New York Times*.

Obviously, no wristwatch in the world could justify a $100,000 price tag by virtue of the accuracy with which it keeps time or the fact that it is waterproof to 600 feet. It must be that the manufacturer who sets the price believes that customers will pay $100,000 for the watch, simply because the watch costs $100,000, and the customer believes that a watch of this price is appropriate for an individual who has the money and good taste that he or she has.

The fact that these companies stay in business and continue to support the *New York Times* advertising department is a clear indication that there must be enough affluent people in the world who do think this way and do buy these watches to keep the companies that make them profitable. Such consumers justify the stereotype of the affluent as materialistic, frivolous, and readily taken advantage of. Such consumers also perpetuate the practice of ripping off the affluent by charging outrageous fees for simple services and goods.

"Don't Tell Me What I Like to Do and What I Don't Like to Do"

I (JT) am certainly not wealthy, but between my professional wife and me, we have a pretty decent income that allows us to engage in many enjoyable activities such as going to the theater, dining in fine restaurants, and taking very nice vacations in some very fancy hotels and spas in different parts of the world. In other words, we have enough money that we have a great many options open to us as to how we want to spend our free time. So I have a question, or rather, I have a bunch of questions:

Why is it that my wife (like the people at *Travel and Leisure* magazine) views golf and tennis as appropriate activities for me, but she views my favorite pastimes of hunting, fishing, and wilderness camping with suspicion? Why is it that she ultimately categorizes these activities as somehow vaguely inappropriate? Why is it that she assumes that the guys I meet at the golf club are okay, but the guys I meet on the party fishing boat must be alcoholics who abuse their wives? Why is it that she asks me not to discuss hunting when we have dinner parties for friends, even though most of the men who attend these parties express great interest in my hunting? Why is it that she asks me to keep my taxidermy animals buried in a downstairs playroom or outbuilding? Why is it that she makes faces at me when a guest asks to go and see these animals?

Along the same lines, why is it that my wife views a soft-collared shirt with a polo player or a pig on the chest as okay, but she thinks that a soft-collared shirt with a deer head on the chest is not okay? And why exactly is it that she finds it so much more desirable to fly to Cabo San Lucas to spend a week at a fancy spa sitting in the sand under the hot sun than it is to spend the same amount of time driving to Black Lake, New York, to sit on a wooden dock where you can feel a cool breeze and catch fish at the same time? The answers to these questions are all the same.

My wife has internalized a set of beliefs and expectations regarding who she is, an affluent professional woman of good breeding, good manners, and good taste. Furthermore, these beliefs and expectations in large measure determine what activities she considers appropriate for a "woman such as herself." These same expectations also go a long way toward determining the people with whom she feels comfortable socializing, the clothes she feels comfortable wearing, and the places she feels comfortable vacationing.

One time I did convince my wife to come with me and spend a week bass fishing at Black Lake, but we left after four days because there "wasn't a good restaurant in the area" and the "novelty" of eating the fresh-caught bass and perch that I caught and cooked for her wore off in two days. She often talks with her friends about going to Cabo. All of her friends have been to Cabo, and all of them stayed at the same spa where we stayed. She does not often talk to her friends about going bass fishing at Black Lake. In fact, she *never* talks to her friends about going bass fishing at Black Lake. Her friends have not been there, and they will never go there. In all honesty, I would have to confess that I believe my wife would be just a bit embarrassed to tell her friends that we went bass fishing at Black Lake.

So I continue to do my bass fishing at Black Lake, either by myself or with my fishing buddy George. We talk about what my wife is missing by refusing to allow herself to appreciate the beauty of nature that we see on each new fishing trip. George and I speculate as to why sunset over the Pacific viewed from a beach chair at a spa in Cabo is beautiful to her, but sunset over Black Lake viewed from a seat in a bass boat just "isn't the same." I do not get it. I think she is missing something.

The other day, we watched a children's back-to-school fashion show on a morning TV program. The kids were dressed in stylish clothes of a type that I have never seen any child actually wear to school, even a rich kid going to a fancy prep school. I mentioned to my wife that if any kid really went to school dressed like these kids were dressed, he would surely be beaten up before the end of the morning. This comment elicited a response from my wife implying that I had spent too much time with my hunting buddies.

But the question I ask is, "Why limit yourself to any one narrow, culturally prescribed set of options for work, leisure activities, clothes, and travel?" If you are fortunate enough to have money, why would you allow it to *circumscribe* your options, rather than *enhance* them? The last time my wife criticized me for not dressing in an "appropriate" manner, she said that I would always be "an L. L. Bean kind of a guy." She viewed this as a mild rebuke. I responded sarcastically that I did not really like paying the high prices at L. L. Bean, since so many of the same types of clothing and footwear are available at Wal-Mart for so much less. She walked away saying that I was a hopeless case, a "redneck wanna-be."

But this is not really true. I do not need to buy everything I wear at Wal-Mart just to demonstrate that I am not a prisoner of the Sunday *New York Times* "Fashions for Men" issue. I just do not want to ever feel that it is somehow inappropriate or beneath my dignity to shop at Wal-Mart, if that is where I can get what I need. I wear Wal-Mart boots. I also wear a Rolex Submariner wristwatch. Neither is a statement regarding who I am. I wear both for the same reason: They work. My wife gave me the Rolex as a present 30 years ago, and it is the only watch I ever owned that I have not been able to destroy. So I keep it. The last pair of boots I bought at Wal-Mart cost me $24.00, and they do what they do just as well as my Rolex keeps time.

8

Raising Confident, Competent, and Connected Children

We have seen that affluence, on its own, can have significant negative consequences for children. As with Briana, the 16-year-old who was devastated because she did not receive the car of her choice on her birthday, affluence certainly can "spoil" children and distort their expectations. Growing up with wealth can leave young people with an unrealistic view of the world, an overwhelming sense of entitlement, a lack of motivation to accomplish anything on their own, and a condescending attitude toward people who have "less."

On the other hand, growing up in the culture of affluence can have the opposite effect. It can lead children to assume that they must be perfect in order to live up to the examples of high achievement that they have observed in their own families, neighborhoods, and social circles. These children may feel that nothing less than straight A's in school is acceptable. They may feel that they must get perfect SAT scores and be admitted to the most prestigious colleges. Yet, if they meet these high standards, they may still feel that they have not accomplished anything special, but have only done what everyone else in their social group has done, and what everyone has expected of them. If they do not meet these high standards, they may feel like failures. Moreover, during the struggle to meet these high standards, the children of the affluent may experience debilitating anxiety and/or other psychosomatic symptoms, or they may respond to the pressure by acting out, using substances, or otherwise rebelling.

The question we address here is, what can affluent parents do to help their children grow up to be confident, competent, and emotionally connected adults? The answer is that parents can do many things to nurture these qualities in their children. Almost every moment presents an opportunity for learning. The key is knowing how to make that learning happen. There are examples to be set, steps to be taken, expectations to be made clear, and agreements to be established.

Parents Can Set Positive Examples

First of all, if we want our children to be confident, competent, and connected in their lives, then we must set positive examples for them. Children learn from what they are exposed to and what we show them of our own behavior. Therefore:

(1) **Model Acceptance of Others and Others' Choices.** If you do not want your child to grow up with a sense of entitlement and superiority, then be mindful not to display these characteristics yourself, even in subtle ways. Don't behave in ways that suggest you and your family deserve only "the best" and that anything less is unacceptable. Even if you have developed a refined taste for certain things, you can share this with your child as just that, a refined taste, not a demand or expectation. Do not boast about expensive clothes or items you or your family may have, and certainly do not put down anyone who either cannot afford such things or chooses something different. Simply help your child recognize that different people have different tastes and different budgets, and everyone should make the decisions that best suit their own needs and circumstances. After all, the primary job of parents is to teach their children to be responsible, self-sustaining adults. So, be a positive role model and do not judge others based on the clothes they wear, the car they drive, the house they live in, or the places they vacation. If you hear your child or your child's friends make such judgments, use the moment as an opportunity to have a conversation with your child (and his or her friends as well) about how important it is to respect others and the choices they make.

(2) **Articulate Your Own Purpose in Life.** We all want our children to be motivated to thrive in their lives. Therefore, it is vital that we display such motivation ourselves. For many families, daily life is structured around children going to school and parents going to work. For some affluent families, there may be no objective need to work. Therefore, the daily structure may not include one or both parents going to work each day. If this is the case in your family, it becomes even more critical that you articulate your own purpose in life so that it is clear to your children and they can understand what drives you and the family.

Making your purpose clear may involve conversations with your children about how you choose into where and what you put your time and energy. What talents and skills do your children see you developing? In what activities do they see you participate? The answers to these questions should reflect values like the importance of lifelong learning and participation in activities that help and benefit others. Family money can be a blessing if it allows you the ability to develop passion and purpose. It can be a curse, however, if it robs you or your children of incentive or the desire to be creative, productive, and self-evolving.

(3) **Take Time to *Enjoy* Life.** Your children will know it is okay to develop a healthy balance between work and play when they see you doing it. You can pass along the ability to relax and appreciate life. This message is crucial to the children of the affluent, because relaxation is essential to the prevention of the performance anxiety, depression, and somatic illnesses that are so often associated with the intense pressure to compete and achieve. You need to let your children see you take "real" time off. You need to take vacations with them and *be* on vacation when you are there. If you are a "self-made person" who has worked very hard and achieved great success in life, then you owe it not only to yourself, but to your children as well to reflect on what you have achieved and the price you have paid for your accomplishments.

(4) **Teach Your Children to Learn from Their Experiences.** You need to have the courage to recognize and accept your own imperfections in order to teach your children to embrace and learn from their imperfections. You need to let them know that it is a part of learning and growing to get *any* score on a test, any grade on a paper, or any result from an audition or interview.

If your child brings home a test having received a mediocre grade, *do not* react impulsively and without further information by telling him or her that he could have done better. Do not say, "You know you could do much better than that if you didn't waste so much time talking on the phone at night." Instead, ask questions. Find out whether your child was disappointed. For example, you might ask, "Is that the grade you expected? How do you feel about it?" If you respond by simply telling your child that he or she could do better, your child will feel criticized and will likely respond defensively. No learning will occur. On the other hand, if you ask your child how he or she feels about the grade, your child is encouraged to think through what grade he or she wanted and how he feels about the result.

Children need us to structure opportunities for their self-discovery. You are better equipped to do that effectively when you are available to help them during homework time and to become familiar with who their teachers are and what they are learning in their various subjects at school. You also must make sure that you have *fun* with your children. If you find that it is difficult for you to do and you have forgotten *how* to relax, then schedule specific times each week when you do not allow yourself to work, but rather force yourself to do different activities and to be present with your family.

(5) Be Open to Different People and Participate in Diverse Activities. If you want your child to have a realistic idea of the world, then you must expose him or her to a great variety of people and experiences. Ask yourself, "Who are the adults that participate in my child's life?" If all the people with whom you or your family associate fall into only a few categories, then how will your child get to know anyone who is different? Critical to a child's ability to accept people of different backgrounds is to see that you do. They can see this when you appreciate, value, accept, and integrate many different people into the lives of your family.

Regarding diverse activities, ask yourself, "Where do we go and what do we do as a family?" If the only place you ever go is out to dinner, and the only thing you ever do as a family is go on vacations together, what message does this send to your children? And to what extent do your family activities contribute to increasing their exposure to people, places, and things? Consider activities that do not require money, such as going for a hike, riding bicycles, fishing, swimming, or "adopting" an older person or older couple in the neighborhood that your family helps because they live alone and do not have many visitors to help them.

Brainstorming with children about different kinds of activities that the family can do both for recreation and community service is a powerful exercise in and of itself. Children usually have better ideas than we do, but they need a forum in which ideas are exchanged and they are asked for input. Children of all ages derive enormous satisfaction when they experience their ideas coming to life!

(6) Be Considerate, Kind, and Respectful to Others. If you want your child to be considerate and respectful of others, then display these characteristics for them. Treat the people who work for you or with you with fairness and respect. If you observe your child, one of your child's friends, or another adult behaving disrespectfully toward an employee, a shopkeeper, a waiter, or any other person, say something! Use these moments as opportunities to talk about the negative effects of disrespect. Say something to your child about how poorly you feel they are behaving. If possible, say something to the disrespecting individual as well. That lets the person know you feel their behavior is unacceptable, and models for children that it is important to develop the *ability to respond* appropriately. It models taking action rather than practicing a passive approach of see nothing, hear nothing, do nothing. The important message for children is that *everyone is everyone's responsiblity.*

(7) Demonstrate Social Responsibility. If you want your child to have a social conscience, show a social conscience yourself. Be an active member of your community, and get involved in civic and/or charitable activities. Make it clear that there are things in life that are more important than only tending to the things you think you need or things you want. Let your children see you go out of your way to help others. Let them see how much satisfaction you derive from participating in such activities. They will follow your example, and they will feel better about themselves as a result.

Specific Steps You Can Take

Beyond setting an example for your children by behaving yourself the way that you hope they will behave, there are specific steps that you can take to help them develop confidence, competence, and connectedness:

(1) **Make Sure Your Children Have Responsibilities.** Regardless of how wealthy you are or how many people you may have working for you, it is essential that children have specific responsibilities and understand how their contribution to the family makes a difference. Children cannot learn responsibility if adults continue to do things for them that they can and should do for themselves. Responsibilities should be consistent with the developmental capacity of the child and should result from conversations and agreements that involve both the parents' expectations, as well as those of the child. Make a list with your child of all the things that need to happen in the house every day to keep it running smoothly. See for what chores your child would like to take responsibility. If they are not forthcoming, tell them you would be happy to choose for them.

Results from such a conversation might include some daily responsibilities for the children such as making their beds, tidying their rooms, taking out the garbage, bringing in the paper, changing the litter box, making lunches, etc. Of course, terms like "tidying" and "changing" the litter box have to be mutually defined and understood. In addition, children need appropriate training for any job they are asked to do. This is often overlooked and leads to a child's failed attempt to help. Agreements from these conversations might also include the child's contributing something they love to do that would also contribute to what needs to happen each day. For example, a child who loves the dog might be the very one to walk or feed the dog. Or a child who loves to cook might help with dinner preparations or coming up with weekly menus.

The specific nature of the responsibilities is not as important as the fact that there *are* responsibilities. While a boy from a less affluent family might be expected to cut the grass, you may have a landscaper who does that. That is okay. Maybe one of the children can work *with* the landscaper to learn about how to maintain a garden. Regardless, there will always be chores of daily living that need to be done, and it is essential that your children be involved in these tasks.

(2) **Give Your Children an Allowance and a Budget.** This becomes the laboratory within which children first learn about money and how to manage it. The allowance should be minimal and commensurate with their

age and household responsibilities. This makes the exchange concrete and understandable to a child. Otherwise, how will the child understand the meaning of money? Children need a frame of reference to understand why their allowance is one amount as opposed to another. The rationale behind the allowance has to make sense and be clear to the child.

Regardless of how wealthy you are, your children should always be aware that there are limits to how much they can spend. Children need structured opportunities to learn about money, how to earn it, how to spend it, and the relationship between the two. Who better to guide that process than you, the parent?

(3) Encourage Your Children to Work. Of course, whatever allowances you give your kids, the amount will not and should not buy everything that kids would like to have. This is okay. They can work. The chances are that if you are wealthy, they will need to work quite a bit to earn as much as their allowance, but that is good, too. As children mature, working for minimum wage or something close to minimum wage will teach them what life is like for most of the people in the world.

There is no other way to understand this except to really experience it. If a child has to work for 25 hours (at $8.00 an hour, the minimum wage in Connecticut) to be able to buy the jeans he wants, he will value those jeans far more than he would if he simply went to the store and used a credit card paid at the end of the month by his parents. Working helps children to appreciate everything that they have. Working outside of the home also introduces them to less affluent people, and it will put them in a position where they have a boss to whom they are responsible. They will need to be somewhere on time, and they will need to schedule their time to accommodate work along with the rest of their activities. All in all, working outside of the house for money that they can really call their own is a win-win situation.

(4) Encourage Your Children to Become Involved in Community Service Activities. When you engage in community service activities, encourage the participation of your children. Their participation in these efforts will not only give you both something positive that you can do together, but will also help your children learn that it is truly rewarding to help others. Given that young people these days tend to have very busy schedules with school and extracurricular activities, and given that we have also recommended that children do some kind of remunerative work outside the home, there may not be a great deal of time to devote to civic and charitable community service. Even a little bit will help. It will not only help them feel good about themselves. It will also enrich their lives by making them aware of how others live.

(5) Spend More Time with Your Children. We have seen that far too often, affluent adults are overextended. Many affluent professionals get to see their children for only a few hours on the weekends. We are certainly aware of the demands on your time and the exigencies of earning a living.

But in this life, balance is everything, and spending time with your children is extremely important. You cannot serve as an example to your children if you are not with them. You cannot demonstrate to them that you love them unless you spend time with them. You cannot share the events of your day with them, and they cannot share the events of their days with you, unless you spend time together. There may be other adults who take care of a variety of daily needs such as cooking, cleaning, or driving, and these can become positive relationships for children, but that is different. They are not *you* and cannot replace time children need with their parents.

(6) Do Not Allow Your Children to Be Alone and Unsupervised, either at home or away from home. Latchkey children get into trouble. Most adolescents who abuse substances get started when they are left home unattended. So even if one or both parents cannot be present when your children are at home, make sure that someone is, or make sure that your children are enrolled in some supervised activity. As children get older, many will attempt to push the limits. They may ask to go out on their own on weeknights, go to the movies with their friends, or sleep over at a new friend's house.

These questions are often asked under pressure at the last minute with a great deal of urgency. They will argue with you and tell you that their homework is done and they are doing well in school and you are "the *only* parent who doesn't allow their kids to do what I am asking." Their arguments can be very compelling, if only by virtue of the passion with which the arguments are presented. Therefore, it can be difficult to hold your ground unless you have your own compelling rationale for maintaining it.

It is a good policy that no decisions about "first-time" activities should be made without advance planning and conversation. If a child is asking for the first time if he or she can go out on a weeknight, you might say, "What do you know about the rules on weeknights?" Let the child tell you that there is no going out on weekdays. Then you could add, "And what do you know about what needs to happen if you want to discuss changing a rule or having an exception to the rule?" It should be established that any changes or exceptions to general ground rules necessitate a meeting with mom, dad, and child. The idea is to have a structure in place that makes clear how and when decisions are made and by whom, so you are not constantly stuck in a situation of deciding yes or no in the heat of the moment.

Just think back to my (OC's) patient Sandra, who found the time to be an honor student and still prostitute herself at the mall on weekday nights. Children tend to do what we expect of them, and Sandra was no exception. Her parents expected her to do well in school, and she did. They did not make it clear to her what they expected beyond that. They allowed themselves to become emotionally distant from their daughter, and they failed to set limits for her protection. Do not make this mistake, no matter how loudly your children protest against your restrictions.

(7) Encourage Your Children and Acknowledge Their Efforts. Children of all ages need encouragement to grow. Always ask your child first how he or she feels about something he has done, whether he has succeeded in an endeavor or failed. This teaches children to evaluate themselves unencumbered by your evaluation of them. Whether you agree or disagree with their self-evaluation, you should always acknowledge and recognize their accomplishments and their effort. Do not tell them that they have done a good job when they have actually done little or nothing, but make sure that you do not fail to recognize them when they have really put in an effort. Then, really make a big deal out of it.

We are not big fans of propping up children's self-esteem by rewarding them or praising them gratuitously when in fact, they have put forth little or no effort. The fact of the matter is that your child will be very much aware of how hard he or she has worked at a particular task, and he or she will be completely aware that a race has only one winner. So you must be honest and real with your feedback to your child. However, when you feel that your child really has tried very hard, tell him or her that you are proud of their effort. And if they actually won a race, tell them that you are proud of their victory. Your rewards will give them the incentive needed to try hard the next time and may very well propel them to another victory.

(8) Support Your Children When They Fail. When your children fail, you should support them. This applies regardless of the reason for the failure. Whether they have come up short because of a lack of effort, because another competitor was more skilled, or because they simply made a mistake, help them understand that failing and making mistakes is a crucial part of learning. The best learning opportunities happen when we spend the time on the mistakes our children have made and help them express and understand what went wrong and how they might do something differently the next time if they want a different result.

The trick, however, is that this reflection has to come from within them. If it comes from the parent, it restricts the learning because it can easily be understood as judgment or criticism. The parent's role here is to facilitate the conversation and provide feedback and support.

It is always important that your feedback is real. If your child did not put forth much of an effort, you should not say that he or she did. Children know when that is not true, and it is a confusing message. If your child tried very hard and was simply overmatched, just be honest and say, "You gave it your best shot. The competition was really good. There will be another day and another opportunity to try your best."

If your child fails at something really important, such as not getting accepted by the college of his or her choice, you should be honest about this as well. You need to acknowledge his or her disappointment, acknowledge his or her effort, and put the setback in perspective. For example, if your son gets into his second-choice school (say, NYU) but not his first-choice school (say, Penn), after asking them how they feel about it, you might say something like: "I know you're disappointed at not getting into Penn, but you're a good student and you worked hard and you got into a great college. I'm proud of how hard you've worked, and I'm proud of what you've accomplished."

(9) Provide Consequences to Your Children When They Misbehave. No matter how good your kids are in general, there will be times when they misbehave. Misbehaving, like making mistakes, is a part of learning and growing. The issue here is not that children should not misbehave, but rather, when they do, how do you help them learn from it? Children need help understanding that there are consequences for their actions. If you do not get this message across early in their lives, it gets harder to learn later on in life, and the consequences become naturally greater. It is important that you establish with your children some basic ground rules and the consequences they can expect when those rules are broken. Consequences should not be unexpected or decided in the moment. The first time a child misbehaves in a certain way, one that has not been taken into account in the basic ground rules, you and the child should establish together that from this point forward, this behavior will have an agreed-upon consequence.

Whenever bad behavior requires a consequence, it is very important to help the child understand exactly what he or she has done wrong and why he or she is receiving the particular consequence. It is sometimes useful to ask the child first what consequence he or she thinks would be appropriate, given the offense. Often a child responding to this question will come up with something more creative and effective than you had in mind.

(10) Teach Your Children to Respect Authority. Given the prevailing stereotype that the wealthy can often *buy* their way out of trouble with the law and/or hassles with regulatory agencies, it is very important to convey to your children when they are young your own respect for the law and for the policemen and policewomen who enforce the law. You want to immunize your children against the idea that they can get things "fixed" because they come from an affluent family.

We know from experience that affluent parents can sometimes behave as if rules do not apply to *them*. They can avoid consequences by paying someone a little extra or accessing an influential person to help them cut through the red tape. When mimicked by children, this way of responding to rules and consequences can be dangerous. You can set a good example by observing laws even if you have reason to think you should not: laws such as wearing your seat belt, obeying traffic laws, complying with various town ordinances, and paying your taxes. It is quite appropriate to teach your children to be assertive and to stand up for their rights, but it is critical that you let them know that there are appropriate and inappropriate ways to assert oneself.

(11) Become Involved in a Religious Congregation of Your Choice and Insist that Your Children Attend as Well. Whatever your understanding of God might be, you and your children will both benefit immensely if you make conscious efforts to incorporate spiritual development into the family. In 2009, Ben Stein lamented on the CBS *Sunday Morning* show that we have become "an atheist country," and that since we have taken God out of our schools, we find ourselves more and more asking "why our children have no conscience, why they don't know right from wrong, and why it doesn't bother them to kill strangers, their classmates and themselves."[1] Stein pointed out the irony that people trash God, but then wonder why the world is going to hell.

But as individuals, we still have the right to expose ourselves and our children to the moral and ethical teachings that characterize the major religions. We believe that this is a very good idea. Studying the beliefs of any religion involves confronting the more negative impulses that we may sometimes feel and considering a system of beliefs that encourages more positive thoughts and actions. We believe that children benefit when they have this opportunity. Even if they chose to reject some of the religious teachings to which they are exposed and ultimately follow a more unique personal path, they have nevertheless had an opportunity to give some serious thought to important moral and ethical questions. In addition, membership in a religious congregation provides a positive social experience for young people. Being a member of a church or synagogue puts children into contact with similar-age peers whose parents are similarly concerned for their spiritual development.

Finally, most religious faiths encourage community service, and we have already made the case that such service is beneficial and enriching to people on many levels. Therefore we strongly encourage affluent parents to become affiliated with their religious communities and encourage their children to participate in the activities that the congregation offers for young people.

MAKE YOUR EXPECTATIONS CLEAR

In the previous sections of this chapter, we recommended a series of fairly specific steps that affluent parents could take to help their children avoid the social and psychological pitfalls associated with affluence and become confident, competent, and connected adults. We suggested that as parents, you should model good behavior by accepting others and the choices they make, while at the same time articulating your own purpose in life, taking time to enjoy life and your children, being open to different people and activities, being considerate, kind, and respectful to others, and being socially responsible. We also suggested that parents take specific steps to encourage the healthy psychosocial adjustment of their children by giving them responsibilities, teaching them to be financially responsible, encouraging them to be socially responsible, spending time with their children, acknowledging their efforts and comforting them in their disappointments, teaching them to abide by the rules and follow authority, and encouraging their spiritual development.

Here we simply wish to acknowledge that actually modeling these behaviors and performing these actions would demand major changes in the lives of many readers, and would concomitantly introduce major changes into the lives of their children. We do not expect that every reader will run right out and implement all these recommendations. However, to the extent that readers do implement some of them, we want to point out that it is important to be clear with your children what is happening and why you are making these changes.

You need to sit down with your children and explore with them what they understand about socioeconomics. What knowledge do they have regarding the differences between the incomes of different families? You should ascertain whether they are even aware that their family is more affluent than the average family, and you should attempt to find out whether they have noticed that this reality makes a difference in how they treat people or how people treat them.

You could say that you have been doing some reading and thinking about this issue, and that the changes you are considering represent your best efforts to facilitate the health and well-being of the family, and especially them, the children. You could propose the idea of a family meeting to brainstorm ideas with them on ways to implement some of the changes you have in mind and to solicit new ideas from them. Once you have enlisted them in the idea of a family meeting and established a time and place for it, you are ready to proceed to the final step.

FAMILY MEETINGS

Family meetings provide an excellent environment to model, teach, and implement many of the recommendations we have made to parents in this chapter. These meetings require that the family spend time together; discuss thoughts, issues, and feelings; problem solve; and establish agreements. The family meeting includes everyone in the family regardless of age. All family members participate as they can, given their ages. These family meetings foster a sense of belonging and the value of everyone's contribution to how the family functions.

Family meetings are most effective when they are held regularly. The younger children are when you start holding meetings, the better. However, it is never too late to begin. The first family meeting might be dedicated to ascertaining the ideas that everyone has regarding the best time, place, and frequency for family meetings. You might elect a facilitator or develop a rotating system. You might also elect a "recorder," someone who writes down those things that are agreed upon in the meetings. This should be done in a special notebook dedicated to family meetings or family agreements.

One way to encourage participation in family meetings is to include fun decisions in the agenda, such as where everyone would like to go on the next family vacation or what sport the whole family would like to learn together, or decisions regarding a family party. Every family meeting should begin with some kind of "check-in" procedure. This procedure might involve going around and having each person either say how they are, or share something that is going on in their lives, or acknowledge someone else in the family for something they have done.

There should be an agenda for each meeting. Generally speaking, having just a few items on the agenda is better than having a large number. Having fewer items allows each family member to have input and allows adequate time for discussion and resolution of differences. Having too many items on the agenda tends to raise issues without resolving them satisfactorily.

Practice over time develops success at these meetings. Do not get discouraged if the first meeting or two feels like it is ineffective or not flowing. It can become a challenge to the family to make the family meetings work. Nuances of how to conduct meetings will vary from family to family, but the central idea remains the same. Below are some ideas for topics to address and examples of what the resulting agreements might look like between you and your children. You should tailor this list to focus on the issues that are the most relevant, given the ages of your children. You should also include other issues not listed here and invite the children to add items that reflect important or relevant issues to them.

Agenda Item 1: What is the family expectation for "acceptable" behavior both among each other and outside of the home?
Agreement 1 (example): All feelings are acceptable and need to be expressed *respectfully*. Respectful means using acceptable language (establish what this is for your family) and using only words. Being physically aggressive, hitting, or bullying is not acceptable. We all agree to be considerate, kind, and respectful to our peers, teachers, parents, and children.

Agenda Item 2: What are the family expectations regarding homework?
Agreement 2 (example): Homework gets started after a short break when kids get home from school. If anyone needs help with homework, Mom or Dad will be home on school nights by 7:00 to be available for helping.

Agenda Item 3: How does our family handle allowance and spending money for kids?
Agreement 3 (example): Mom and Dad (parents) will give kids an allowance of _____ (agreed-upon amount depending on age) each week, to be used for _____. (Allow your child to think through what they want to spend their allowance on—it provides an opportunity to discuss and think

---

through what they value.) Kids agree to live within the budget afforded by our allowance. If we want something special that we cannot get with our allowance and we are old enough, we will work (at home or outside home) to earn money and save the money for what we want.

Agenda Item 4: What are the family rules about curfew, going out, and sleepovers?

Agreement 4 (example): Kids (applicable to teens) are not allowed to go out after dinner during the week. Kids need to give a day's notice to ask about going out or having a sleepover. Mom and Dad will not give permission at the last minute (if kids ask, they will say no). Mom and Dad have to know and confirm there is adult supervision wherever kids are going.

Agenda Item 5: What are the family expectations about chores?

Agreement 5 (example): All kids have two or three household chores, which change each month at family meeting. Chores include (for example) helping to prepare dinner/set the table, helping to clean up dinner/load dishwasher, feed cat, feed dog, walk dog, take out recycling, take out garbage, and empty dehumidifier. Kids get their allowance only if their chores are done.

Agenda Item 6: What are the family expectations about going to church/synagogue or other house of worship and participating in their youth program?

Agreement 6 (example): Kids agree to attend house of worship regularly and participate in the youth program (or another youth program if the religious institution does not have one). When kids are at the appropriate age for their given faith, they can choose if they want to be confirmed (have a Bar Mitzvah, etc.) and continue their involvement.

Agenda Item 7: What are family expectations about school performance and grades?

Agreement 7 (example): Kids will do their best to do well in school and in their extracurricular activities. They will work hard to develop their talents and to accomplish meaningful goals. We will also accept any limitations we may have that make any of us feel less than perfect in certain areas. We will not get down on ourselves if we are not "number one" at everything. We will allow ourselves to have fun!

Agenda Item 8 : What are family expectations about what to do when something is bothering or upsetting you (or if you are in some kind of dilemma/crisis)?

Agreement 8 (example): Kids agree to let one of their parents know if they are having a problem or are upset by something.

Obviously, depending on your child's age and personality, and depending on which of our suggestions you feel might work for your family, the agreements that are reached will vary. We are simply saying that it is a good idea to discuss with your children the fact that you have had some insights regarding the issues associated with the fact that children are affected (sometimes negatively) by their family's income level, and that you would like to take steps to deal with these issues as a family. Family meetings are a great way to begin and guarantee that there is a forum where all family members have a voice, and mutual expectations will be discussed, be agreed upon, and be unambiguous.

It is our sincere belief that your choosing to follow some variation of the suggestions in this chapter will improve your children's chances of growing up confident, competent, and connected.

9

Relationship Issues among the Affluent

In Chapter 4, we mentioned that the affluent often experienced problems in connection with interacting and socializing with less affluent persons. These issues included: (1) the possibility of being viewed in terms of negative stereotypes of the wealthy by community members and associates with whom one naturally interacts; (2) possible awkwardness in socializing that could occur when you can clearly afford to spend much more than those with whom you are spending time; and (3) doubts regarding the motivations of individuals who might approach you socially, including the idea that "he (she) only wants me for my money."

These issues may become even more significant when one focuses on developing and maintaining close long-term relationships. Moreover, relationship issues may arise within affluent couples as a result of wealth itself, even when both parties are affluent. In this chapter, we want to consider how affluent individuals can minimize the negative impact of such problems. We have structured the chapter in such a manner as to reflect the life span, with sections on relationship-oriented issues that may arise in relation to: (1) dating; (2) marriage; (3) raising children; (4) repartnering or remarrying; and (5) your estate.

Dating

When to Reveal One's Affluence

We mentioned in Chapter 4 that many affluent college students make it a point to hide the fact that their families are wealthy, because they feel that members of the opposite sex may approach them socially for the wrong reason. They are afraid that they will be approached or treated nicely not because they are interesting and attractive, but simply because they have money. We have worked with young people who consciously choose to live in a more modest apartment than they can afford, or drive a more modest car, or avoid spending much money on clothes or on entertaining, specifically because they do not want to give potential romantic interests any hints regarding their actual financial status.

This strategy does seem to provide some reassurance to affluent young people when they are just meeting new people, or when they are going out on a first or second date. Clearly, however, as dating relationships develop and progress, it will become more and more difficult to avoid having one's financial status become apparent. People naturally ask you questions about where you grew up and where you went to high school. At some point, your date will probably ask you about your parents—maybe just about how you like them, but also more than likely about who they are and what they do. New friends are also quite likely to ask you what you like to do for fun, and they will be curious about the places you have been.

These are perfectly normal questions, and you certainly should not interpret them as a specific effort to extract data from you on your family's financial status. Although we certainly understand any desire you may have not to flaunt your wealth as a means of attracting attention, we strongly believe that you should be honest when you answer such questions. To be less than honest is to convey the message that your distrust of others' intentions is your paramount concern in making new acquaintances, and this would be likely to be perceived as reflecting poorly on you. So if you have gone to a fancy private school, if your dad is a partner in a major investment banking house, if your primary leisure activity is racing yachts, or if you spend summers in the south of France, you should not lie about these aspects of your life. It is better to be truthful from the start. In any case, it will become clear soon enough that there is money behind you.

So when a new friend asks questions about your background and interests, be candid. At this point it will be up to you to get to know your new friend better and to make judgments regarding his or her entire personality and character, including a judgment as to whether or not there might be any hidden agenda in his or her interest in you. It is really important as you get to know someone that you are not paranoid regarding their motivations. You should realize that it is not necessarily a bad thing if a potential partner considers your wealth a plus. All other things being equal, your wealth *is* a plus.

It is a plus not only to a potential partner who is less affluent than you, but also to a potential partner who is similarly affluent. So the point of not flaunting your wealth specifically to attract someone is not to find a partner who is looking to establish a relationship with a poor person. The point is simply to avoid attracting anyone who would want to develop his or her relationship with you *primarily* because of your wealth. And if you have not made your finances obvious at first glance, you have probably already weeded out any potential partners who might be attracted to you solely on the basis of money.

For this reason, as you spend more time with someone, getting to know them and discussing the things that are important to the two of you, you should not hesitate to include in these discussions what it means to have money and what each of you would hope to do with your life. By really getting to know a potential partner's values and goals, you will be able to make a judgment as to whether or not this is someone with whom you might want to spend time, perhaps the rest of your life.

By the way, there is another reason why an affluent individual might wish to avoid making flashy displays of his or her wealth early in the course of a relationship. If a potential partner is not affluent, your affluence may make him or her *un*comfortable. Your new friend may not be used to going to fancy restaurants or black-tie parties. The friend may feel out of place if you take him or her to expensive clubs or restaurants, and as a result, the friend may shy away from developing the relationship. Here again, as you get to know someone, you need to feel them out regarding such possibilities. You need to find out what wealth means to them down deep. Do they regard wealth as a mere external aspect of one's life that is nice if you have it, or do they regard wealth as defining one's whole personality and worth as an individual? Are they so wrapped up in locating themselves along the continuum of affluence that they neglect to define themselves in terms of other aspects of personality, such as health, having a happy outlook on life, having goals to work toward, and having causes to which they can devote their creative energies? Obviously, you want to cultivate your relationships with people who have a balanced perspective regarding the meaning of wealth. You do not want to get too close to individuals who regard wealth as a character flaw, and you do not want to get too close to individuals who consider wealth to be an absolutely essential characteristic of anyone who would become a friend or love interest.

WHO PAYS FOR WHAT?

Both before and after your affluent status is clear to a new friend, the question of who pays for what will come up. We live in an age of gender equality, and many women feel that they should pay their own way on a date. They feel that it is demeaning to them and unfair to their date if they do not share the expenses of the evening's entertainment. This issue is one that needs to be worked out by all dating couples, since both females and males vary in terms of how traditional they are or how modern and politically correct.

The issue is compounded when one or both of the two members of the couple are very wealthy. In the case where the male is very affluent, a female dating partner may feel doubly obligated to share in the expenses, both as a statement of gender equality and as a statement that she intends to pull her own weight financially, despite his wealth. Alternatively, some women who might feel strongly obligated to share in the entertainment expenses when they were on a date with a man of modest means might not feel so strongly about this if they perceived their date as very rich. And what if the female in the dating couple is very wealthy? It is possible that she might feel as if she wants to carry the greater burden in regard to entertainment expenses. If this is the case, how does the less affluent male feel about being "taken out"?

Obviously, this is a complex issue with many permutations, as dictated by the combined effects of: (1) his financial status; (2) her financial status; (3) his position along a traditional vs. modern continuum; (4) her position along this same continuum; and (5) the degree of communication and compromise in effect between the couple. We cannot give you guidelines to follow, because we cannot know where you and your dating partner(s) of the moment might fall with respect to any or all of these dimensions. What we can do, however, is to urge you not to take the question of who should pay for what for granted. Do not just assume that you will pay, or that your dating partner will pay, or that you will split the bill. These are things that need to be discussed. After all, these discussions may well pave the way for discussions of much weightier financial decisions that might need to be made, should your relationship progress to the point that you decide to cohabit or marry.

MARRIAGE

ALLEN AND TRISH

Allen, a 20-year-old who had just completed his junior year at Dartmouth College, was the son of a wealthy manufacturer from Nashua, New Hampshire. He and his two brothers had attended a prestigious private preparatory school, and all had been very good students. The oldest brother, Jack, had decided at an early age that he wanted to become a physician. He had graduated from Dartmouth last year and now was attending a first-rank medical school. Allen was the middle brother. He was less cerebral than Jack, but still a very good student. He was gregarious and a fine athlete, and he was the president of his senior class in high school. He was majoring in economics and preparing for a career in international banking. Allen's younger brother Seth was more artistically inclined. He had just graduated from the same preparatory school that his father and brothers had attended. He had flirted with the idea of going to the Rhode Island School of Design for college, but in the end he chose to continue the family tradition of going to Dartmouth, because he was really not sure what he wanted to do professionally, and he felt that Dartmouth would allow him to keep all his options open.

All three of these brothers had been raised with the expectation that they would work during their summers. Their father had turned his father's small company into a very large company, and he considered himself to be a self-made man. He did everything in his power to teach his sons the value of hard work and the feeling of satisfaction that comes after a productive day. He had obviously succeeded in the sense that the boys all did work every summer and did develop a good work ethic. They had worked at various summer jobs in and around their father's manufacturing plant. They had shown up regularly and done whatever work had been assigned to them. They had earned money that they used as discretionary spending money. Over the years, they had been assigned positions of increasing responsibility, and they had responded well to the challenge. Their dad reasoned that this aspect of their upbringing must have been a success, because they were all doing very nicely academically, and they all appeared to have bright futures.

This was the first summer that Jack would not be working around the factory, since the medical school he was attending was on a 12-month schedule. Allen had sufficient experience with the company that his summer job was now that of coordinating the company's public relations activities, including the organization of a large company-sponsored charity golf event that took place over Labor Day weekend.

In the course of his summer work, Allen met Trish. Trish was a summer intern in the company's art department, and they worked together developing the posters that were used to promote the tournament. Trish would be entering her junior year at Colby College. She planned to go to graduate school in design, and she hoped to work in the advertising industry. Trish had obtained her summer job at the company with the help and encouragement of her father, who was a long-time employee of the company in the manufacturing production division. Her dad ran a computerized circuit board fabrication machine. Allen's dad was his boss, although they were so many levels apart in the company hierarchy that they had never actually met.

Allen and Trish fell in love almost at first sight. They had a great deal in common. They were both attractive and intelligent. They were both very sociable. They both liked sports, both participating in sports and watching sports on TV. They were both Red Sox fans. They had great chemistry and were insanely attracted to each other. It didn't take long before they realized that their relationship was serious, and they began talking about the future. They both wanted to settle down in a big house in the country, and they both wanted to have a large family. They wanted to teach their kids to love sports as they did.

Allen brought Trish home, and his parents liked her very much. They did not want Allen to rush into marriage, but they felt right away that he could do a lot worse. Trish brought Allen home, and Trish's parents liked him very much as well. They told Trish from the start that it made them a bit uncomfortable to think that her boyfriend was so wealthy and that his dad was her dad's boss, but they also said that they could not help but like him.

Allen and Trish became engaged during Christmas vacation the year they met, and they were married shortly after Trish graduated from college. Allen applied to business school in New York, because they knew that if they lived there, Trish would be able to attend the Parsons School of Design. He had originally hoped to go to Wharton in Philadelphia, but New York worked out better for the two of them. Following his graduation from business school, Allen worked for a year for an international bank in New York. When Trish had completed her master's degree in design, the two of them moved back home, where they both worked for Allen's father's company. Allen gave up on his idea of the career in international banking, partly because his year working for a bank in New York was not nearly as exciting as he had hoped, but primarily because he and Trish could both get great jobs with his dad's company. Also, given the different vocational interests and plans of his brothers, Allen anticipated that in due course he would assume the responsibility of running the family business. Allen and Trish went on to have a very happy life together, with the home they wanted and the children that they hoped for. In short, they lived happily ever after.

However, their path was not an entirely easy one, nor did they travel it without incident. In addition to all the normal decisions that new couples need to make after they marry, such as the question of how to accommodate the educational and career plans of both spouses, Allen and Trish had to deal with issues related to the differences in their families' circumstances. Of course, they had to contend with the awkwardness associated with the meeting of the future in-laws. All new couples experience this. But here, the normal questions as to whether their parents would get along were compounded by the great differences in wealth of the two families, and by the fact that Trish's dad was an employee of Allen's dad. Their engagement party and their wedding were very different from what Trish's family would have done had she married a young man of more modest means. The guest lists were huge, and the functions were far more lavish than anything that Trish's family had ever even attended, much less hosted. And of course, Trish's mom and dad were in no position to pay for these events. Therefore everyone had to sit down and discuss why the events had to be as large and lavish as they were, and all had to agree that Allen's dad would pay for the events. Fortunately, the in-laws got along rather well and worked everything out without any ruffled feathers. Allen and Trish were very fortunate in this regard. Sometimes pride takes over and in-law relations become very rocky.

Similar issues surrounded the choice of a honeymoon location, the purchase of the couple's first home, and eventually the gifts and contributions that Allen's parents made to the grandchildren. While it was quite obvious that both Allen and Trish would get jobs in the company because of their relationship to the owner, there were also some delicate questions that arose later on when Trish's dad got a promotion. Trish's dad had to deal with comments from his fellow workers implying that he was receiving preferential treatment, which indeed may well have been the case. Certainly he was a good deal more visible to the company management hierarchy after his daughter's marriage to the company's heir-apparent than he had been before their marriage.

The experience of Allen and Trish illustrates a number of concerns that affluent young people must address when they begin to think about marriage. Obviously, any young adult contemplating a first marriage will have a large number of issues to consider and work through. However, a young adult who is wealthy will have not only these "regular" premarital issues, but also important additional issues to consider and work through.

These wealth-related issues are serious. We have even heard some affluent young people express doubt as to whether they would ever marry, given the difficulties that they felt could arise as a result of their wealth. These included the idea that they must take steps to protect themselves in the event of a future divorce, as well as the idea that they would need to discuss with parents and/or other sources of family wealth almost every aspect of their family financial life, including such issues as determining their household budget, determining the extent to which their potential new spouse would be involved in major financial decisions, and establishing trust funds for children they might have.

The issue of a potential divorce somewhere down the line is certainly worth considering. No one goes into a marriage with the idea that it will fail, but the reality of the situation is that the majority of marriages do not last a lifetime. This reality raises the issue of a possible prenuptial agreement. Of course, no one contemplating a marriage wants to bring up this subject with a prospective spouse, for fear of raising the question of whether they are experiencing doubts regarding the long-term future of the marriage. However, it may be unrealistic to fail to consider all eventualities. We will consider further the topic of prenuptial agreements later in this chapter.

Assuming that an affluent individual does decide to marry in spite of these annoyances, additional issues arise. There is the question faced by Allen and Trish regarding who will decide what type of wedding there will be and who will pay for it. There is the issue of where the new couple will honeymoon and where they will live. There may be an issue surrounding the question of whether one or both spouses will work, and there may be related issues such as whether one or both of the new spouses will be expected to join in an existing family business.

When children arrive, there will be other wealth-related questions to be answered. Will there be a nanny? Will the children attend public school or private school? Will the kids be expected to go to the same summer camps that the children of the family have attended for generations? Will they be expected to attend the same schools? And, in connection with all these questions, the question of who will pay may arise. The whole issue of how much personal wealth each spouse has and how much financial support is available from wealthy family members comes into play. Will one or both of the members of the new couple attempt to assert their independence by assuming the financial responsibility for their household, or will a flow of family funds be required and/or expected to supplement their expenses? If such a flow is anticipated, is anything expected in return?

When kids arrive, the whole issue of the role of the grandparents will surface. This issue may be complicated if one set of grandparents is rich and the other set is poor. The couple will therefore have the standard question that most couples have regarding how heavily involved the grandparents should be in caring for grandchildren, and in paying for things for the grandkids such things as toys, vacations, camps, and school tuition. But then on top of this general question, they may well have the additional questions that arise when one set of grandparents can give the grandchildren so much more than the other set. Will the poor grandparents feel that the wealthy ones are buying the affections of the grandchildren and in so doing alienating the grandchildren from themselves? And what about family functions where both sets of grandparents are present? Will they have common ground? Will they get along?

In the paragraphs that follow, we consider some of these issues surrounding first marriages that affluent individuals must consider.

WHETHER TO MARRY AT ALL

More and more affluent young people are simply deciding not to marry at all. Marriage is certainly not a prerequisite to sex these days, and many couples simply choose to move in together without benefit of marriage. Given the extra hassles that the affluent may face in connection with getting married, living together at his place or hers may constitute a path of least resistance that enables young couples to avoid dealing with the many issues that would arise with the decision to get married. This is particularly the case among affluent young professionals who are anxious to pursue their careers and have no immediate interest in having children. When couples begin to feel that they would like to have children, this situation may shift in the direction of marriage, but some couples have children before they marry, and some couples with children never marry at all.

We do not presume to advise anyone on issues of personal morality, and we are not in the business of promoting matrimony. However, we do point out that whether you actually get married or not, once you make the commitment of living together and particularly the commitment of having children, most of the wealth-related "couples" issues we are considering here will come into play anyway.

When affluent young people elect not to marry and use the complicating effects of wealth as the rationale for this decision, they are quite often manifesting much more than simply a desire to avoid working out a bunch of difficult financial issues. Very frequently, they are displaying a more deep-seated desire to avoid the intimacy and closeness of a committed relationship. Therefore, if you are a wealthy young adult who has had a steady relationship for a long time but has not considered marriage, you might well wish to give some thought to your conscious and unconscious motivations. You might even want to consider going for some professional advice to help you either carry this relationship to a more committed level, or move on to another relationship that you can carry to such a level.

PRENUPTIAL AGREEMENTS

Prenuptial agreements may be used for many purposes. A prenuptial agreement can be used to avoid potential arguments in the event of a divorce by specifying in advance how property would be divided and whether or not either spouse will receive alimony. (A few states do not allow a spouse to give up the right to alimony; and in most other states, a waiver of alimony contained in a prenuptial agreement will be scrutinized heavily by the court.) Prenuptial agreements can be used to keep family property within the family. Such property may include heirlooms, shares in a family business, and property that you expect to receive in a future inheritance. Prenuptial agreements may also be used to keep some or all of the assets that one spouse accumulates individually during the course of a marriage as individual property, as opposed to marital property or community property.

A prenuptial agreement can be used to protect spouses from each others' premarital debts. Creditors sometimes turn to marital or community property to satisfy debts incurred by just one spouse. A prenuptial agreement can be used to limit each other's liability for each other's debts. Prenuptial agreements may be used to specify agreements made with respect to such questions as: (1) whether the couple will file separate or joint tax returns; (2) who will pay the household bills; (3) whether the spouses will have joint or individual bank accounts; (4) how credit card bills will be managed; (5) what major purchases will be made, including a new home or a new business; (6) what will be done regarding future savings; (7) how to handle a situation in which one of the spouses puts the other through college or professional school; (8) how future disputes will be resolved, such as through the use of mediators or arbitrators; (9) how retirement benefits will be handled in the event of a divorce; and (10) to whom your property will be left when you die.

Attorney-mediators Irving and Stoner have suggested that prenuptial agreements are desirable for couples in which one or both spouses fall into any of the following categories: (1) own real estate; (2) own assets other than real estate valued at over $50,000; (3) own all or part of a business; (4) earn over $100,000 per year; (5) have already earned more than one year's worth of retirement benefits; (6) plan to pursue an advanced degree while the other spouse works; plan to leave all or part your estate to someone other than your spouse.[1]

The major questions surrounding the use of a prenuptial agreement are: (1) whether both spouses are comfortable with making such an agreement; and (2) if you do decide to make a prenuptial agreement, making it valid and legally binding. With respect to the first question, if one prospective spouse would like to make a prenuptial agreement but fears starting an argument or offending his or her fiancé by asking for one, then you might try to regard addressing this issue as an opportunity to practice your skills in discussing difficult issues in a loving and considerate manner. It may help to enlist the services of a professional counselor who specializes in premarital counseling to help the two of you work on your communication and negotiation skills. It may help to go to premarital counseling in any case, in order to learn more about what you and your prospective partner want and expect from the relationship. In this way, opening up the topic of a possible prenuptial agreement may strengthen your relationship, rather than threaten it.

With respect to the question of making your prenuptial agreement valid and legally binding, you are well advised to use the services of a good lawyer. In fact each prospective spouse should have a separate attorney. The reasons why lawyers are necessary include the fact that the laws governing marriage contracts are complicated, and they vary greatly from state to state. You will not want to invest your time in trying to become knowledgeable regarding the details of your state's matrimonial laws. Each spouse should have an attorney, because the state courts still tend to scrutinize these agreements very carefully to make certain that neither spouse is taken advantage of. The best way to make sure that the court ultimately views the agreement as fair and valid is for each spouse to be represented individually.

In order to minimize the time and expense involved in crafting the prenuptial agreement, it is advisable for you and your fiancé to come to substantial agreement on the terms of the agreement, perhaps with the assistance of your premarital counselor, prior to going to the attorneys. In this way, the attorneys can focus on making the agreement state what you have agreed upon in a manner that is clear and legally binding, rather than get involved in the negotiations.

The Wedding Itself

Obviously, family wealth will have an impact on the nature of the wedding you have. If one or both of the families are involved in extensive networks of business and social contacts, the guest list may be large. There may be people there that the bride and groom do not even know. Affluent parents may feel obligated to put on a wedding that is more lavish than either their child or his/her fiancé might normally want. Making these plans is often a delicate matter, and it is not unusual for frictions to arise. Our advice to the prospective newlyweds regarding differing ideas about the wedding is to defer as much as possible to parents and simply let them have their way.

Difficult issues may arise when the spouses' respective families differ considerably in terms of wealth, so that the wedding the more affluent family might expect to have is a far more lavish and expensive affair than anything the less affluent family would ever think of putting on. This situation requires that the prospective spouses get everyone together and discuss the issue openly, including who will be paying for what and why. Parents of modest means may feel very uncomfortable with serious black-tie attire and elaborate gourmet meals. To the maximum extent possible, an effort should be made to make everyone comfortable. However, it may well be necessary to ask each set of parents to do things a bit differently from how they might otherwise do them. Everyone needs to remember that the wedding is just one day, and they will all live through it.

When the social differences between the respective families are extreme, consideration may also be given to having some events collateral to the wedding itself in which the respective families entertain their own friends and families, separately from the friends and family members of the new in-laws. We are not talking about events that are so large as to rival the wedding celebration itself, but rather smaller gatherings at which the closest friends and associates of each of the families can share some intimate moments.

Issues surrounding the wedding may also arise when the two families are both affluent, but to differing degrees. Surprisingly, this situation may actually generate more conflict between the prospective in-laws than the situation in which the families are vastly different in terms of wealth. When the two families both have considerable resources, it may not be clear that the more affluent family needs to pick up the bigger portion of the cost. This is particularly likely to become a problem when the relatively less affluent family is that of the bride, since the bride's family is traditionally expected to pay most of the wedding expenses. It may be that the more affluent family has expectations that the less affluent family does not share; or it may be that the less affluent family feels that they need to put on an event that will impress the more affluent family.

Our advice here is the same as that for the situation where the two families are of vastly different levels of wealth, namely, to sit down as a group to discuss the whole issue like adults. The prospective spouses should take the lead here. They should bring up the need for a discussion in a matter-of-fact manner, for indeed such discussions should be considered normal, appropriate, even indispensable. It may be that these discussions could amount to a de facto negotiation regarding who wants what, how much of what each family wants they will actually get, and who will pay for the various parts of the entire package. If the couple or one or both of the families have a trusted counselor or therapist, it may even be necessary to employ this person as a facilitator and arbitrator. Both families should be honest and open about what they would like to do, and especially about how much they feel comfortable paying.

THE DUAL CAREER ISSUE

These days, most women want careers, whether they need the money or not. If one or both spouses are wealthy, the wealth may give one or both the option of not working, or the option of pursuing non-remunerative employment of some kind. However, two young people contemplating marriage should always be clear on what they each intend to do with their lives from the point of view of education and employment, and how much their educational and vocational objectives will impinge on the plans that their spouse may have.

If a young man is independently wealthy or has an extremely high-paying job with the family company, he may want to marry a woman who is free to focus on being a wife and mother. Even if both partners expect to have careers, the type of careers they each choose may be crucial to the practicability of their plans. In the situation where one spouse is definitely committed to working for the family business in a particular location, it would be fine if the other spouse wanted a career in nursing or family medicine, since nurses and general practitioners can work pretty much anywhere. However, if one spouse is tied to the family business in a particular location and the other spouse intends to pursue a career in some relatively obscure academic discipline, it could pose difficulties. In some fields, only a very limited number of positions are available, and someone involved in one of these fields may be required to relocate in order to be employed. This might well be a major issue, requiring the couple to have a "long-distance relationship" for some time before things can be worked out so that they can be together full time. Obviously, such a situation would have an impact on the timing of having children.

In-law Relations

Issues surrounding in-law relations may begin with the wedding planning, but they may also continue on well into the marriage. Once a couple has gotten married, there will be numerous occasions when the in-laws from the two sides of the new family will be thrown together. The formal occasions that will bring the new in-laws into contact with each other include birthday celebrations, baby showers, anniversaries, and various holiday celebrations. Obviously, these occasions will be much more pleasant if the two sets of parents get along. They can be quite stressful if there is any substantial degree of discomfort or acrimony between the new in-laws.

Therefore, it is quite important for newly married couples to foster good relations between their respective sets of parents. Ideally, the parents will have something in common other than their children and grandchildren. However, in some cases where the two sets of parents come from very different worlds and very different socioeconomic levels, this may not be the case. In this event, the children can still help to make the situation work. The young couple can help by entertaining their respective parents with activities that everyone can enjoy. In addition, the couple can plan activities that encourage their respective sets of parents to focus their attention on those things that are important to the new couple, including their careers, their homes, and, of course, their children. If the two sets of parents differ on politics, then by all means, the children should steer clear of activities that emphasize these differences.

Of course, each set of parents will also be the hosts of certain events, and decisions will need to be made about when to invite the in-laws. In addition, one of the issues that affect all newly married couples is the question of where to spend the holidays. Often this issue amounts to nothing more than making decisions regarding which holidays or parts of holidays will be spent with each set of parents. These decisions can be difficult for any newly married couple, but they can be complicated considerably by substantial differences in wealth between the two sets of parents.

If the parents of an affluent young husband have made a habit of spending a week in the Caribbean over the Christmas holidays, they may very well choose to continue this tradition by inviting the new couple along for the trip, just as they invited their own child before he or she wed. Of course, this may well be a very nice gift that the new couple can share and enjoy. But what if it means that they will not be spending time over the holidays with the other, less affluent in-laws? This can generate resentment. The less affluent parents may feel that the children's affections and attention are being "bought." Young couples need to be sensitive to this issue and to make sure that they give enough time to each set of parents to avoid the possible development of such resentments.

Another "in-law issue" that can arise has to do with the opposite situation, where a young couple assumes a degree of responsibility for one set of parents, perhaps because they are ill, or perhaps because they have fallen on hard times. This responsibility may take the form of spending a great deal of time with this set of parents, or it may take the form of helping them out financially. In either case, this behavior can lead to resentment on the part of the other set of parents. Moreover, if the less affluent set of parents is receiving financial assistance from the young couple, while at the same time the couple is receiving financial assistance from the more affluent set of parents, the resentment factor can be exacerbated. Once again, we do not have any formula for you to use to determine what you should or should not do for one set of parents or the other. We are only noting that such actions, however well intentioned, could become a source of resentment. Therefore, you would be well advised to communicate your intentions and your reasoning to the other set of parents, so as to keep them in the loop and enlist them in your good works.

CHILDREARING DECISIONS

When you have children, you may find that you and your spouse have different ideas about how to raise children. You may also find that your parents and your spouse's parents have still different ideas about what is appropriate and what is not appropriate for the children. These differences can occur with any couple; but they are likely to be greater when the two spouses come from vastly different financial backgrounds.

An affluent spouse may envision the children going to private schools rather than public schools, and may deem appropriate a completely different set of social activities from those that a less affluent spouse might contemplate for the children. The more affluent spouse might assume that the children will spend their summers at the same exclusive summer camp where he or she spent the summers. The less affluent spouse might assume that the children should work in the family business. These issues all need to be discussed, and the children need to be involved in these decisions.

In the last chapter, we considered the question of how affluence can affect the value system of children who grow up wealthy, and we have provided the reader with some advice regarding how to raise children who appreciate what they have and do not assume that they are automatically entitled to have anything that they want. Childrearing decisions have much to do with achieving this objective, in particular decisions that are made with respect to children adhering to a budget and getting along on a fixed allowance, as well as decisions regarding whether and how much children will be allowed or expected to engage in remunerative work.

When spouses come from very different socioeconomic backgrounds, they may not see eye to eye on just how strict they want to be with their children in terms of discretionary spending. The two spouses need to share their respective personal experiences with respect to working when they were children and what they feel they learned from their experiences. Then they need to work out an agreement on what their children should be given and what they should expect their children to earn on their own. This agreement should be structured so that the children can reap the social and intellectual benefits of activities that are made possible by the family's wealth, but at the same time still learn that they are capable of providing some things for themselves through the sweat of their own brows.

If a decision is reached that involves the expenditure of substantial sums of money, such as sending the children to a very expensive private school, this decision needs to be shared with all the concerned family members. Once again, if the affluent grandparents are going to foot the bill for the private school, the less affluent grandparents may need to be reassured that they are still important to the lives of their children and grandchildren.

Issues Surrounding Grandparents

The possibility of sending the grandchildren to private school is just one of many issues that will affect both the more and the less affluent members of the family. Similar issues may arise with expenditures for camp, school clothes, horseback lessons, and electronic devices. Parents may in any case seek to limit the extent to which grandparents are able to "spoil" their grandchildren, but they may need to be particularly vigilant in this regard when one set of grandparents is very wealthy and very intent on providing their grandchildren with all the best things in life.

The two parents and/or the two sets of grandparents may also have very different ideas about the activities they consider appropriate for the grandchildren. One set of grandparents may be vegans, while the other set of grandparents may like to hunt and fish. This could potentially cause friction when the grandparents invite their grandchildren to join them in their favorite pastimes. Once again, the issue of differing resources may exacerbate an already difficult situation. The vegan grandparents may find it particularly difficult to deal with a situation where the hunting grandparents are in a position to take all the grandchildren on safari to Africa for three weeks. The vegan grandparents might feel that they cannot in good conscience object to the grandchildren taking the trip, since it will be exciting and educational, yet they may also feel that the affluent hunting grandparents will have an unfair advantage in transmitting their value system to the grandchildren, by virtue of the glamorous and exciting adventures that they can provide.

REPARTNERING AND REMARRIAGE

When affluent individuals find a new love interest following a divorce or the death of a spouse, another set of issues comes into play. The question of protecting one's children is often paramount. The children may be worried that all of mom's or dad's affection and all of her/his money will be directed toward the new love interest, leaving them empty-handed. Meanwhile, the divorced or widowed parent may have been lonely for some time and may well be head over heals in love with the new partner. In fact, he or she may not be thinking very much about the children at this point, and may interpret any efforts on their part directed toward clarifying the new family roles and/or receiving reassurance that they will still be taken care of as selfish and intrusive. In this regard, we have several pieces of advice.

ALLOW YOURSELF TO BE HAPPY

Always remember that you have a right to be happy. That means that you have the right to have a partner with whom you can share your life, and from whom you can derive comfort and care. If you have divorced, do not allow a bad experience with one marriage to turn you off marriage altogether. While divorces certainly can be both emotionally and financially difficult, having a life partner may be a critical element in your psychological well-being and even your physical health, so you should look ahead rather than behind. If you have been widowed, do not feel that you have an obligation to the memory of a deceased spouse to remain single for the rest of your life. Do not feel that you need to give up your life to work for the causes that your deceased spouse supported. You can respect his or her memory without allowing it to dominate your existence now.

Your wealth is definitely an issue that must be addressed when you are considering a commitment to a new partner. However, you can be prudent with respect to protecting your wealth for yourself and your children and still have a new life partner. You should not under any circumstances allow your children to make you feel guilty for finding a new partner. If you are sensitive to your children's feelings, you can take a new partner and still give your children sufficient attention to keep them from feeling shut out. Taking a new partner may actually prove to be a relief for them, since it will alleviate any burden that they might have felt to fill the void in your life. Moreover, if you are careful with respect to your finances, your children need not worry about the implications of the new partner in relation to any ongoing financial support that they are receiving from you, or in relation to what they might expect to inherit from you when you die.

EXERCISE CAUTION

Although you absolutely have the right to be happy and the right to repartner, you should exercise caution, for a number of reasons. First, you do not want your loneliness to lead you to become committed precipitously to a person who is superficially attractive, but may in fact not have a great deal in common with you. This potential problem is exacerbated by the fact that there are members of the opposite sex out there who may be just as lonely as you, and who may for that reason be as likely as you to act precipitously. This could represent a prescription for unhappiness. You do not want to rush into a marriage with someone whom you barely know. If such a marriage ends in divorce, it is possible that there will be bitterness on both sides arising out of disappointment. This could prove expensive as well as emotionally stressful.

Second, there are members of the opposite sex out there who are either consciously looking for an affluent individual on whom they can rely for financial support, or at least unconsciously insecure enough about their own financial position that your wealth may make you far more appealing to them than you might otherwise be. Potential partners who fall into this category might present serious problems down the line. If you marry someone with a strong financial motivation and the marriage does not work out, the ensuing divorce could cost you a great deal of your wealth.

SPENDING AND LEAVING BEHIND

Repartnering and remarriage raise the potential issue of differences between you and your new partner in terms of how much of your wealth you wish to spend, how much you wish to pass on, and to whom you want your wealth to go. You may be quite comfortable living modestly until you die, leaving the bulk of your wealth to your children. But your new spouse may feel that it is appropriate to spend as much of what you have as you can before you die, like the couple in the quarter-million-dollar recreational vehicle with the bumper sticker that says, *"I'm spending my children's inheritance."* Part of the reason for not rushing precipitously into a new marriage following a divorce or the death of your spouse is that you need time to learn what your potential new spouse's values are. You need to share your respective goals for the future and decide how compatible you are. Of course, you may be willing to compromise your goals to some extent to conform to the wishes of a new partner, but you need to know what you are getting into and how much you may be expected to conform to his or her ideas.

THE WEALTH YOU LEAVE BEHIND

Assuming that you are happy with your new partner, and that the two of you live happily until you die, there may still be potential problems associated with passing your wealth on to your children. If your new partner has children, these children may end up making a claim on your wealth, which will be harmful to your children. If your new partner outlives you, there is the potential for your wealth to pass first to the partner and then from him or her to his or her children, leaving your children out in the cold. Of course, these issues can all be handled by means of an appropriate prenuptial agreement and sound estate planning, but the point is that you need to be careful and take the necessary steps.

A related issue is the question of giving some or all of your wealth to a favorite cause or charity. You may feel that you can take care of your children and still give a large portion of your estate to a charity, and you may wish to do so. Your new partner may have other ideas. He or she may want to keep all the money in the family. Your new partner may feel that he or she should have the money after you die, or that your children should have it, or that his or her children should have it.

Another issue that may arise concerns the possibility that at some point during your lifetime you might wish to make a gift to one of your children or to a favorite cause. If you have a new spouse, he or she may object to your giving anything away. They may want all that you have to be available for the two of you to spend, or they may want the money to be available to be divided up between your children and their children. This kind of thinking can get rather petty. I (OC) recently had occasion to work with a couple who had just such an issue:

NED AND KAREN

Ned and Karen are affluent, but not fabulously wealthy. They are both retired professionals. They each have very substantial retirement funds, and they own two homes free and clear, a large suburban home and a smaller summer home in a lakeside community in the country. They had each been married to other partners before they were married to each other. Ned has two daughters from his previous marriage. These daughters are 37 and 39 years old, respectively. Karen had no children from her previous marriage. Ned and Karen also had one child together, a son aged 25.

Ned and Karen had discussed what they wanted to do with their money. They were pretty well agreed on how they wanted to live during their retirement—namely, modestly—so as to preserve the principal that they had accumulated over their lifetimes and leave this to their children. When they initially discussed how their estate would be divided up, Ned had simply assumed that they would leave one-third to each of the three children. However, Karen had other ideas. She did not feel any obligation to look after the interests of Ned's children from his previous marriage. She sought to look after the interests of her own son. She insisted that the half of their combined estate that she regarded as her own should go directly to her son, and that the other half of the estate, which she regarded as Ned's, should be divided equally among the three children. Thus she wanted her son to receive a total of two-thirds of the total estate (his half plus one-third of the remaining half) whereas each of Ned's daughters would receive one-sixth of the entire estate (one third of his half). This was the way that their will was written; and there were provisions for preserving this allocation regardless of whether Ned or Karen died first.

This decision generated some ill will on the part of Ned's two daughters, but since their father agreed to these terms, they had little choice but to "grin and bear it." However, a problem arose when one of the two daughters asked her father for some financial assistance. She was married and had two children. She did not work, and although her husband had quite a good job, they were certainly not affluent. Nevertheless, they lived in the same affluent suburb as Ned and Karen, in a home just a few blocks away. The problem was that their home was really too small for their family, yet they could not afford to purchase a larger home in that town.

But then Ned and Karen decided to sell their large home in that town to purchase a small retirement condominium in Florida. They planned to divide their time between Florida in the winter and their small lakeside home during the summers. Ned's daughter, who was in need of a larger home, asked her father if she and her family could take over their large house that Ned and Karen planned to sell. She and her husband would sell their smaller home and pay the proceeds to Ned and Karen in exchange for the larger house. Since the proceeds from the daughter's smaller home would be more than enough to cover the cost of the Florida condominium, everyone could move to a suitable place without anyone making any new, out-of-pocket expenditures. Ned felt that this was a perfectly reasonable proposition, particularly in view of the fact that both his second daughter and the son he had with Karen were doing quite well financially and really did not need any inheritance at all.

However, Karen objected vehemently to the proposition, because the market value of their larger home was considerably greater than the value of the smaller home that Ned's daughter and her husband would be selling. Karen reasoned that the proposed arrangement was simply removing about a half a million dollars from their estate and giving it to one of Ned's daughters, when in fact she was actually entitled to only one-sixth of this money.

This issue became sufficiently contentious that it brought the entire family into therapy with me. Eventually a compromise was reached, but it was no easy task. It took a good long while to work out, and eventually a compromise was reached, primarily because the other two children were extremely accommodating and anxious to help out the less affluent sister. In the end, the other children had to convince Karen that this was the right thing to do under the circumstances, and even then she insisted that the daughter receiving the home take on an additional partial mortgage, so that she did not end up with as large a portion of the estate as she would have, under the original plan.

This case illustrates how complicated these finance- and inheritance-related relationship issues can become.

In this example, Karen was quite protective of her own son, something less than solicitous of the exigencies of Ned's less affluent daughter, extremely dogmatic in terms of her idea of the proper way to divide the family fortune, and quite stubborn in her intention to see to it that her ideas were enacted. Of course, we recognize that Ned and Karen were remarried long before they were old enough to really give very much thought to the allocation of the estate that they would eventually accumulate. When they married, they had not yet conceived the son whom they would have together. Therefore, it is not likely that they would have sat down and had a long discussion of what they might do in the eventuality that they did have children of their own, and much less the eventuality that one of Ned's children by his previous marriage might at some point need a bit of financial assistance. Yet it would not have been a bad idea for them to have had such a discussion, had they been able to anticipate any of these events. Certainly it would not have been a bad idea for them to have a general discussion about how they might feel finances should be worked out in the situation where there are "his kids and our kids."

So if you think that at some point you might want to give some of your wealth to one of your children, or if you think you might want some of your wealth to go to a favorite cause, you will be better off if you discuss this wish in advance. We recognize that it may not be possible to anticipate every possible eventuality, but it would be a good idea to anticipate as many such eventualities as you can. In addition, you should make sure that you have your wishes firmly set forth in binding legal documents. We give additional attention to the details of estate planning in Chapter 12.

10

The Midlife Crisis among the Affluent

BRENDA'S MIDLIFE CRISIS

Brenda was 48 years old when the last of her three children went off to college. At the time, Brenda was working as a school psychologist, a position that she had held for nearly 20 years. Brenda was quite wealthy and really had no need to earn a salary. She had inherited a substantial trust fund from the estate of her maternal grandfather, and she was in line to inherit her parents' considerable fortune as well. In addition, Brenda's husband came from a wealthy family, and he also earned a great deal of money as a partner in a major Manhattan law firm.

Brenda had gone to graduate school and had gotten a PhD in psychology for several reasons. First, her family had always placed a great value on education, and they had instilled in her the value of work and the importance of making a meaningful contribution to society. Second, Brenda had gone to college during the height of the women's movement, and she had been thoroughly convinced that no woman should ever put herself in a position where her husband's career took precedence over her own career. She had inherited resources, but she also felt that she needed to be earning money of her own in order for her to be an equal partner in her marriage.

It had been quite difficult for Brenda to complete her graduate studies while starting to raise a family. Her first child was born when Brenda was in her first year of graduate school, and her third child was born the year that Brenda began her full-time position as a school psychologist. Once she had settled into her job, the task of fulfilling her responsibilities at work and her responsibilities toward her children had become a bit easier. She had child care help while the children were still very young, and once they started school, her own work schedule permitted her to be present at and participate with her children in most of their after-school activities when they were young.

Brenda and her husband got along pretty well when they were together, but they were together less often than she would have wanted, due mainly to the demands of his position at the law firm. He was away all day each day, from early in the morning when he took the train to work in the city, until fairly late at night when he got back after working quite late. He really loved his work, and he never thought that staying at the office until 7:00 or 8:00 at night was much of a burden. Brenda's husband was hardly involved at all in the school-work or the after-school activities of the children, although he did love them, and he did have a good time with them when he actually could spend time with them—occasionally on weekends and on family vacations.

On the other hand, Brenda was not terribly invested in her work. She had chosen the field of school psychology with the idea in mind that her workday would typically end early each day, so that she would be able to have children and to be involved in their activities while continuing to work. As the years went by, Brenda came to view her job as mundane rather than challenging. She felt as though she could write more or less the same report regarding one child as she could write about another. She felt that she was working primarily for the school district rather than for the students that she saw, since a large portion of her time was dedicated to convincing parents and their attorneys that the district was doing as much as it could to meet the special needs that a particular student might have.

When Brenda's last boy left for college, she found herself with a good deal of time on her hands. She still finished work around 3:00 PM most days, and her husband did not get home from the city some nights until 9:00 or 9:30. Even then, he was usually making phone calls or reading briefs, or he was simply flat-out tired from his long day at work. Brenda filled up her time at first with tennis lessons and trips to the gym. But these activities were only mildly interesting. She really did not have very many women friends, because she found most of the women her age in their social circle to be pretty boring. Most of them had no careers at all, but busied themselves with shopping, decorating their homes, and hanging out at the tennis club (doing more gossiping than playing).

So Brenda got a little bored, a little depressed, and quite introspective. She began to wonder whether anybody really gave a damn if she lived or died. She asked herself why anyone would care, since she had hardly made much of an impact on the world. She asked herself what exactly it was that she was getting out of her marriage at this point. She realized that she was not happy with her life, yet she did not know what to do to make herself happy.

She did some reading on spiritual subjects and went on a few retreats to conferences aimed at encouraging participants to get in touch with their inner selves and make changes in their lives aimed at achieving self-actualization. She thought about going back to school to study oriental medicine, but she never quite got organized sufficiently to actually visit an appropriate school or to fill out an application. She gave more thought than she had before to the tentative sexual advances that she occasionally received from a coworker at school, from one of her tennis instructors, and from the divorced parent of one of the students with whom she was working. But she never followed through on any of these thoughts, because the men involved were really not that exciting, because she felt an obligation to be loyal to her husband, and because she realized on some level that she was experiencing a midlife crisis, and she would probably be served best by not rushing headlong into any actions that had obvious potential to cause trouble for her and her family.

Brenda remained in this state of mild malaise for two years, until one day she happened upon the Web site of an organization intended specifically for women and men who were experiencing midlife crises. She read the materials on the site and took a little diagnostic quiz that confirmed her status as involved in a midlife crisis. Then she signed up for a workshop sponsored by the group that aimed at developing participants' skills for coping with the stresses of this period of life. She attended this workshop, and she found that: (1) the suggestions provided were very helpful to her in her efforts to sort out her values and find a purpose in life; and (2) she was very much drawn into the life stories and the midlife experiences of the other participants of the group. Brenda left this workshop so fired up about the issue of midlife crisis that she signed on to work as an assistant to the facilitator for the next weekend workshop session to be given near her home. She also established e-mail and telephone relationships with several of the individuals whom she had met at the two workshops she had attended. In short order, Brenda had become very much engaged in the midlife crisis group. She became a principal workshop facilitator, and she began to do some traveling around the country to conduct workshops in different cities.

Fortuitously, the emergence of her midlife crisis led Brenda to the Web site of a self-help group for those undergoing midlife crises, and the Web site led her to a workshop aimed at addressing such crises. Brenda's initial participation in this workshop ended up doing much more for her than simply providing her with suggestions regarding how she might cope with her midlife malaise. Ultimately, her stumbling upon the Web site of this group and casually signing up for one of their workshops led Brenda all the way back through the resolution of her midlife crisis, by providing her with: (1) a new purpose in life that had meaning for her (helping others who were also experiencing midlife crises); (2) a vehicle through which to pursue this purpose (the midlife self-help group); and (3) a new form of activity that she found to be both socially significant and completely engrossing intellectually and emotionally (the workshops in which participants shared their experiences with their midlife crises and brainstormed ways in which they could begin to live lives that they perceived as purposeful and fulfilling).

The existence of self-help groups such as the one with which Brenda became affiliated is a testament to the ubiquity of the midlife crisis in our society. Having a midlife crisis has almost become a normative developmental event. In this chapter, we consider the broad issue of midlife crises as manifested among the affluent. We believe that midlife crisis has particular significance for affluent individuals. While one certainly does not need to be affluent to experience a midlife crisis of significant proportions, our experience working with wealthy clients has convinced us that: (1) the most affluent members of our society are more likely than individuals of more modest means to experience a midlife crisis; and (2) when affluent individuals do experience midlife crises, their wealth is likely to exacerbate the crisis and complicate the already difficult process of achieving a satisfactory resolution. The chapter begins with a discussion of midlife crises in general. Then we consider why the affluent individual appears to be relatively more vulnerable to midlife crisis than the average, not-particularly-affluent individual. Next, we discuss the potential impact that one's wealth may have on the effort to get through the midlife crisis. We contend that wealth may have both positive and negative effects on the resolution of midlife crises. However, whether the overall impact is positive or negative, affluence is likely to complicate the resolution of these crises.

WHAT IS A MIDLIFE CRISIS?

A midlife crisis has been defined as an internal conflict that emerges at around the age of 40, when we become increasingly aware of our mortality. The conflict is between, on the one hand, a set of externally imposed social values that instruct us as to the "right" goals to pursue and the "right" ways for us to act, and on the other hand, the deep personal values that define who we truly are and what makes us happy.[1] All of us are influenced strongly by the society in which we grow up to "do the right thing." It is made clear to us from a very early age that it is right for us to go to school, to be polite to our teachers and to follow their instructions, to study hard, and to get good grades.

Depending on the cultural groups and the socioeconomic class to which we belong, social values may also include the mandate to attend a prestigious college, get good grades there as we did in secondary school, obtain admission to a prestigious professional or graduate school, and go on to pursue a successful career in business, law, or medicine. All of these socially derived mandates are viewed by society as leading to the socially approved rewards, which include a large income, a big house, a fancy car, nice clothes, and vacations at fancy resorts.

We are also socialized to believe that once we master a profession, we really should stick to that profession for all of our lives, since changing professions would require additional training and would therefore be inefficient from the point of view of society as a whole. The pressure to remain in the profession in which we have invested substantially to obtain training tends to be reified in phrases such as "I am a physician," or "I am a lawyer." That is, one does not say "I am currently employed as a physician," or "Right now I'm working as a lawyer."

In contrast to the values that society instills in us, we also have deep-seated personal values. We have the personal knowledge of the activities we have pursued over the course of our lifetimes that have made us the most happy, brought us the most joy, and/or transported us deepest into to a state of total absorption in which we are completely wrapped up in a particular activity, and completely oblivious to what may be going on around us that is not a part of this activity. These personal values determine what really makes us happy. These are the values that, on our deathbeds, will determine whether we regret that we have not done enough of something else instead of what we are doing right now.

A midlife crisis occurs when the process of aging and the occurrence of normative life passages make us increasingly aware of the reality that we will not live forever, and this awareness raises the question of whether we have spent our lives aimlessly pursuing externally imposed, socially mandated values, to the neglect or exclusion of deep-seated personal values. When we send the last child off to college, when we begin to plan for retirement, when a parent dies or a friend develops a serious illness, we are forced to recognize that we are not, in fact, immortal. At this point, it is only natural to wonder whether we have gotten the most out of life that we could possibly get. At this point also, it is natural to ask whether our life to this point has had any meaning, whether we have made a contribution to the world, whether we have helped any of our fellow men. Quite often, these introspective questions are answered in the negative, and the realization that we have not, in fact, lived the fullest possible lives that we could precipitates an existential crisis.

The Center for Midlife Crisis has stated that the important question asked during the midlife crisis is, "If you had an unlimited choice, what would you rather do that you will be proud of at the end of your life."[2] This question not only summarizes the existential dilemma posed during the midlife crisis, but also provides an excellent transition to the next section of this chapter, in which we argue that midlife crises are more prevalent and often more difficult to resolve among affluent individuals than among less affluent individuals. The key element of the question in this regard is the part that specifies, "If you had an unlimited choice." This is crucial, because affluence certainly does expand one's range of choices, and with a broader range of choices, midlife options are more plentiful. This may well complicate the course that affluent individuals must negotiate in their efforts to assess their lives to date, reassess their goals, and possibly redirect their endeavors.

THE IMPACT OF AFFLUENCE ON MIDLIFE CRISES

We believe that affluence is likely to increase the likelihood of a midlife crisis, due to the greater difficulty that affluent people may have in regarding the accomplishments they have made during their lives as really special and worthy of enhancing their pride and self-esteem. We also believe that affluence complicates midlife crises when they do occur, because wealth gives individuals at midlife a great many options that the less affluent simply do not have.

WHY AFFLUENCE MAKES A MIDLIFE CRISIS MORE LIKELY

We have already argued that, despite the natural tendency to believe that wealth makes our lives easier, in point of fact, wealth often creates problems. Here we carry forward this argument to point out why various problems associated with affluence and with the culture of affluence tend to increase the likelihood that one will experience a midlife crisis. Such problems include the intense pressure to succeed faced by individuals who grow up in affluent families who live in affluent towns (see Chapter 2); the great potential for affluent, overworked professionals to become disconnected from their children (see Chapter 3); the impact of negative social stereotypes that are held with respect to the wealthy (see Chapter 4); and developing the belief that one should be completely in control of one's life and that there is no excuse for having a life that is anything less than perfect (also discussed in Chapter 4). These problems have the aggregate effect of making it more likely that affluent individuals will tend to devalue their actual life accomplishments, castigate themselves for not having "done enough," and blame themselves for not constructing a perfect life.

The Culture of Affluence and the Expectation of Success. Suppose that you are a guy who came from a wealthy family residing in an affluent suburban community. You pleased your parents by working hard and getting admitted to an Ivy League college. You pleased them still more by being admitted to a well-known graduate school of business. You took a job with a major investment bank. You worked hard, and at the age of 48, you are earning a seven-figure salary. Your response to all of this now is, "So what?" Most of my close friends from high school also went to Ivy League or similarly prestigious colleges; and most of them went on to earn graduate degrees from prestigious professional schools or graduate faculties. All of them are pursuing socially acceptable careers, and all of them are doing just fine financially. So what have I done that sets me apart, even a little, from anyone else? What have I really accomplished?

The reality of the situation for a man in such a position is that he has probably done quite a bit of work to succeed academically and professionally; but in all likelihood, most or all of his peers will have also worked hard and achieved similar levels of success. They have all been driven by the same demands and high expectations that have been placed upon them by the culture of affluence. They have all conformed to these demands. They have dutifully done what was expected of them, even though it was a very great deal indeed that was expected of them. Even the few who have not done well will not provide a point of reference against which our investment banker can measure his accomplishments, because in the culture of affluence, failing in one's education and career is viewed as a sign that there is something wrong with you. In that culture, remarkably high levels of academic and career success do not really raise an eyebrow. They are simply expected. Therefore, when our midlife investment banker looks back over his life, his very real accomplishments will not appear particularly noteworthy, and he may view his life as uninspired, ordinary, and mundane.

In contrast, a young man who grew up in a poor or middle-class family, and who had the same aptitudes and achieved the same or similar outcomes as our investment banker, would most likely regard himself as a great success. He would look about him and see among his peers from high school a much greater variety of outcomes, perhaps ranging from people who dropped out of high school and ended up very poor, through people who wound up in jail or rehabilitation facilities, all the way up to a relatively small proportion of individuals who did very well academically and professionally. Even a midlife individual whose achievements were substantially less than those of our investment banker might develop a very positive self-concept, based on his comparison of his accomplishments to those of other individuals who grew up in the same neighborhood, with the same advantages and disadvantages, and the same expectations from parents, teachers, coaches, and peers.

Workaholism and the Disconnect with Your Children. Referring once again to the midlife investment banker we described above, what do you suppose the chances are that he typically gets home from work in time to see his kids' soccer games? What are the chances that he is home each night for a family dinner at which he can discuss the day's events with his wife and children? In the culture of affluence, dedication to work is expected, and as a result, most successful professionals end up spending far too little time with their children. The result is that these workaholics often fail to develop meaningful and satisfying relationships with their children. This can reduce the level of satisfaction that these affluent individuals will have with their lives when they get to midlife.

In one scenario, the kids may react to the distance from their parents by acting out and getting in trouble. This outcome would give affluent midlife parents one more reason to feel like failures. In another scenario, the kids are well behaved and successful, as were their now-midlife parents, but the kids go off to college without looking back over their shoulder. Perhaps the kids are angry at their parents for not being there for them. Perhaps the kids are simply not very close to their parents, because they never had a chance while they were growing up to develop close and confiding relationships with their parents. In either case, the young adult and adult behaviors and attitudes of the children will not allow their parents to derive any real credit for raising up good and successful kids. In addition, these parents will be able to derive little or no satisfaction from a continuing close relationship with their grown-up children. In extreme cases, kids may go off to college and

from that point on have very little contact with their parents. All of these outcomes of the workaholism that is associated with the culture of affluence provide fuel for midlife dissatisfaction and malaise.

Negative Stereotypes of the Affluent and Midlife Distress. The popular
stereotype views the wealthy as indolent, ineffectual, and entitled. It is
common to think of the wealthy as lying around a pool, sipping champagne,
trying to fight off the boredom that derives from never having to strive for
anything in life, but rather, having everything given to you. Although most
affluent midlifers would swear that they have worked very hard to achieve
whatever they have achieved in life, they are nonetheless impacted by these
stereotypes.

For example, the investment banker we described above might have a tendency to dismiss his accomplishments because "everything was handed to
me." He may reason that he would not have been admitted to the Ivy League
college that he attended if he had not been a legacy applicant, or that he
might have been unable to afford to go there had his parents not been in a
position to pay the hefty tuition and fees. He may feel that family contacts
were crucial to his obtaining his position in the investment bank where he
has worked. And there may be just enough truth in these internal misgivings
that they interact with and amplify the externally conveyed stereotypes of
privilege. This may lead our midlife investment banker to feel guilty for his
success, rather than proud of it. He may wind up feeling that he has not done
nearly enough to make a positive contribution to the world, and that he
needs to turn his life around and to begin to do good works in order to justify
his existence on the planet.

In contrast, an investment banker who got to the same place in life without
the benefit of family money or family connections may simply feel unashamedly
proud of his success. He may feel that he has accomplished quite enough in
his lifetime simply by insuring that his family will be provided for well, and
by helping his own children follow an easier path than the one he had
to follow.

Buying into the Expectation of Control and Perfection. Finally, we
have discussed the notion often developed by some affluent people that their
wealth should place them firmly in control of their lives, so that there is no
excuse for allowing any rough spots or loose ends to persist in their lives. This
type of thinking will obviously contribute to your midlife crisis, in that any
misgivings you might have with respect to how perfect your life is or how
meritorious your contributions to society have been will be compounded
by the belief that anything less than absolute self-actualization and prodi-
gious, even saintlike efforts on behalf of mankind will be interpreted as total
failure. The idea that a midlife crisis can be generated by a perception
that one's life is anything less than perfect has prompted one expert to
observe that:

The fact is that very few, if any, of us truly have it all. Even famous, wealthy people get unhappy . . . so instead of wondering if it's too late to have the life you've dreamed of and doing something drastic, how about simply considering if you're happy. Not delirious, can't wait for the sun to rise happy, but find your life gives you mostly joy, despite the hardships that just come as part of everyday life.[3]

What this means is that you are more likely to have a significant midlife crisis if you expect nothing less than perfection in your life. What our expert is saying is that such an expectation is unrealistic, even if you are financially independent. We think back to the example of the professional baseball pitcher that we provided in Chapter 1. He correctly observed that his fabulously lucrative contract solved just one problem for him, i.e., the money problem. Other than that, his expectations regarding happiness in life were no better than those of any other person.

WHY THE MIDLIFE CRISIS OF A WEALTHY PERSON MAY BE PARTICULARLY COMPLEX

Let us assume now that in spite of the foregoing cautions, you are experiencing a midlife crisis. Why is it that we argue that if you are wealthy, you may have a more difficult time getting through this crisis than an individual who is less affluent? The answer is very simple: you have more options. If you are financially independent, you are in a position to respond to midlife dissatisfaction by quitting your job, taking a trip to India for spiritual enlightenment, or starting a foundation to do good works that will make your life worthwhile. The average midlifer probably does not have such options. He might want to quit his job and go to Africa to become a professional hunter or to Alaska to become a bush pilot, but the chances are that he simply cannot afford to quit his job before his kids have finished college or before his retirement savings are in place. He cannot afford to suddenly sell his home and move his family halfway around the world to pursue a risky and most likely (at least initially) low-paying new career. On the other hand, if these same thoughts were to occur to a wealthy individual, they would represent actual potential courses of action. So the chances are that individuals of modest means will conceptualize their midlife discontent in entirely different terms than wealthy individuals.

Individuals of modest means are likely to respond to their midlife crises in a measured fashion. They might begin to take courses in an area that interests them on a part-time basis, or they might begin to cut back a bit on work and spend more time engaging in enjoyable leisure-time activities or personally rewarding charitable or humanitarian work. They might begin to develop their spiritual side, by attending religious services more regularly or by pursuing personal spiritual-growth experiences. They might sit down to start writing the book that they have had in the back of their mind for ages. Or they may plan to do some traveling that they have always wanted to do. But the chances are that they will not act in a precipitous manner that involves a total makeover of their lives. In effect, the limitations imposed by financial exigencies will provide a natural brake on the impulse to "chuck it all" and start over.

Affluent individuals are not so constrained. If they wish, they can actually quit the law firm or sell their medical practice and move off to Montana to raise llamas, or go to volunteer to build homes for Habitat for Humanity. Of course, it is good to have options. But having a broader range of options involves making more decisions, and particularly more decisions that could radically transform your life. Therefore, our first caveat to affluent individuals in the throes of midlife crises is that when you are sitting down to make decisions about how you want to spend the second half of your life, avoid acting precipitously. You have been leading this life of yours for some time, and even if you are feeling increasingly dissatisfied, you can still take a bit of time to weigh your alternatives and make thoughtful, informed decisions regarding changes you might wish to make.

The next section of this chapter provides you with some hints for coping with midlife stresses and making midlife decisions that will help you to achieve greater satisfaction with your life and your accomplishments.

Making Good Midlife Decisions

The freedom that affluent midlifers have to alter the course of their lives can prove to be a trap. Suppose you are a partner in a major New York law firm. In a moment of frustration with a particularly difficult and tedious negotiation at the law firm, you might think back to what a great time you had when you were scuba diving in St. Croix last year. You think about the magical night dive off the pier in Fredricksted, with the full moon illuminating the pilings, the luminescent plankton in the water, and the fish, mesmerized in the beam of your lantern, seemingly tame enough to allow you to touch them. Because you can, such thoughts might lead you to decide to quit your job and move to St. Croix. You might decide to open a scuba diving shop, or you might simply decide to live there and go diving each day. Alternatively, you might decide to spend your time traveling around from one diving venue to another, simply pursuing your hobby on a full-time basis.

But before you make one of these choices, consider what such an action would involve. It would involve moving, or at a minimum being away from home for long periods of time. Unless your spouse was as much in love with scuba diving as you, if would involve major changes for her (him). Either your spouse would be uprooted to follow you, or your spouse would be separated from you for long periods of time. The same would apply to your children, if they are still at home. Would they move? Would they go to school in St. Croix? Would they continue to live at home and attend their present school? If so, they would probably see less of you than they already do. And what about your colleagues at work? It is one thing to come to the decision that you are not much interested in the work that you have been doing and that you would like a change. But it is quite another to simply pick up and quit. Would you be harming your partners? Would you be placing an unnecessary burden on fellow workers? And what about your new plans? Are they realistic? If you open a dive shop in St. Croix, will you find that in short order you are working just as hard as before and feeling just as bored as before? Will the main difference between now and then simply be that you are making a lot less money? Or if you choose to simply travel around the world and dive in different places, would that lifestyle itself soon become tedious and boring? Will you find yourself in six months feeling just as hassled as you did when you were spending 60 hours a week at the law firm?

In order to avoid such possible disappointments and negative outcomes, we strongly advise anyone contemplating a major midlife change (regardless of how wealthy they might be) to be guided by the flowing rules:

(1) Take the time to think through the course of action that you are contemplating. After it has taken you half a lifetime to realize that you are not satisfied with what you have, you still have another half of a lifetime ahead of you. So give yourself some time to weigh your options.

If you are aware that you are not satisfied with what you are doing, do not just pick some other activity that you have enjoyed in the past and decide to turn this into your life's work. Be a little more systematic in your assessment of your deepest personal values and your search for activities that will be intrinsically rewarding. Here are some steps you might take in this direction: Begin by making a list of all the "peak experiences" that you have had in your lifetime. These are the occasions when you have felt completely involved in an activity and completely at ease. Try to remember occasions during which you have lost track of time, when you have forgotten yourself and you have become completely absorbed in a particular activity. When you have recalled as many such experiences as you can, look over your list and ask yourself, "What do these experiences have in common?" The chances are that there will be one or two major themes that run through most or all of these peak experiences, and these themes should point the way toward one or more areas of endeavor that you might find intrinsically rewarding and self-actualizing.

Once you have identified one or more activities that appear to be compatible with your true self, try to develop some strategies aimed at putting you in a position in which you will engage in these self-actualizing activities regularly. Once you have developed a list of such strategies, think about the factors that have been contributing to your discontent. Try to anticipate how the various courses of action that you are contemplating will address these sources of dissatisfaction. Try to estimate the probability that this each possible course of action will succeed in helping you to overcome your malaise and achieve self-actualization.

Next, consider how each of the alternative approaches to the problem might change your life. One or more of the alternative courses of action that you have identified may involve relatively small changes to other aspects of your life. For example, some might not require relocation, while others certainly will. Also, you might be able to implement one or more of the alternative courses of action gradually, whereas others will call for drastic changes in the short term. If possible, make the changes you are envisioning in a gradual manner, and in such a manner that you do not necessarily need to burn all your bridges behind you.

(2) Consider the impact of the changes you are considering upon your loved ones. Consider the impact of your changes on your spouse, your children, and other significant individuals in your life. Obviously, you have a right to pursue happiness on your own behalf, but to the extent that you have made commitments and assumed obligations with respect to others, you owe it to them and to yourself to consider their happiness as well. Develop and weigh alternative courses of action that might give you a better chance for happiness, yet have a lesser or more favorable impact on your significant others. Most important of all, discuss the changes you are contemplating with these significant others. Share your frustration and your ideas regarding how you might increase your level of satisfaction with your life. Get some input from your loved ones, and allow them to verbalize their apprehensions regarding the possible outcomes of the course you are contemplating. Be ready to compromise if necessary. Enlist professional help from a family counselor or mediator if necessary.

(3) Consider what you are giving up. Often dissatisfied midlifers tend to "throw the baby out with the bathwater." That is, they respond to the dissatisfaction they feel with their current work by quitting everything. They leave their job. They leave their profession. They may even leave their country. But this may be giving up more than is necessary to alleviate your midlife dissatisfaction. It may be that there are still aspects of your profession that you find rewarding, and it may be that there are ways in which you can alter your specific work assignment to find a much more rewarding mission within that profession.

For example, if you are an attorney working for a large law firm, you might be able to reconfigure your work to include more interesting cases. If that is not possible within your particular firm, you might at least be able to find more exciting work in another position within the profession. If you are socially conscious, you might move from your traditional position in corporate law over to a position involving environmental issues, or you might take a position in the legal department of some nonprofit foundation whose work you support. Whatever your profession, the chances are very good that there will be ways in which you can use your credentials and the skills that you have developed to pursue more rewarding objectives.

We are not necessarily saying that you should confine yourself to the "safest" alternatives. Indeed, it may be necessary for you to make radical changes in life circumstances in order to find satisfaction and purpose in your life's work. However, we are saying that some midlife career changes are more disruptive than others; and very few offer any guarantees. Therefore, it is best to take the time to anticipate all the possible consequences of major life changes, and to proceed with due caution. We encourage you to listen to your true self and identify courses of action that will lead you to work that is intrinsically rewarding. We also urge you to have the courage to change the aspects of your life that need to be changed. However, we also strongly suggest that you avoid the temptation to use your wealth to effect far-reaching changes that may have unanticipated negative consequences for you or for members of your family.

(4) Be Careful about Giving Money Away. Affluent midlifers who have succumbed to socially induced guilt regarding the privileges that they may have received by virtue of being born to wealthy parents are sometimes tempted to rectify the situation by giving away large amounts of money to charities. This tendency is particularly common among midlifers who have not pursued careers that may be perceived as contributing to the betterment of society. We are not here to tell you not to be charitable. Charity is good. However, we can tell you from our experience with wealthy clients that giving money to charity is a poor substitute for engaging in paid or unpaid activities that allow you to provide "hands-on" service to humanity. We have had more than one client who has been honored by an organization to which he or she has made substantial contributions tell us that the honor felt hollow, since all they did was give money, and the money had been given to them based on no particular effort on their part.

In addition, just giving away money, particularly large amounts of money, can generate animosity on the part of one's spouse and children, who may feel that what is being given away is basically coming from family wealth to which they have a claim. Therefore, to the extent that you do give money to charities, it is a very good idea to discuss the gifts with concerned family members. Involving them will make them feel that they are participating in the gift, and this will tend to reduce any level of resentment that they may have regarding the gifts.

If you are going to become involved in a worthy cause, you and your family will both be better off if your involvement includes participation as well as giving. For example, if you have a favorite cause, you might consider establishing a foundation of your own to raise money for the cause. You can donate some of your own money, and you can engage in activities aimed at raising additional funds. You can also enlist your family members in the foundation's activities. This will have the additional benefit of instilling a sense of community in your children, and giving them the sense of accomplishment that one feels when one has done a good service.

If you do not feel up to starting a foundation of your own, you can consider volunteering some of your time to a charitable organization like the Community Chest or the Red Cross, or a charity sponsored by your church or temple. This will enable you to get the "hands-on" experience of doing service to the community, without making such extensive demands on your time and energy as might be required if you established a foundation.

Substance Abuse among the Affluent

We have seen that affluent men, women, and children may all be subject not only to the same stresses that everyone else experiences, but also to unique forms of stress that are related specifically to having wealth. This stress can contribute directly and indirectly to substance abuse. We have already noted that, contrary to what one might expect, research indicates that substance abuse is actually more prevalent among affluent suburban youth than among inner-city youth. Affluent adults are also vulnerable to substance abuse disorders, as indicated by the growing number of "executive" drug rehabilitation centers that have sprung up specifically to provide drug treatment for affluent families and celebrity clienteles.[1] In this chapter, we consider the problem of substance abuse among the affluent, including both the etiology of substance abuse within this group and the special problems associated with substance abuse treatment for the wealthy.

John's Drinking Problem

John is a 51-year-old attorney who is a partner in a large New York law firm. His specialty is dealing with litigation surrounding issues of bankruptcy in large corporations. He is one of the very few experts in the country in this field, and he is extremely well compensated for his work. However, he has reached a point where he finds the work boring and frustrating. John once described his typical case as "interminable ... grinding on forever toward an inevitable foregone conclusion, with progress toward resolution interrupted frequently by the petulant objections of one or another interested party who is ignorant of the legal constraints involved and angry because he feels he is getting screwed."

Much of John's work consists of getting parties to disputes and the legal representatives of these parties to understand the law, which allows little room for negotiation or litigation. In order to facilitate this work, John spends a good deal of time having lunch or dinner with clients, other attorneys, and various financial and accounting professionals. A good deal of drinking goes on at these meetings.

In addition to this work-related lunchtime drinking, some years ago, John began frequenting a bar just across the street from his office. He and some of his colleagues became "regulars" at the bar, to which they would go for an hour or so each evening when work was over before heading home to their families in the suburbs. Typically, John would arrive home around 8:00 or 9:00. At first he seemed okay when he got home. He would have a drink with his wife before dinner, then eat with her and go to bed. He was generally exhausted by the time they had finished dinner, and since he got up each morning at 6:30 to get into work by 9:00, it seemed perfectly reasonable that he would go to bed before 11:00.

As the years went by, however, John arrived home more and more inebriated. Lately, he was often so intoxicated that he could not carry on a conversation with his wife. He often skipped dinner altogether. He almost always had even more to drink after getting home, and he typically passed out on the couch each night and dragged himself into bed some time in the middle of the night. In addition to being intoxicated, John seemed depressed. He complained that he dreaded going to work each day.

John also drank on the weekends, when his mood was a little better. He fancied himself a gourmet cook and wine connossieur, and he had a substantial wine cellar that he loved to show off to his friends. He and his wife Janie did a lot of entertaining on Saturday nights, and many bottles of wine were consumed. In addition, John had football season tickets to both the New York Giants and the New York Jets, and every Sunday in the fall he went to a game with his male friends. They generally arrived at the game around 11:00, and they did an elaborate tailgate lunch party before the game. They began drinking Bloody Marys while cooking the tailgate meal, and they continued with beer throughout the game. John had on several occasions been unable to drive home after the game, and had to enlist the assistance of one of his friends who tended to consume much less alcohol.

John and his wife came into marital therapy with me (OC) following an argument that they had one Saturday night while they were entertaining. They had both had quite a lot of wine, and they acknowledged that they were pretty well sloshed. They got into an argument about something trivial that neither could recall the next day, but they did remember that their argument became mutually abusive verbally and ultimately physically, so that their friends had to literally stop them from hitting each other. The next day, John's wife accused him of being an alcoholic and not being able to control his drinking or his temper, and she said that if he did not do something about his drinking problem, she was going to get a divorce.

John loved his wife very much, and he agreed to come to therapy to discuss the issue. He argued that he was not an alcoholic, though he did occasionally overindulge. He also argued that he was no worse an alcoholic than his wife, and that her complaints about his drinking were the pot calling the kettle black. I used the Michigan Alcohol Screening Test to assess the drinking behavior of both John and his wife, and the results clearly indicated that both were pretty far along in the progression of the disease of alcoholism.

I explained to them that they both had drinking problems that needed to be addressed immediately, although this was by no means the only issue in their relationship.

I suggested that they should both begin attending Alcoholics Anonymous (AA) meetings, but at that early point in the therapeutic relationship, both denied that they needed to go to AA, or even to quit drinking altogether. Even Janie, who had accused John of being an alcoholic, thought that the solution to their problems lay in simply cutting back their alcohol consumption, i.e., learning "when to stop." She said that there was no way that John could ever give up his wine. He was too knowledgeable a wine expert to abandon this aspect of his personality, and the fine wines that he served with dinner were too big a part of their social life to simply give them up. Janie was afraid that their friends would not know how to relate to them.

John attempted to cut back on his drinking in a variety of ways. He resolved to give up going to the bar by work each day, and to come directly home instead. This resolution came as a result of Janie's revelation in therapy that she had deeply resented this aspect of John's behavior, which she interpreted as a statement that he would rather spend time with his friends from work than with her. John also promised to limit his drinking when they entertained and when he went to his football games. He promised to always stop after two glasses of wine or two beers. Janie promised to do the same.

John's efforts to cut back on his drinking had only limited success. He did stop going to his watering hole after work, and Janie liked it much better when he came home earlier and less intoxicated. I use the term "less intoxicated," because Janie said that it seemed to her that John had still been doing some drinking somewhere before he got home each day. Later, John admitted that he kept a bottle in the office and a flask in his briefcase, so when he stopped going to the bar, he started having a drink at the office just before leaving, and another in the train or in his car on the way home from work.

John's drinking reached a low point one Saturday night when he had a minor traffic accident. He had been drinking, but this probably would not have been discovered had he not flown into a rage and threatened the driver of the other car. John tended to lose his self-control when he had been drinking, and this had been the primary cause of the physical fights with Janie that had brought them into treatment. Because John was screaming at and threatening the other driver, the police officer who investigated the accident suspected that John had been drinking, and he ended up getting arrested for driving under the influence of alcohol. This was the wake-up call that John needed to bring home to him the severity of his problem. He was fined heavily and had his driver's license suspended for a year. He was told by the judge that he was fortunate that he had not been charged with making terrorist threats or with assault, which could have put him in jail. He was also told by his wife that if he did not seek treatment for his alcoholism, she would leave him.

John went to a psychiatrist who specialized in addictions. He told John that he was clearly an alcoholic and that there was no solution to his problem short of abstaining from all drinking. He referred John to an AA group near his office, and another in his hometown. John agreed to attend at least one AA meeting each day for 90 days. The psychiatrist prescribed Antabuse, which would make John sick if he did drink alcohol. The psychiatrist also prescribed an antidepressant, on the theory that John's depression surrounding his boredom at work was a factor that contributed to his substance abuse. Although John had always resisted taking medication, at this junction, he was willing to comply with pretty much any prescriptions that might help him to overcome his drinking problem.

With these efforts, John succeeded in stopping his drinking. His wife also stopped drinking and began to attend AA meetings, although she did not go so far as to see an addictions counselor or take Antabuse. She stopped drinking, partly because she recognized that she also had a problem, and partly to support John in his efforts to quit.

When John and Janie stopped drinking, they both felt better—better physically, better about themselves, and better about each other. John eventually gained enough confidence in himself that he was able to take an early retirement from his position at the law firm and apply his legal expertise to help several environmental groups that he supported. Janie stopped worrying so much about John's self-destruction that she could not think about her own interests. The result was that she finally turned what had been an intermittent unpaid hobby into a successful interior design business. The two of them felt much better about each other. Their arguments became less frequent. Their sex life improved immensely.

This case example is extremely valuable, because it illustrates both aspects of the culture of affluence that are conducive to the development of substance abuse issues, and aspects of substance abuse that are common to all socioeconomic strata. John's job, like the jobs of many successful and highly paid individuals, made it very easy for him to develop a drinking problem. Going out to lunch and dinner with clients was part of the job; and drinking is widely regarded as part of the job of entertaining the clients. Of course, you do not have to consume alcoholic beverages with your meal; but some people feel that if they do not order alcohol, they may make their drinking clients uncomfortable. The problem, of course, is that alcoholism is a progressive disease, and if you drink at lunch and dinner most days throughout a career, you are increasing the chances of developing full-blown alcoholism. This is particularly true if there is a history of alcoholism in your family, but it is true even if you have no genetic predisposition to the disease. This is why more and more older individuals are being diagnosed with alcoholism. We are living longer these days, and the longer we live and consume alcohol, the better the chance that our consumption will become an addiction.

John's drinking problem was also facilitated by his midlife crisis and the accompanying depression. In the previous chapter, we noted that the affluent have a greater likelihood of developing a midlife crisis than individuals of more modest means. They may also feel trapped in their jobs by virtue of the extensive professional training that they completed in order to prepare for those jobs, the high salaries they are earning, and the narcissistic notion that they cannot be replaced.

In addition, John's drinking history includes the influence of the wealth-related cultural norm of drinking fine wines. There is a great emphasis in our culture on the pleasures of fine food and wine. These are viewed as a part of the rewards one receives for hard work and success. Knowledge of fine wine is viewed as a mark of distinction, a sign of "good breeding." John considered his knowledge of wine and his ability to serve fine wine to his guests to be a major part of his identity, and one of the reservations that he had about abstaining from alcohol consumption was the impact that this might have on his reputation as a host.

We have heard from a number of clients who have quit drinking that one of the most dangerous situations that can tempt one to relapse is being present at a dinner party or a wine tasting where particularly fine wines are being consumed. Our clients report that they are tempted enough by the wine, and they are doubly tempted because those who are imbibing tend to tell them over and over how good each new wine is, and to encourage them to "at least have a small taste." Of course, John's alcoholic progression was also facilitated by other social activities that are less closely connected to wealth. Drinking at tailgate parties and football games is certainly not confined to the wealthy, even though the price of season tickets would suggest that there are few really poor people there. The bottom line is that our culture glorifies substance abuse, and in affluent circles, the methods of glorification may be particularly tempting.

John's history also illustrates a number of aspects of substance abuse that you should be aware of, in the event that you are worried that you may have a potential problem. First, like most alcoholics and substance abusers in general, John engaged in heavy denial of the extensiveness of his problem until the DUI and road rage incident brought it all home to him. Second, during the period that John was struggling with the idea of accepting the fact that he was an alcoholic, he made unsuccessful attempts to limit his consumption of alcohol. This is usually a good test for anyone who thinks he has a drinking problem, because the chances are very good that such efforts will be largely or wholly unsuccessful.

Other aspects of John's story that are instructive include the changes that occurred when John and Janie both stopped drinking. Not only did they feel better physically, but they began to see life more clearly. John realized that he was not stuck in the job that he hated, and Janie realized that she could take the plunge and start the business that she had always considered simply a fantasy. They argued less. Well, of course they argued less—most of their arguments had been about John's drinking. What is more, they no longer had the alcohol to make them argumentative and to remove their inhibitions regarding verbal and physical abuse. Their sex life improved. Again, of course their sex life improved—now that they were not fighting, they could once again focus on the things that had attracted them to each other. And now they could have sex, because they were more often awake. It is not possible to have sex when one is passed out drunk.

KELLY'S PRESCRIPTION DRUG ABUSE

Kelly was born into a wealthy family in Atlanta, Georgia. The wealth had been accumulated five generations back through lumbering and paper mills; and the family tradition of acquiring wealth had been continued in subsequent generations through real estate development. Kelly's family was very traditional with respect to social roles. The control of the family enterprises was passed, generation to generation, to the male children. Women were expected to be well educated, charming, beautiful, fertile, and involved in church-related charities. The female heirs were always provided for with substantial trust funds, but it was quite clear that they were expected to "marry well," so as to increase the social, economic, and political power of the family.

Kelly dutifully adhered to these social expectations. She attended a fine southern finishing school, and she graduated with honors from the University of Virginia, majoring in art history. During the course of her studies, she spent several semesters abroad, and she became fluent in French. She had a number of appropriately well-bred suitors, and during her senior year, she became engaged to a handsome University of Virginia law student whose family was also prominent in Atlanta social circles. Kelly taught for a year while her fiancé Brad completed his last year in law school. She taught at the same private school in suburban Atlanta from which she had graduated. She and Brad married immediately following Brad's graduation from law school. He began working in the legal department of her family's corporation.

Kelly never worked following college. She spent most of her time during the first year of her marriage decorating the home that her parents had given to her and Brad for a wedding gift. She became pregnant within a few months of her marriage and gave birth to their first child right around their first anniversary. She had a full-time nanny, which allowed her to participate in a variety of charitable activities. Over the next 10 years, Kelly and Brad had three more children. Kelly was very involved in their lives, very involved in the social life of her family, and very involved in the local United Way charity and in a foundation that supported the arts. She spent much time keeping fit and playing golf at the exclusive club that her family had helped to found.

From time to time, Kelly thought that she might like to become involved in her own business, perhaps an art gallery. Each time she raised this possibility with Brad, however, he suggested that she was far too valuable to him as the mother of his children and the director of their social life to be able to take the time that would be required to run a business. Besides, she had all the money she needed in her trust fund, as did he, and he was making even more money for them, since he was now the head of the legal division of her family's corporation. Whenever Kelly would make noises about wanting her own business, Brad always proposed a trip abroad to visit some of the famous art museums of the world. This would occupy Kelly's attention for a time and take her mind off her career ambitions.

Over time, Kelly developed a bit of a problem with performance anxiety associated with the speaking that she sometimes did in connection with her charitable work. This anxiety progressed to the point that it became a mild form of agoraphobia. Kelly became nervous in public and nervous about traveling alone. With some trepidation, she mentioned her anxieties to her family physician, who prescribed Valium. As time passed, Kelly became more and more dependent on the Valium to keep her anxiety from overwhelming her.

She also tended to drink a bit too much alcohol, often combining it with the Valium to obtain a desired state of equanimity.

Then, 16 years into her marriage, at the age of 38, she suffered a torn ligament playing tennis. The injury required surgery to correct, and during her recovery her surgeon prescribed Oxy-Contin for her pain. Having already developed the habit of self-medication, Kelly became addicted to this powerful drug very quickly. She continued to use it long after she needed it as a painkiller for her surgery. Kelly tried several times to stop taking the Oxy-Contin "cold turkey." However, she found that when she discontinued the use of the drug, she almost immediately began to experience discomfort, diarrhea, abdominal pain and cramping, vomiting, sweating, agitation, and restlessness. The latter two withdrawal symptoms were particularly difficult for Kelly, since they reminded her of the anxiety reactions that led her to begin taking Valium.

So Kelly continued to crave and to use the Oxy-Contin. She obtained prescriptions for the painkiller from several different physicians, some of whom were close family friends. She also used closely related painkillers when she could not obtain Oxy-Contin. These included Vicodin and Percocet. Kelly was extremely circumspect regarding these doctor visits and prescriptions, because she dreaded the possibility that anyone in her family should discover her secret.

However, within a year, one of the physicians she saw must have broken her confidentiality, because her father learned of her addiction. This resulted in a family intervention and a trip to a very exclusive and very discreet detoxification and rehabilitation facility located in Michigan. These problems are not tolerated in her family's social circles, and they were dealt with accordingly. Kelly successfully underwent detoxification and spent two more weeks in a post-detoxification rehabilitation program at the facility.

This rehabilitation effort was at first welcomed by her family, but later the rehabilitation process generated some further family problems, because the rehabilitation counselors convinced Kelly that she should attend local meetings of Narcotics Anonymous (NA) when she returned home. Kelly's family objected strongly to this. They feared that everyone would learn about her addiction, and they were extremely apprehensive about the people in NA with whom Kelly would be rubbing elbows. However, Kelly went to NA in spite of her family's objections. She had gained a bit of perspective during her rehabilitation, and she realized that her affluence and the attending expectations of her family had played a role in her developing a dependence first on Valium and alcohol, and then on Oxy-Contin.

Kelly also began private therapy with a woman psychologist who had some feminist leanings. This step also resulted in some fallout within the family, because eventually it led Kelly to insist on beginning her own business when her youngest child entered prep school. There were a number of adjustments to be made by all concerned. Fortunately, the story has a happy ending, because today Kelly is completely drug free and has almost completely overcome her problems with anxiety. She feels much better about herself because she runs her own business, and the confidence that she has gained from this effort has given her a much higher standing within the family circle. She is no longer just Brad's wife and her children's mother. She also has an identity of her own as a gallery owner and the proprietor of an art/antique auction barn.

Kelly's story is typical of a great many wealthy women who come from very traditional families and are expected to behave in a manner that is appropriate to women of fine breeding. Feminist therapists have made a great deal of the plight of such women, stressing the insidious nature of the "gender oppression" experienced by the women of the upper classes. For example, Wolfe and Fodor have described wealthy women as bored, frequently lonely and depressed, utterly lacking in personal survival skills, hopelessly dependent upon their husbands, and totally lacking of self-respect. These correlates of gender oppression among the wealthy are seen as creating fertile ground for the blossoming of anxiety, somatic illnesses, and substance abuse:

> Silently suffering and afraid to expose their husbands—often the ruling class— [wealthy women are] most likely to come to therapy when the bubble seems in danger of bursting. Most typically it is because they find out that their husband is having an affair, and they panic at the thought of losing it all; or they have developed medical or psychiatric problems (e.g., bulimia or alcoholism) related to their desperate attempts to fit the class mold lest they be replaced by a younger model. Another reason they may appear in our office is they have begun to tire of being only an "adjunct," wishing instead to develop a life or economic base of their own.[2]

Of course, not all wealthy families engage in gender oppression, and not all affluent women exist only to bear children "who become the vehicles for perpetuating the power and privilege" of their families," as Wolfe and Fodor argued.[3]

As we have already pointed out in Chapter 6, this feminist perspective may in fact be viewed as a manifestation of the negative stereotyping of the wealthy that characterizes our society in general and elements of the social work profession in particular. Nevertheless, it is said that there is a modicum of truth in most negative stereotypes, and here we certainly do acknowledge that many women of wealth and privilege (and some men as well) drift toward substance abuse at least in part because they find little meaning or fulfillment in their lives. Furthermore, many of those who do turn to substance abuse experience an even greater tendency to deny the problem than the average substance abuser, because of the perception that one's wealth should make everything all right, and because of the fear of being ostracized socially should one's addiction become public knowledge.

JASON THE GARBAGE HEAD

Jason is 21. He is currently in the middle of a six-month residential rehabilitation program for drug-abusing young adults. When he introduces himself at the NA meetings that take place in the treatment facility, he tells everyone that methamphetamine was his favorite drug, but really he was a "garbage head," which means that he would take anything that anyone gave him and anything that he could buy or steal that he thought would get him high. Jason landed in the residential program by virtue of a court mandate following his arrest for auto theft, driving under the influence of a controlled substance, and resisting arrest.

Jason had been at a house party where everyone was taking drugs. Jason had been taking a combination of alcohol, crack cocaine, and methamphetamine. Then he decided that he needed to go shopping for an iPod. He took a friend's car without asking. His own car was parked at the party as well, but it was blocked by another car, so he took the first one he found with keys in it. He wrecked the car in the parking lot at the mall, severely damaging several other parked vehicles. Then he had a fight with the security guard who came to investigate, which led to the state police being called in and ultimately to his arrest. When Jason realized that he was going to be arrested, he cursed out the troopers and told them that they would be sorry for arresting him when they found out who his father was. He refused to be handcuffed, and had to be restrained. This led to the charge of resisting arrest.

Jason's father is an extremely wealthy businessman and a member of the county legislature in the county where Jason resides. Under other circumstances, his father's influence probably would have benefited Jason in his legal troubles, but the incident in question was so public that his hands were tied, and his dad was also so furious with Jason that he had just as soon see the judge throw the book at him, which indeed he did.

Jason had graduated from the local high school with a respectable average and the highest SAT scores of any student in his class. He had never studied very much. He was simply very bright. He did not get into any really prestigious colleges, but he was admitted to the state university nearby. He went for one semester before dropping out with a grade point average of 0.0. He failed every course, because he never went to any of them. Jason had started doing a variety of drugs in junior high school, and by the time he went off to college, he was a serious drug abuser. He spent his one semester in college stoned all the time, mostly on methamphetamines. He would often go on tears where he did not sleep for a week at a time, running on meth alone, with an occasional candy bar thrown in.

Jason had been raised by his father and stepmother. His dad was and still is a workaholic, and his stepmother, only 10 years older than Jason, had no interest whatsoever in "playing mom" to the stepson who was older than her youngest brother. Jason's own mom had left his dad and Jason to open a pottery studio in a local artists' village. This was made possible by her own trust fund, for she was also from an extremely wealthy family. Jason's mom had her own drug and alcohol problems, although she had not begun to conceptualize her substance use as a problem. So Jason had grown up as a very rich latchkey child, and his substance abuse took place primarily in the afternoons while he was home alone. As long as he had decent grades, everyone seemed to assume that he was okay. No one was aware of how heavy his drug use had become. He had totaled two cars while he was in high school. His father's response to these earlier accidents was simply to buy Jason a new car each time. Jason stated once during an NA meeting that he believed the unconscious reason why he had stopped attending classes when he got to college was to let his father know that everything was not all right.

In his rehab, Jason has begun to see that his drug use is a problem that will ruin his life and might very well kill him. He has also begun to see that his family life has been neither normal nor healthy for his development. He is aware that he has the resources to pick up the pieces of his life and resume his education. He has adopted the goal of being sober, but has not yet developed any degree of confidence that he will be able to meet this goal. He is engaged in his treatment program, which is certainly a good sign, but the ultimate outcome remains very much in doubt.

Jason is representative of an epidemic of substance abuse among affluent suburban youth. As we pointed out in Chapter 1, the rate of substance abuse among affluent suburban youth is considerably higher than the corresponding rate among inner-city young people.[4]

A number of explanations have been offered for the relatively high rate of substance abuse among affluent young people. It may be related to wealth directly, in that affluent young people are quite likely to have disposable funds that they can use to purchase drugs.[5] It may also reflect the fact that suburban youth are less likely than inner-city youth to witness major negative consequences of substance use. Inner-city young people are more likely to witness drug-related violence, to observe drug dealers being arrested, or to see the negative consequences of drug abuse affect the everyday lives of their parents or other family members.[6] Still another explanation for substance use among affluent suburban youngsters suggests that the affluent youngsters simply have greater psychosocial adjustment difficulties than inner-city youth, and therefore, the suburban youngsters are more likely to use alcohol and other drugs to self-medicate for their experienced distress.[7] This stress is derived from many factors already considered in this volume, including the tremendous pressure to succeed that they experience, the likelihood of parental absence, and the isolated nature of affluent suburban homes.[8]

Bogard has reported that adolescents experience increased rates of both depression and substance use as they enter their teens, that both depression and substance use are higher among affluent adolescents than among less affluent youngsters, and that a significant positive relationship exists between depression and substance use.[9] It follows from these findings that steps that can be taken to reduce depression among affluent youth would likely tend to reduce the likelihood of substance abuse.

Included among these steps is increasing the amount of contact and the perceived emotional closeness between parents and adolescents. It has been reported that in families earning over $150,000 per year, the proportion of youth between the ages of 12 and 17 who report that they have close relationships with their parents is lower than the corresponding proportion in the same age range in less affluent families.[10] Research has also demonstrated that an adolescent's psychosocial adjustment is related positively to perceived closeness with his or her parents.[11]

Also important is the availability to adolescents of sources of social support outside the family.[12] Such sources of support include teachers, coaches, clergy, Boy Scout or YMCA leaders, camp counselors, neighbors, and members of the extended family. Although we certainly recommend that affluent parents do everything in their power to maximize the amount of contact that they have with their children and to develop the closest possible relationships with their children, we also recognize that other adults can aid in the effort to support young people, to bolster their sense of self-worth, to keep them motivated and engaged rather than apathetic and depressed, and to minimize the chance that they will engage in self-destructive substance abuse. Therefore, it is good to encourage your children to participate in school activities, to play sports, to be a member of a religious community, to go to camp, and to become involved in public service activities.

Although the research is less clear with respect to the relationship between peer relationships and substance abuse, we strongly recommend that affluent parents make every effort possible to encourage their children to form close relationships with peers who are also engaged in positive activities. I (JT) recall specifically the tremendous positive influence on my daughter that came from the friends and competitors she met while participating in equestrian events. Riding a hunter-jumper is no trivial endeavor. It requires hard work training, time-consuming effort to prepare the horse for showing, a considerable degree of alertness in learning courses and planning jumps, and the courage to perform in public in an activity where it is quite possible to falter badly or even fall. The kids that engage in this activity tend to be mutually supportive and encouraging, even when they are in direct competition with each other. This experience was truly character building for my daughter, and I am quite certain that she never thought about using alcohol or drugs while she was preparing to ride.

Of course, the ideal situation is the one in which parents can be involved with their children in such activities. We realize that it may be difficult to find the time to go to your children's games, take them fishing, or help them braid the horse, but there is no better way to give them a positive orientation toward life and a strong sense of subjective well-being. Such positive psychosocial adjustment will also help to avert the possibility that they will succumb to culturally driven pressure to drink or use other drugs.

Conclusions Regarding Substance Abuse

In view of the epidemic nature of substance abuse, the widespread social acceptability and even the glorification of drinking and even using other drugs, and the prevailing tendency of those who have substance abuse problems to deny that they have a problem or to minimize the severity of whatever problem they may have, we have chosen to include in this chapter a few questions that—*if you have read this far*—you should probably ask yourself these 10 simple questions:

1. Do you sometimes have more than two alcoholic drinks on one occasion?
2. Do you think you are drinking more (or more often) lately than you did before?
3. Has anyone ever suggested to you that you act differently when you have been drinking?

4. Have you ever missed work or canceled an appointment because you felt "hung over"?

5. Has anyone ever suggested to you that you have "had enough" to drink?

6. Do you become argumentative or aggressive after drinking?

7. Do you sometimes have a drink to help you fall asleep?

8. Have you ever made an effort to stop drinking or to cut back on your drinking?

9. Have you ever found yourself looking forward to having a drink when work would be done or when a certain time of day would come along?

10. Have you ever been unable to remember part or all of an evening when you have been drinking?

Each of these questions represents an indication of alcoholic drinking, and an affirmative answer to more than one or two of these questions is an indication that perhaps you need to see a professional for a more complete evaluation.

If you are beginning to wonder whether you might have a problem, but you are not yet ready to go to a professional for an evaluation, try the following experiment: make a promise to yourself not to drink any alcohol for a month. If you have no problem, you should have no difficulty fulfilling this promise. If, on the other hand, you find that you cannot keep the resolution, or that keeping the resolution is a struggle involving discomfort, subjective distress, and/or a clear craving for alcohol, then the chances are that you do have a problem. In this case, we recommend that you see an addiction specialist.

Remember, despite the culturally bound myth that only people on skid row are alcoholics or junkies, substance abuse problems can affect anyone. Remember, too, that the idea that one must drink fine wines and cognac in order to qualify as a full-fledged member of the affluent elite class is nothing more than an advertising strategy employed by the liquor industry. It is true that some people can drink without their drinking ever becoming a problem. But most people cannot do this. Many people are genetically prone to alcoholism, and these folks typically will begin drinking alcoholically quite soon after they take their first drink. Moreover, people who are not genetically prone to alcoholism can still develop the disease over time. This is because our bodies gradually build up a tolerance to alcohol that eventually requires us to consume more and more to obtain the same subjective effect. Because of this insidious characteristic, and because alcohol is legal, it may be even more dangerous to the public health of the nation than the many illegal drugs that are available.

It is your life to live, and only you can determine the substances you put into your body. We are confident that you will be most likely to enjoy life and to feel good about yourself if you avoid introducing the problems surrounding substance use.

Problems with Inheritances

Like having wealth in general, inheriting wealth is nice, but it can present problems as well. If you are wholly or even substantially dependent upon inherited wealth for the maintenance of your lifestyle, you may find yourself feeling somewhat embarrassed or inadequate when people ask you what you do for a living. If your neighbors in your affluent neighborhood and the other members of the country club have attained financial success on their own by virtue of extensive professional training or creative entrepreneurship, there may be a tendency for you to feel inferior to them, or to feel that what you are doing with your life is inconsequential

If you have been born into a wealthy family and have led a pretty privileged life in which someone else has taken care of most of your needs (financial and otherwise), inheriting wealth may place you in a position in which you are suddenly called upon to participate in the management of your finances. You may feel unprepared to do this, particularly if your parents have neglected to provide you with any experience or training along these lines. You may, in fact, be unprepared to manage a large inheritance. You may be unprepared psychologically, because you have never learned to plan ahead; and you may be unprepared academically, because you have never learned the difference between a stock and a bond, or the difference between a revocable living trust and a living will.

If you are unprepared to manage newly inherited wealth prudently, you may well wind up dissipating your inheritance, perhaps by reckless spending on pleasures of the flesh or thrill-seeking activities, perhaps by making foolish investments, or perhaps by simply giving the money away to various legitimate or questionable causes or charities.

In this chapter, we will provide you with some guidelines on how to avoid such potentially negative outcomes of inheriting wealth. Because inheriting wealth raises many of the same issues as having wealth, in the course of laying out these guidelines, we will revisit some of the topics considered in earlier chapters, including coping with negative stereotypes of the wealthy; handling the pressure to achieve that characterizes the culture of affluence; raising decent, competent, and happy children; socializing with those who are less affluent than you; and protecting yourself from those who would take advantage of you because of your affluence.

JUSTIFYING YOUR EXISTENCE AND YOUR LIFESTYLE

Those who have inherited substantial amounts of wealth frequently report that they tend to feel a bit uncomfortable or embarrassed when they are asked, "What do you do?" This discomfort is particularly common among individuals who are living on inherited wealth who have chosen not to pursue careers that would generate an income, but it is reported as well by individuals who do work but do not earn enough from their jobs to support the lifestyles that they are living, made possible by income derived from their inheritances. For example, consider the case of Laura.

LAURA

Laura is a 34-year-old social worker. She is unmarried. She works in a Veteran's Administration hospital doing discharge planning for disabled vets. She makes $68,000 a year at her job. Laura lives in Chappaqua, in a $3 million dollar home set on eight acres. She inherited this home from an aunt who died nine years ago. The aunt also left Laura a fortune worth roughly $12 million. The annual income that Laura derives from her inheritance is approximately $600,000.

Laura came into treatment with me (OC) primarily because she was depressed. She had extremely low self-esteem, and she was lonely. This seemed a bit odd to me at first, because she is clearly intelligent, reasonably attractive, and (of course) very rich. However, it did not take long for Laura to get across to me the sources of her discontent.

One of her primary complaints had to do with her home and her neighbors. Laura had visited her aunt frequently during her childhood and in the years preceding her aunt's death. She had loved her aunt very much, and she had always had a very good time when she stayed at the house in Chappaqua. She still loved the home, and she was reluctant to sell it and move elsewhere. However, she said that she had problems living there. First of all, she said, since the house was situated on an eight-acre estate, she felt isolated. She did not often see her neighbors, and when she did see them, she always felt that they were looking down on her. The neighbors included two investment bankers, a brain surgeon, and a rather well-known novelist. Laura felt that all of these neighbors were people of immense substance and accomplishment, and she felt that they would have no reason to want to socialize with her, a lowly social worker. She said that this feeling was corroborated by the fact that none of the neighbors had ever invited her to their homes to have dinner or for parties, even during the holiday season.

Laura attributed what she perceived to be her neighbors' snubs to her inferior intellectual and career achievements. She felt that it did not require any particular intelligence to become a social worker, and she was certain that her neighbors were all part of a monolithic, highly intellectual social group in which she could never be accepted. She recalled a brief meeting that she had with one of the investment banker neighbors shortly after he and his family moved into the home next door to her own. She told me that within five minutes of meeting the man (at her mailbox), he had informed her that he was a graduate of Wharton and a partner in Credit Suisse, and that his year-end bonus of $400,000 was a bit disappointing. She said that her conversation with this man began with an oral presentation of his resume, and concluded with a quiz on her own. She said that when she told her neighbor that she was a social worker at the VA hospital, he immediately discerned that she was living on inherited money, because he remarked that she must be either very compassionate or very patriotic, since she could not possibly be doing that job for the money.

Rather than focus on how impolite her neighbor had been in making these judgments, Laura focused on the aspect of his remarks that she viewed as representing a criticism of her for her failure to choose a more competitive field of endeavor, a field that demanded expertise rather than just compassion, a field in which the risks and rewards were much greater.

Another issue that Laura raised when she came into treatment was the difficulty that she had developing relationships with men. She said that there was little opportunity to meet men at work, since the staff members at the VA hospital were almost all married, and she did not consider it appropriate to socialize with patients. She had tried dating services, but she was extremely apprehensive about meeting strangers, primarily because of her wealth. She thought that she would make an ideal target for an insincere "gold digger." She said that she found it difficult to believe that anyone that she would want to have a relationship with would also want her, or at least that anyone would want her for herself and not for her money. On the rare occasion when she did meet someone who was potentially interesting, she was very careful not to have him over to her house or to let on in any way that she was rich. She said that she feared that she gave off the impression of being "standoffish," when in fact she was simply trying to protect herself.

First of all, I (OC) would like to point out that Laura was a great patient to work with, and that after the application of a considerable amount of cognitive restructuring, she began to realize that in fact, her accomplishments as well as her compassion were quite substantial; and that some people, despite the fact that they have achieved great success by virtue of their intelligence and competitiveness, are nevertheless assholes.

Laura also responded enthusiastically to my suggestions that focused on developing a new social network of individuals involved in diverse charitable and philanthropic endeavors, a network that would likely include other individuals who were affluent by virtue of family wealth, as well as individuals whose motivations extended beyond the size of their year-end bonus or the annual profits of their company. Making these new contacts helped to solidify Laura's new way of thinking about herself and her value as a member of the human race. These contacts also developed into new social relationships with individuals with whom Laura did not need to feel so vulnerable.

Nevertheless, when Laura entered treatment, she manifested many of the insecurities that often plague those who are living on inherited wealth. She was surrounded by individuals who had similar wealth to her own, but who had earned this wealth through their own efforts and intelligence. She compared her own accomplishments to theirs and found herself to be wanting. She assumed that they would not be interested in anyone of modest abilities and accomplishments such as her own. She assumed that she had not been invited over to her neighbors' homes because they looked down upon her. She did not recognize the sociological reality that individuals living on estates in the suburbs tend to be relatively isolated from and indifferent to their neighbors, forming their social circles based on professional connections and shared avocational interests rather than simple geographic proximity.

Laura also suffered from apprehension regarding the motives of potential friends and suitors. As we saw in Chapter 4, many wealthy individuals go out of their way to avoid letting potential social contacts know that they have money, because they fear that the potential friend will stereotype them as entitled and demanding, or helpless, or because the potential friend may be drawn to them by their wealth rather than by any real interest in them as persons. Laura was desperate enough to meet men that she used online dating services, yet she was fearful about revealing her wealth to strangers. This conflict was apparently sufficient to make her appear paradoxically standoffish to any new men that she met through a dating service. This was apparently a sufficient turnoff to severely impede the development of close relationships with new dates.

The only advice that we can offer to individuals whose lifestyles are supported in substantial measure by wealth that they have inherited is to remember that being lucky enough to get some extra money in this manner may change where you can live and the type of things that you can do, but it does not change who you are. If you became a social worker because something about this profession appealed to you, then by all means, continue to do the work that you enjoy. Continue as well to associate with the people that you associated with before the advent of the new wealth, and continue to evaluate yourself, your accomplishments, and your satisfaction with living in comparison to the people against whom you have always measured yourself. If your new wealth places you in the company of individuals who appear to be very intelligent and very high achievers, just think of these new acquaintances as you would anyone else, and do not be afraid to tell them who you are and what you do. You do not need to explain to anyone how you can afford the lifestyle you are living. Among the new acquaintances that you might make as a result of inheriting money, those who pry into your personal finances and those who make inconsiderate and thoughtless remarks like those made by Laura's neighbor will probably not be people with whom you would like to develop friendships, anyway.

You have nothing to be ashamed of because you have inherited some money. You have nothing to be ashamed of because this money allows you to live a more sumptuous lifestyle than would be possible on the basis of your current personal earnings. You have nothing to be ashamed about with respect to what you do for a living, as long as it is legal and socially acceptable. Who says it is not morally superior to be a social worker in a VA hospital than to be an MBA investment banker or a personal injury (slip-and-fall) lawyer? Remember that our society places a premium on achievement as measured in annual income, but this is not the only measure of an individual's worth. You may very well be in a position to live without doing any remunerative work whatsoever, and you may choose to do exactly that. It is okay. You have only yourself to answer to with respect to how you choose to spend your life.

We do strongly suggest that everyone needs to be engaged in some meaningful activity that requires real effort and has a purpose, but you have no obligation whatsoever to accept as your own the standards against which your neighbors, your friends, or the other members of your family evaluate their own success. In the service of feeling that one has a purpose in life, we suggest that all individuals, wealthy as well as poor, invest in themselves by getting a good (and by that we mean higher) education. You may never need a college degree to enable you to earn a living, but you may well benefit from a college education in terms of broadening your horizons and making you aware of possibilities for living life with a purpose and feeling that you have accomplished something in life.

It may turn out that what you perceive to be an interesting and rewarding area of interest turns out to involve the need for extensive higher education and carries with it the possibility of substantial financial remuneration. This might lead you to undertake a career quite similar to what you might have chosen if earning a good living were also a necessity. The only difference, then, is that if you are wealthy, you will not need to apply for scholarships, and you will probably have a nicer home to live in while you are completing your studies. On the other hand, your college education may make you aware of possibilities for personally rewarding and socially relevant vocational activities that do not involve any graduate-level training and perhaps do not result in significant earned income. This outcome would be fine as well. If you have inherited enough money that you never need to engage in paid work, there is no rule that says you must. We are simply suggesting that you probably do want to do some meaningful work that will give you a reason to get up each day and a sense of accomplishment. Without work, we lack purpose. Without purpose, it is easy to fall into an existential malaise that may wind up in depression, substance abuse, and/or self-deprecation. We are also suggesting that a college education may well be the best way to explore the various paid and unpaid options that lay before you, affording you the best possible opportunity to discover the vocation that will give meaning to your life.

Understanding Your Finances

Many individuals who inherit money are completely ignorant regarding financial matters in general and the nature of their inheritance in particular. In some families, wealthy parents make a conscious effort to give their children knowledge of personal finance and the nature of investments and the tax system. In these families, also, parents may take steps to insure that their heirs will be familiar with what they are inheriting. This may involve giving children experience working in the family business that they will be inheriting and are perhaps expected to run. It may involve teaching the children about investment portfolios or real estate investments. It may involve making sure that they are familiar with the tax codes. In some families, wealth is managed by professional financial planners. In this case, it is still important for potential heirs to have basic knowledge of investments, so that they can ask the planners the appropriate questions about how the money is being invested. Children who will inherit substantial wealth also need to know exactly what they have inherited. If trusts have been established, heirs should certainly know what is in the trust and when it is possible to take distributions from the trust(s). They should also know whether the trusts have any special conditions, such as providing incentives for certain accomplishments or behaviors. For example, an individual might leave money in trust for a child, with the incentive clause that the child will receive a certain sum of money upon completion of his or her college or graduate degree.

Unfortunately, many heirs lack either general information regarding personal finance and investing, or specific information on the nature of their inheritance. There are many reasons for this. It may be that the heir does not have and has never had any aptitude for or an interest in finances, and has therefore avoided asking questions or taking courses that would provide relevant financial knowledge. Perhaps the heir is a woman who was socialized to believe that finances are an appropriate area of interest for men, but not for women. Perhaps the heir is simply a man or woman who has a math phobia and therefore avoids any subjects involving the use of mathematics.

Perhaps the heirs have had all their needs met by parents or their operatives over the course of a lifetime, so that they are only vaguely aware of where the money comes from or what needs to be done to insure that it will continue to come. In some families, parents tend to shield their children from knowledge of the family wealth, perhaps thinking that it is better for the child not to know how wealthy they are. They may think that a child who is aware of the extent of his or her wealth may tend to reveal their financial status to others, thereby making himself or herself an easy mark for a predatory gold digger. Or they may think that they have worked very hard to earn their fortune and to understand how to manage it, and that they would be doing their children a favor by insulating them from such mundane and boring concerns. If there are financial planners and/or estate trustees involved, they may be reluctant to provide heirs with a complete picture of the family fortune, for fear that the heirs will attempt to manage it themselves or dissipate it.

If you have an inheritance and you are uncertain as to exactly what you have inherited, you need to be assertive with the lawyers and/or trustees who are handling the estate. You need to get them to sit down with you and go over the entire inheritance. You need to have them tell you what your options are with respect to taking distributions and using the funds obtained in this manner. You should not simply accept whatever payments you see coming to you. The trustees may have a vested interest in maintaining the principal, or they may seek to invest some or all of the funds in areas that may be of greater benefit to them as individuals than to you. Of course, none of this may be going on. But it could be, and you need to know what is there, how much it is earning, and what alternative investments might be available.

As much as you might hate doing so, it would not be a bad idea to obtain some tutoring in personal finance. It may be possible to enlist the aid of a trustee and/or financial planner who is working directly with your inheritance. In this case, you might be able to tailor your financial education specifically to your holdings, which may save you time. If you do attempt this route, make sure that you ask your tutor to explain each technical and financial term that he or she mentions and that you do not fully understand. Remember, financial professionals, like professionals in any other field, have a large amount of technical jargon that they understand completely and use freely. It may not occur to your advisor that he or she is using terms that need to be explained. You need to be sufficiently assertive to stop your tutor and ask for clear and concise definitions that will enable you to understand completely what he or she is trying to tell you about your investments.

It might also be useful for you to take a college course in basic personal finance, or to attend one of the many commercially produced seminars that are offered for this purpose. A number of good resource books are also available to which you might turn. These range from large comprehensive texts such as *Personal Finance* by Kapor, Dlaby, Hughes and Hughes, to simplified volumes such as *Personal Finance for Dummies* by Tyson.[1]

HANGING ON TO YOUR INHERITANCE

JEREMY'S $11 MILLION

Jeremy is a 52-year-old bush pilot working in the Queen Charlotte Islands of British Columbia and along the southeastern Alaska coast. Twenty-eight years ago, just two years after he graduated from Dartmouth, he inherited a lump sum of $11 million following the tragic death of his father, which occurred when his private plane crashed in a storm. At the time of his father's death, Jeremy was working as an Outward Bound leader. He was making very little money there, but he liked working with kids. Besides, he did not think he really needed to make money since his family had money.

Jeremy had always been outgoing, athletic, gregarious, and socially conscious. He was bright, but not a scholar. He had never worried very much about choosing a profession or a career path, because he was always quite aware of his father's wealth. Furthermore, his father had himself inherited the wealth. He had spent a small part of his own life coaching lacrosse at the prep school he had attended, but he had spent the greater part of his life pursuing various adventures around the world. He had circumnavigated the world in a sailboat, climbed Mt. Everest, and spent several years guiding National Geographic tours of the headwaters of the Amazon. He had passed on his sense of adventure to Jeremy. He had also taught Jeremy to fly. Before graduating from college, Jeremy had become certified to fly both fixed-wing aircraft and helicopters.

Jeremy really had very little idea about just how much money $11 million really represented. He just knew that it was a great deal of money. In fact, it seemed to him that it was an inexhaustible sum of money. But it turned out that this was not the case. Amazingly, at the age of 52, Jeremy has very little of his inheritance left. He has managed pretty much to dissipate his fortune, and he has done so without succumbing to the stereotypical temptations that are available to wealthy young people, such as alcohol or drugs, gambling, or fast women.

Jeremy spent a big chunk of his inheritance almost immediately financing a company that he hoped would compete with Outward Bound. While he loved the concept of the Outward Bound program and the work he did with young people there, he had issues with his superiors regarding administrative policies, particularly centered around the question of providing additional outside counseling and support services to program participants, as well as rules governing retention in the program. Jeremy thought that the program as it existed did not provide kids with enough extra support, and that the administration was too willing to let a participant go when they had real problems fitting in.

Therefore, Jeremy formed a company, hired a bunch of people in various capacities, and set about the task of doing the work of Outward Bound "the right way." Unfortunately, he knew nothing about management and had no idea how quickly an endeavor such as he envisioned could eat up money. Rather than use some of his own money to get started and then focus on fund-raising, he just muddled along, spending more than he took in. It took Jeremy about 10 or 12 years to exhaust most of his inheritance in this way. He got to a point where all he had left was around $400,000 plus some assets, including a small ranch in Idaho, a small private plane, and a couple of cars. At this point, he realized that his Outward Bound–style boot camp idea had gone belly-up, and he closed it down. Realizing that he would need to work, he took a job as a bush pilot with an air service in Alaska. That is where he is working now.

In the course of running his failing business and seeing his inheritance dissipate, Jeremy has become much more knowledgeable regarding personal finances. He has invested the remainder of his inheritance wisely and leased out his ranch while he is working up north. He is pretty content using his flying certifications to make a living, and he is well prepared for retirement now, although his retirement will certainly not be as luxurious as it might have been, had he managed his inheritance wisely from the start.

Jeremy is an example of a very common problem among heirs who have grown up in families with wealth. Depending upon their parents, heirs to family fortunes may either be carefully groomed and prepared to manage the family wealth when the time comes, or they may be completely unprepared. If you have inherited money or will inherit money, you should ask yourself whether you know how to handle it. This has to do in part with the knowledge of personal finance referred to in the previous section of this chapter, but it has to do also with your general outlook on life. If things have simply "been taken care of" for your entire life up to this point, it may very well not even occur to you that inheriting money implies that you have things to take care of. It is very easy to spend a large amount of inherited money, even if you have the best intentions regarding how to use it.

If you suddenly find yourself in control of an inheritance, and you do not feel completely qualified to manage it and to handle your personal finances in general, it is probably best for you to strive for the time being to maintain the money in low-risk investments, using only interest income until such time as you feel you have gotten a handle on the situation. By "getting a handle," we do not mean that you need to have an MBA and be fully prepared to manage all your own affairs. You may still use the services of a financial advisor or broker. However, before you contemplate any major spending or any major investments, you should be confident that between you and your advisors, you should be able to make sound decisions. Just go slowly and exercise due caution. We are *not* saying that you should never spend inherited money. Inheriting money should be a good thing, and sometimes it makes sense to spend some money to improve your lifestyle. But you need to be aware of the costs and benefits of the decisions that you make. You need to have sufficient foresight to avoid the type of outcomes that Jeremy experienced.

FAITH'S UNFORTUNATE MARRIAGE

Faith was recently divorced following a marriage of 11 years. Faith and her ex-husband Hal were married right after college. They both came from wealthy families. Faith's dad had made a fortune owning mobile home parks and recreational vehicle campgrounds around the country, while Hal's family had a successful chemical company that made and marketed products for swimming pools. Following their marriage, Hal completed an MBA, while Faith had two children and settled down to the life of a wealthy suburban wife and mom. Faith inherited the bulk of her family's fortune when her dad died, approximately two years after her marriage. Because he had an MBA and was the working partner in the couple, Hal took over the management of the inheritance, along with the rest of the family finances.

Their marriage was happy for seven or eight years. Then they seemed to drift apart. Faith was focused on the children, while Hal was focused on business. He spent more and more time at work, and less and less time at home. Then Faith found out that he was having an affair. She began to make some inquiries, and found that, in fact, he had already been involved in several previous affairs. She confronted him, and in fairly short order they agreed to divorce.

While the divorce settlement was being drawn up, Faith found out that most of her inheritance had been invested under Hal's name or both of their names in a variety of ventures, some of which were good and some of which were dubious. Much of her money had actually been channeled into his family's business, which had first undergone a bit of a difficult period, and which Hal had subsequently expanded into a large home and resort pool construction business. The upshot of all these dealings was that Faith ended up with only about 20 percent of the fortune that she originally inherited. She was not left out in the cold starving or penniless, but she clearly suffered substantial losses. None of this took place as a result of intentional or premeditated fraud on the part of Hal, although it was clear in retrospect that he was always looking out for his own interests and those of his family throughout the course of their marriage. It was also particularly irksome to Faith that some of their combined fortunes had been spent on the women with whom Hal had been having his affairs.

Faith's story illustrates another way in which inherited money can be dissipated. An heir can be taken advantage of, either by a spouse, or by friends, or by investment advisors who may propose investments that prove more beneficial to them than to the heir doing the investing. Here again, the operative word is caution.

In the case of any heir to a substantial fortune who is contemplating marriage, we strongly recommend that you draft a prenuptial agreement. Even in the case where both prospective spouses have wealth, use a prenuptial agreement. The two spouses will probably not have equal fortunes, and if one spouse takes charge of running the family business affairs, there will always be a temptation, conscious or unconscious, to place his or her own interests ahead of those of the less involved spouse. Should a divorce ensue, this can generate unfair outcomes. It can also have the concomitant effect of increasing resentment and the level of acrimony that may be attendant upon the divorce. It can also complicate the settlement process, and it may make planning the succession of wealth to children difficult. This issue of succession can be particularly troublesome in second marriages, where the respective spouses may have separate heirs for whose interests they are looking out.

Of course, the above example does not encompass the possibility that an heir could marry someone who purposely sought out a wealthy spouse, either for his or her wealth alone, or because wealth was high up on some mental "checklist" of factors that a potential spouse had to have to qualify. In either case, an individual who has inherited a substantial amount of money would be well served by drafting a prenuptial agreement. The bottom line is that one never knows whether a marriage will work out and last a lifetime, and it is best for those who have inherited considerable wealth to operate on the assumption that there is at least a possibility that the marriage will not endure. A well-drafted prenuptial agreement may actually promote the success of a marriage, if it frees the wealthy heir from the burden of worrying about whether he or she is protected financially.

The final caution we raise for heirs is the possibility that people will ask you for personal loans or will ask you to make donations to various charities. While we have nothing against your helping a friend and nothing against charitable donations, the problem for the wealthy heir is that there is potentially no limit to these requests. Therefore it is up to you, the potential giver, to set limits. Specifically, we recommend that you do not make "loans" to friends. Make this a firm decision, and explain to any friends that ask that you simply cannot make any exceptions to this rule, because making an exception would unleash the floodgates. You can cite any number of literary quotes to justify your decision, from "Good fences make good neighbors," to "Neither a borrower nor a lender be." If the petitioner is a real friend, he or she will understand. Of course, you may have a friend who is genuinely down and out and needs money to pay hospital bills or to live for a time while he gets his finances in order following some disastrous setback. You may feel that you really need to do something to help out. If this is the case, just give him or her some money, with no strings attached.

So far as the solicitations of charities is concerned, the best course of action for the wealthy heir who receives many such requests is to establish a foundation and to direct all such requests to this foundation. You can decide how much giving you wish to do, and you can either decide for yourself how these funds will be divided up, or you can delegate someone to handle this chore. The idea is to maintain the status of your inheritance as a positive event in your life, rather than allow it to become a burden, as it quickly can become if you feel obligated to deal personally with every request for a donation that comes in.

None of the problems considered in this chapter is insurmountable, yet they are problems. If you have inherited money or will inherit money, you would be well advised to give the issues raised in this chapter some serious thought. Try to anticipate these problems before they come up in your life. In that way, you can derive the maximum possible benefit from your inheritance, with the fewest headaches possible.

When We Lose Our Wealth:
A Postscript for a Bad Economy

On March 8, 2009, a long-standing and extremely affluent client of mine (JT) came into my office and announced that he was at his wit's end because "everything that I have worked for all my life is going down the tube." His name is Jerry, and this is his story:

JERRY'S FINANCIAL LOSSES

Jerry is a handsome and vibrant 51-year-old entrepreneur. He is pretty much a self-made man. His parents were both physicians before they retired, and they could afford to send him to the best schools and give him some financial support when he began his first business, but Jerry had taken the advantages that his parents had afforded him and raised the financial status of the family to a whole new level. He had gone to Cornell, where he majored in business. Initially, his plan was to get an MBA. However, during his undergraduate years, he began a marketing business aimed at fellow students, and this venture was an overnight success. By the time Jerry graduated from the college, he had a six-figure income, plans for additional businesses, and no interest in pursuing an MBA.

For 20 years following graduation, Jerry had worked very hard to establish a number of different companies, almost all of which were successful to one degree or another. He had a unique gift for identifying potentially profitable business opportunities and putting them into operation. Over these years, Jerry had accumulated not only a great deal of wealth, but also a very large network of trusted associates and competent employees whom he viewed as "making it possible for me to act quickly to take advantage of any new business opportunities that I am able to identify." In short, Jerry was pretty close to the point where one might consider him to be the head of a modest "business empire."

But now, Jerry said that it seemed as if all that he had worked for was under attack, and he was feeling threatened. When he came into my office, Jerry explained that he had lost $14 million in the stock market since Election Day last November, and that his present income was only about 30 percent of what he had been making fairly regularly over the past decade. Jerry said that his market losses were primarily the result of the recent market downturn. However, he had lost more than an amount proportionate to the decline in the Dow Jones average, because he had made a pretty big investment in the Bernard Madoff ponzi scheme. He said that in retrospect, he could not believe how stupid he had been in getting involved in such an unlikely investment. He knew better. He had allowed himself to "get lazy," and "take the easy road." His total investment portfolio had been around $21 million less than a year ago. Now it was only worth about $7 million. Of course, his overall net worth was a good deal more than that. He still had considerable equity in his various businesses, and Jerry and his wife owned four residences, which together were possibly worth another $6 million. On the other hand, Jerry was quite aware that these holdings had also lost considerable value over the past several months.

Furthermore, Jerry's current business ventures were not doing well. Jerry said that he had just laid off half of the salespeople and office workers at his commercial real estate agency, because there was "nothing at all going on out there right now." He also said that he had decided to shut down another business altogether. This was a discount warehouse that specialized in high-end billiard tables, poker tables, and custom-built furniture to be used in home game rooms, libraries, and home theaters. Jerry said that the wealthy people who had such rooms were not redecorating, and the people who might otherwise contemplate including such rooms in their new homes were either scaling back on what they were building, or postponing their building plans altogether. Jerry said that it had killed him to have to let people go, because he felt responsible for these employees. They had been loyal to him, and he felt like a failure.

Jerry lamented that he was so stressed by his financial difficulties that he couldn't "eat, sleep, or make love." He said that he was very reluctant to share these adversities with his wife or his children, because he did not want to worry them, and because he did not want them to think of him "as a failure." Jerry felt that if he could not guarantee their financial security, he would be "letting them down." He recognized and stated that he felt as if his whole sense of worth as a man and a breadwinner was in danger.

On the positive side, Jerry was quite aware that he was still a very wealthy man. He explained that things had not yet gotten anywhere near the point at which he might have to ask his family to scale down their personal lifestyle. On the other hand, such steps were certainly "not out of the question" if the economy did not improve. Jerry said that he had already considered selling two of their four homes and their private plane, but he had held up because he knew that there was very little demand these days for ski houses in Vail, summer homes on Martha's Vineyard, or executive jets.

Jerry also said that his teenage son Jeff had been hearing about the bad economy from his friends at the expensive private school that he attended, and that Jeff had asked his father if it might be necessary for him to go to a state university, because the tuition would be cheaper there. Jeff told his father that he and his friends understood the economic downturn. They had discussed the issue, and they had all agreed that it would be okay if they had to modify their educational plans for the sake of the financial security of their families.

Jerry told me that on the one hand, it made him feel good that his son had enough awareness of the value of money that he could think in these terms, but he still felt badly that his son had to be considering such issues at this point in his life. Jerry felt that kids in high school had quite enough to worry about in terms of performing well academically and being accepted socially. They did not need to worry about money as well.

Jerry said that one of the things he had always been most proud of was the good life and the sense of security that he had been able to provide for his family. But now he felt that the foundations of the secure life that he had built were under siege and in jeopardy. Jerry said that after Jeff had spoken to him about the discussion he had with his friends, Jerry had taken great pains to reassure his son that they would still be able to send him to whatever college he wanted to go to, and that all he had to worry about was continuing to do well in school and thinking about what he might want to do with his life.

When Jerry shared these feelings and symptoms of anxiety with me, I responded first by acknowledging how difficult it must be for someone who had always been so very successful in virtually every business endeavor to experience the difficulties that he had described. I told him that one of the biggest problems with being a winner is the disappointment, dissonance, and confusion that results when adversities and setbacks do occur. I complimented Jerry for being able to share his concerns with me. I explained that I knew that this was not an easy thing for him to do. Many affluent men and women are quite able to share intimate aspects of their personal lives and problems, yet are extremely reluctant to reveal difficulties that pertain to their wealth and success, since their success is such a big part of their self-concept.

Once I felt that I had made clear to Jerry that I understood his anxieties and the internalizing symptoms that he was experiencing, I began to work toward making absolutely certain that he had a realistic view of his current circumstances, so that he could maintain both a healthy self-concept and an optimistic outlook for the future. I suggested that when Jerry evaluated himself and his accomplishments, he needed to take into consideration the entire picture, rather than focusing solely on the recent losses and setbacks. I did not bother suggesting to him that most people would love to have his net worth, because: (1) I knew that he was fully aware of the fact that he was still extremely wealthy compared to most people; and (2) I also knew quite well that "most people" was not a reference group to which Jerry typically compared himself. However, I did suggest to him that he had accomplished a great deal over the course of his lifetime, and that in point of fact only a very successful man could lose as much as he had just lost. This got a bit of a laugh, so I figured I must be on the right track.

I also made it a point to compliment Jerry on how he had raised his son, as well as on the manner in which he had reassured his son that there would be no need for any changes in his plans for college. I pointed out that in spite of his very real worries, it was clear that Jerry was still firmly grounded in reality. He knew that his family's basic lifestyle was not in imminent danger of being disrupted by the financial difficulties he was experiencing, and he had not allowed his own anxiety to interfere with the goal of making them feel secure. I told him that he should be proud of the manner in which his son had responded to the economic downturn and the anxious discussions that were taking place among his peers in school, in that Jeff had demonstrated concern for the family rather than selfish entitlement. I observed that our strengths are revealed during times of adversity, and it was clear to me that Jerry had done a very good job raising his son with a good set of values and priorities. I also suggested that the concern that Jerry had expressed for his employees seemed to be reflected in his son's concerns for the welfare of their own family.

Having made these positive observations, I also made it clear to Jerry that I believed the symptoms that he reported were problematic, and that we needed to deal with them. I said that losing sleep, losing his appetite, and losing interest in sex were understandable short-term reactions to stress, but they should diminish in intensity as it becomes more and more clear that: (1) the setbacks he had experienced are not a significant threat to the fundamental well-being of the family; (2) these setbacks are temporary in nature and will be resolved satisfactorily in due course; and (3) these problems were not primarily problems of Jerry's making. I reminded him of something that he certainly knew far better than I, i.e., that the economy runs in cycles that are beyond the control of any one individual. I also told him that he could choose to castigate himself for investing with Madoff if he chose to do so; but if he did so, he would be in very good company.

Interestingly, Jerry responded very enthusiastically to the latter suggestion, confirming that he had many friends and associates who had made that same bad investment. I found this response very interesting, in light of the point made earlier in this volume that high achievers tend to use wealth less as a means to gratify desires than as a means of "keeping score" in the competition for success. I realized that Jerry was not nearly as concerned with the several million dollars that he had lost through this poor investment as he was with the poor judgment that he had shown in making the investment. The fact that other businessmen whom he respected had made the same mistake was truly comforting to him.

With a little time and frequent reminders that the problems were not the result of his ineptitude, not catastrophic, and not permanent, I am quite certain that Jerry will be just fine. He is too bright, too strong, and too resilient to allow himself to be overwhelmed by these adversities. Nevertheless, the problems that he has experienced make it clear that financial loss can be extremely difficult for the affluent.

Jerry's visit also made it quite clear to me that the present draft of this book was lacking this chapter on the impact on the affluent of losing part or all or their wealth. When I e-mailed Orla to see how she felt about adding a chapter, she came back immediately with several similar stories from her practice, as well as a bunch of recent newspaper articles she had saved dealing with problems experienced by the wealthy during the recent economic downturn. One of the families that Orla has been seeing appears to be experiencing even worse problems arising out of loss of wealth than my client Jerry, as you will see below:

I (OC) work with a family who lost approximately 90 percent of their family wealth in the Lehman Brothers failure. At the same time, the primary breadwinner in this family lost his source of income, putting the family into a very serious financial crisis. Unlike the case Jim presented above, this family's losses were such that they have already had to make significant changes in their lifestyles:

A Wealthy Family Is Forced to "Cut Back"

Barbara, a 46-year-old client with whom I have worked for several years, recently tearfully informed me that she would need to greatly cut back on her visits to me, because she and her husband were nearly broke. She explained that they had "lost pretty much everything" that they had saved over the last 20 years as a result of the Lehman Brothers failure. In addition, her husband, Sam, who had made a great living over the years as the owner of a successful powerboat dealership, had recently been forced to shut down the business and declare bankruptcy. Barbara said that until her husband could find new employment, the family would be forced to make do living on her salary as a special education coordinator in the local public school system.

The upshot of these adversities was that the family simply could not maintain its previous luxurious lifestyle. Barbara's salary barely covered the mortgage and tax payments on their $2 million home in an affluent Connecticut suburb. Barbara's husband had managed to scrape together a small cushion through the liquidation of some of the assets of the powerboat company, but they felt that they needed to hold on to this money in case of an emergency. They were up in the air as to what their future earnings and expenses might be, and they felt that until they got "back on an even keel," they should not spend any money at all that was not absolutely necessary. Complicating matters still further was the fact that they had three children ranging in age from 13 through 17, all of whom would be needing money for college. They had a little money set aside in special college funds, but not enough to cover a substantial portion of the costs of school.

So they had cut back. Barbara and Sam stopped going to New York City for the "theater weekends" that they had always loved. They cut out all expensive dining and most of their use of local convenience restaurants and take-out food. They cut out their spa visits and the masseuse who came to their house once a week. They also sold the two horses that they had kept in a local stable for their two daughters. This was done not so much for the money the horses brought (which was almost nothing), but to eliminate the expenses associated with keeping the horses (which were great). They sold the family's third car (a large SUV) and they put the family's lake house in New Hampshire on the market (though it had not sold yet). They canceled all their plans for vacations, even the trips that they had routinely taken by virtue of their ownership of several vacation time-shares.

They had considered selling the time-shares, but they found that the market was so bad they would really just be "giving them away." Therefore they had postponed the use of the shares to the extent that they could, in hopes of either using them or selling them when times got better.

Barbara and Sam had completely discontinued any retail purchases of clothing or luxury items, and they asked their children to cut back as well. This request brought forth howls of anguish from the kids, who had previously been given pretty much carte blanche to use their credit cards at the mall to buy whatever they needed, including clothing for school, school supplies, sporting goods and sneakers, and electronic devices such as cell phones and MP3 players.

Barbara indicated to me that the kids had always done reasonably well in school, but she was genuinely fearful that these changes might cause them to act out. They had never been in a position where it was necessary to be careful about spending or to deny themselves a new pair of jeans or a CD, and in this unfamiliar situation, the children felt put upon and victimized.

Barbara said that she and her husband had also suggested the possibility that the kids get some part-time work after school to help with their expenses and perhaps save some money for college. However, to the complete surprise of Barbara and Sam, all three of the children rejected this idea out of hand. Their 17-year-old son said that he simply did not have time to work, keep up his grades, and apply to colleges all at the same time. Their youngest daughter said that she would not be "caught dead" flipping burgers or running a cash register for minimum wage. After all, what would she ever do if her classmates ran into her while she was working? It would be "so humiliating."

I (OC) told Barbara that the issues associated with having to economize were quite serious, more for the children than for the parents, since the children did not know any life other than the life of ease they had experienced previously. I pointed out that kids who grew up with few constraints in terms of money were quite likely to interpret the family's economic adversities as a tragedy of monumental proportion, and they were likely to be angry at the parents who could no longer provide everything to which they had come to feel entitled. I told Barbara that her apprehension regarding possible acting-out behavior on the part of the children was justified, and we should be very careful to explain to the children what had happened and to monitor their coping responses.

I suggested to Barbara that, despite the money crunch, this did not seem to be the best time to cut back on seeing me. I took great pains to reassure her that over the years, I had come to care a great deal for her welfare and that of her family, and I promised that we would be able work something out in terms of my fees that would enable her to continue to see me over the next few months, while everyone was getting adjusted to their new circumstances.

It remains to be seen how everyone in this family will adjust to the adversities they are facing, and it remains unclear for how long the financial distress might continue. I do feel optimistic regarding the family's future, because

Barbara and Sam have always had a thoughtful approach to the various issues that have arisen over the course of their marriage, and I feel confident that they will approach this new challenge in the same spirit. But make no mistake about it: It is not easy for affluent people who have prided themselves on their success to come to grips with significant loss of wealth.

Issues Associated with Loss of Wealth

The cases we have considered above provide pretty good illustrations of some of the problems that wealthy individuals and families may encounter when they suffer a serious loss of wealth. However, these illustrations do not exhaust the wealth loss issues that may arise. In order to identify other potential problems that may accompany a loss of wealth, we went back over the previous 12 chapters of this book and identified a series of observations that we had made with respect to the meaning of wealth in the culture of affluence. Each of these observations on the meaning of wealth has a corollary that pertains to the loss of wealth:

Success Is Relative, and the Loss of Wealth Is Therefore Relative as Well. We have noted that the affluent use money as a means of keeping score in the competition of life. Success is not measured by the absolute value of one's wealth, but rather by the comparison of how much we have acquired relative to others. Furthermore, in the culture of affluence, the fact that your wealth may be in the 99th percentile of all the adults in the United States means very little. What matters is how your success (i.e., your wealth) compares to that of your peers from business school or your professional colleagues. Therefore, paradoxically, a large loss of wealth that affects us along with many of our peers, such as a loss caused by an unavoidable downturn in the economy, may not be as devastating as a loss that is unique to the individual. This is why my (JT's) client Jerry was cheered by the fact that many people had lost money in the stock market. It is almost as if the losses that he had suffered could not justifiably be counted against him in the competition that comprises the culture of affluence. Jerry was even comforted by the fact that the mistake he had made by investing in the Madoff ponzi scheme had also been made by a number of other affluent and presumably savvy investors.

I can also attest to the greater importance of relative success than absolute success among the affluent based on the experience of my (JT's) son-in-law. He is a very successful investment banker. During the recent difficult times, he has certainly not been making as much money as he had been making over the preceding decade. However, in comparison to many of his peers, he has not been hurt nearly as badly. Many of the investments that he made have proved to be relatively recession-proof, so the downturn in the economy did not impact him as hard as it impacted many. Therefore, paradoxically, my son-in-law is now just as proud as a peach that he has come out of this economic downturn looking "not so bad." When he tells you how small his losses have been and how little his income has fallen off, you would think from his affect and tone of voice that he had just quadrupled his net worth. Well, he has not increased his net worth in an absolute sense, but he has clearly won the competition that counts. He has beaten his peers.

Affluence Is Addictive. Affluent individuals, whether they are born into money or become wealthy on their own, can become addicted to wealth. Even though the most competitive individuals among us use money more to keep score than as a means of acquiring tangible rewards, we all have the tendency to get used to being pampered. This aspect of affluence is almost like a substance abuse disorder. We know that there are some people who are born alcoholics, but even among those who are not born with the problem, it can still sneak up on us. Most people who drink alcohol over the course of a lifetime will eventually develop a degree of tolerance, followed by some degree of dependence, sometimes followed eventually by a full-scale addiction.

It is the same with the substance called money. As we are becoming affluent, the first few times we purchase something really expensive, we really appreciate what we have bought. However, over time, we get used to "having the best," and eventually we feel deprived if we are forced to settle for anything less. When Barbara and Sam had to give up their spa treatments and the weekly massages at home, they felt deprived—really deprived. The loss of wealth can be truly devastating.

Although there is no way of knowing exactly what his greatest source of pain may have been, it is worth noting that after losing most of his wealth, the German industrialist Adolf Merkel committed suicide on January 5, 2009. He was 74 years old. He had been the 94th richest person in the world in 2008, with a net worth of $9.2 billion. A *New York Times* report (January 6, 2009) indicated that poor investment decisions concerning his Volkswagen shares had pushed his business empire to the brink of disaster.

We have all heard the stories of the many suicides following the stock market crash of 1929. Suffice it to say, the loss of wealth can be devastating. It should not be taken lightly, either by the affluent individuals who are affected by the loss, or by any professional with whom they might consult.

Financial Adversity Is Worst among Those Who Have Never Known It. The affluent individuals who are hit hardest by the loss of wealth are those who have always been affluent. A teenager who has never lived without a full-time housekeeper to clean his room and iron his shirts will have a much more difficult time adapting to life without the housekeeper than his father, who worked his way up from a blue-collar family to become a successful investment banker.

We have all heard stories from men who told us that over the course of their lifetimes, they had "made and lost" a dozen fortunes. These men speak with authority, based on the experience of having nothing and living off very little. If you have been poor, then you know that you can survive being poor. If you grew up in a modest middle-class family, you probably did chores around the house. You probably had some experience with part-time work, even if it was only to earn spending money. When you applied to college, you knew that you would have to apply for a scholarship, and you knew that you would most likely go to the school that gave you the most money, rather than the one to which your more affluent friends are going, the friends who did not even apply for a scholarship.

On the other hand, if you have always been wealthy, the world without wealth is an uncertain and frightening place. If you have used the credit cards your parents gave you since you were old enough to sign your name, the possibility of not having them is a real threat. If you are a teenager who has never had to say "no" to yourself when you wanted to buy something, it may be difficult to learn to say no for the first time, all of a sudden, when you have reached the age of 18. From the other side of the family, if you are a self-made, successful, affluent parent who has suffered recently from financial adversity and plans to react reasonably by cutting back, keep in mind that what is clearly reasonable for you may be very strange and very frightening for your children.

It Is Difficult to Talk about the Loss of Wealth. Affluent people who lose much of their wealth may be devastated, yet unable to tell anyone how upset they really are. They may be reluctant to share their anxieties with their spouse and children, because these are the very people that the affluent achiever has been trying to protect. Also, these are the people whose opinions matter the most to us, and we do not under any circumstances want to be viewed as failures by those for whom we are responsible.

Affluent persons who seek professional help from mental health workers may be embarrassed to reveal the extent of their distress. This is particularly the case among the affluent who have lost much, but still have a great deal. They may think that they cannot confide their anxieties to their therapist, because "He doesn't have nearly as much money as I do even after my losses, so he'll think I'm crazy." Unfortunately, it is quite true that many mental health professionals tend to minimize the impact of the loss of wealth among their wealthy clients. This is a very big mistake that indicates a serious lack of empathy on the part of the professional. The first thing that the professional must do when he or she senses the pain that a client is experiencing in connection with the loss of wealth is to acknowledge the reality and the severity of this pain. This in no way precludes the introduction of a reality check on the patient's relative wealth at some point in the intervention. But it is important for wealthy clients and their therapists alike to recognize that the distress of significant financial loss can be quite real.

Changes in Activities Can Have Both Negative and Positive Effects. If you are a wealthy individual who has lost wealth and given up some of your more expensive hobbies and activities as a result, keep in mind that these changes can have both negative and positive effects. If you give up golf, tennis, and skiing because they are costly pursuits, you should recognize that you still need exercise, and that there are many ways of getting exercise that do not require the expenditure of vast sums of money. You might need to give up the ski house in Vail, but you probably still have a gym nearby or a treadmill in the basement. So do not let the loss of wealth be compounded by the loss of health associated with the lack of exercise.

On the other side of the coin, changes in activities made necessary by the loss of wealth can open new interests and avenues for enjoyment. Cutting back on visits to four-star restaurants might give birth to a new or renewed interest in gourmet cooking at home. Cutting back on foreign travel could lead to the development of a healthy interest in hiking local trails or fishing in the local reservoir.

The bottom line here, of course, is that individuals who are flexible and open to new experiences may have a much easier time adapting to the stress of a major financial setback than individuals who lack flexibility.

The Experience of Adversity Can Help Develop Resiliency in Kids. One of the greatest fears that some affluent individuals experience in connection with a significant loss of wealth is that the financial difficulties will remove the mantle of security from their children, leaving them vulnerable to insecurity and possibly resentful of the father or mother who can no longer provide everything they want without hesitation. But you need to think of the other side of the coin here as well. A degree of travail can help to make kids strong and resilient. It may help them learn a bit about impulse control, and it may help them to develop a work ethic that they otherwise would not have had. Kids who have to work for some of what they have tend to appreciate it more; and often in the long run they feel better about themselves. They begin to realize that they can do something for themselves.

The Loss of Wealth Triggers Control Issues. The reader may recall that one of the problems of the culture of affluence is the misguided belief that one can be in control of every aspect of his or her life, as if money can eliminate all our problems. This is the misconception to which we referred in the first chapter of this book, where we referred to the major league baseball player who recognized that his multimillion-dollar contract did not solve all his problems, despite the assertion of a reporter that he no longer has any problems. That pitcher correctly observed that money did not guarantee good health or satisfactory personal relationships. It only paid his bills.

While this is certainly true, affluent individuals who experience a significant loss of wealth often have the perception that, "My world is falling apart." If you have lost a lot of money in the stock market or your business has gone belly-up, you probably feel that life is out of control. But the reality is that *you never had life under control.* This was an illusion and a reflection of unrealistic delusions of personal power, based in large measure on the sacrosanct status awarded to wealth in the culture of affluence.

It may not be a pleasant experience to recognize of the reality that we are never completely in control by the advent of a major financial setback, but in the long run, the reality check may prove highly useful to our personal development. The fact is that we are not often either as much in control as our wealth might lead us to believe, nor as out of control as the loss of significant wealth may make us feel. The only folks who have some genuine idea regarding what we can control and what we can never control are those who have made and lost fortunes several times. These folks know that there are many forces in life that are beyond our control; yet they also know that we are resilient, and we can pick up the pieces, start over, and recover from losses. Even among these folks, many do not know anything at all about what we can and cannot control with regard to our health, or about what we can or cannot control with regard to our personal relationships.

Appendix: An Empirical Study of Professional Social Workers' Attitudes toward the Affluent

Lest any reader question our assertion that professionals may hold negative attitudes toward the affluent that might impact the services they provide to affluent clients, we present here the results of an empirical study of social workers' attitudes toward adolescent clients from families of different income levels. The results of this study clearly indicated that social workers tend to consider an adolescent from a wealthy family as more selfish and entitled than an otherwise similar adolescent from a low income family. The results of this study also suggested strongly that these negative attitudes toward the affluent client are reflected in the quality of service that social workers provide to clients of different income levels.

THE STUDY METHOD

I (OC) surveyed 359 members of the Clinical Division of the National Association of Social Workers. These respondents comprised approximately 20 percent of a random sample of 1,800 NASW members whose participation in the survey study was solicited by mail.

The responding clinicians read a vignette that described an adolescent client who comes to a social worker to begin psychotherapy. The adolescent's presenting problem was described as depression, based on a perception of personal worthlessness and a view that life is meaningless. In the vignette, the adolescent client was described in general terms as intelligent, articulate, and attractive. The client was also described as coming from an intact family. The income level of the family was manipulated in the description contained in the vignette. The client was described as coming from a family having one of three different levels with respect to annual family income: (1) under $20,000; (2) about $50,000; or "in excess of $400,000." The client was also described as being either female or male. The gender of the client was manipulated so as to: (1) make the findings of the study generalizable to clients of either gender; (2) allow the investigator to test for the significance of the effect of gender on social workers' attitudes toward the client; and (3) indicate any possible interaction between the client's gender and family income level in terms of the social workers' attitudes toward the client.

Each social worker who participated in the study read and responded to only one vignette. This vignette had one of the six possible combinations of client family income (three levels) and gender (male vs. female). Approximately equal numbers of respondents read a vignette representing each of these six combinations. The exact number of respondents who rated clients with each of the six combinations of family income and gender are presented in Table 4. By employing a between-subjects design (i.e., by having each respondent rate just one vignette) we made it impossible for any one respondent to determine that the study would be making comparisons of the attitudes expressed toward clients with differing income levels or clients with different genders. This eliminates the possibility that respondents might rate adolescents of different income levels similarly, in an effort to appear unbiased.[1]

After reading the vignette contained in his or her survey, the responding social worker was asked to rate the client described in the vignette on a series of 15 adjectives. Ratings were made on seven-point scales with response options ranging from "not at all like the client" to "exactly like the client." The adjectives on which the respondents rated the client are presented in Table 1. Some of the adjectives are positive descriptors, while others have more negative connotations. The ratings assigned by respondents on these adjectives were examined through a procedure known as factor analysis, which enabled us to identify the attitude dimensions that underlie the ratings that respondents assigned on the 15 different adjectives.[2] The use of adjective rating scales that are factor-analyzed to identify attitudes makes the attitude measurement procedure "nonreactive" in nature. This means that respondents are unlikely to assign ratings based on their perceptions of what responses might be considered socially acceptable or appropriate for a social work professional. Instead, the ratings are more likely to reflect the respondents' unconscious attitude toward the client described in the vignette.

Scores were obtained for each respondent on each of the attitude dimensions identified in the factor analysis.[3] These scores became dependent variables, which were compared in terms of the income level of the client described, the gender of the client described, and the gender of the responding social worker. The specific statistical procedure employed for this purpose was a multivariate analysis of variance. Client income, client gender, and respondent gender were the independent variables in this analysis.[4]

The research instrument also measured the respondents' perceptions of the seriousness of the adolescent's problem and their prognosis for the case. Finally, the survey included measures of the responding social worker's background characteristics that might be related to attitudes toward the wealthy. These included that income level of the responding worker's family of origin, the respondent's experience with pre-service and/or in-service training relative to the culture of affluence, and the extensiveness of the respondent's experience working with clients of various income levels. Items relating to training in the culture of affluence and experience working with clients of various income levels were embedded in sections of the survey that covered many different types of training and client groups. In this way, the items that were concerned with affluence were rendered less obtrusive. In addition, the responding social worker's theoretical orientation, employment setting, length of experience in clinical social work, and personal income level were assessed.

RESULTS

Table 1 indicates the mean and standard deviation of the ratings of the 15 adjectives on which the respondents rated the clients in the vignettes. Note that some of the adjectives have a positive connotation, while others

Table 1   Descriptive Statistics for Respondents' Ratings of Adolescent Clients on 15 Adjectives

Adjective	Mean	Standard deviation
Compassionate	4.01	1.08
Arrogant	2.62	1.31
Vain	2.64	1.30
Self-reliant	3.64	1.23
Aimless	4.10	1.54
Interesting	4.58	1.26
Sober	4.06	1.22
Prejudiced	2.99	1.28
Entitled	3.58	1.50
Selfish	3.43	1.35
Superficial	3.27	1.37
Hardworking	4.09	1.22
Competent	4.35	1.20
Motivated	3.63	1.34
Fragile	4.77	1.49

have a negative connotation. On the seven-point rating scale employed here, a mean rating of 4.0 would correspond to the midpoint of the scale, indicating neither a positive nor a negative view of the client. Thus, across the entire sample, and regardless of how the client's family income was described, the respondents tended to view the client as relatively fragile (mean = 4.77), interesting (mean = 4.58), and competent (mean = 4.35). They tended not to view the client as arrogant (mean = 2.62), vain (mean = 2.64), or prejudiced (mean = 2.99). There was substantial variability in the ratings on all 15 items.

Table 2 presents the results of the factor analysis of these ratings. Based on various statistical criteria, it was determined that the ratings could best be described in terms of two attitude factors that respondents held with respect to the clients described in the vignettes.[5] The numbers listed under each of these two factors in Table 2 are called loadings. They constitute the correlations between each of the two factors and each of the 15 attitudes. For each factor, the adjectives having the strongest correlations have been underlined. These adjectives serve to describe the factors.

Table 2   Rotated Factor Matrix for Principal Components Analysis of Client Ratings

	Loading on	
Adjective	Factor 1	Factor 2
Compassionate	.474	.479
Arrogant	.652	.396
Vain	.653	.431
Self-reliant	.373	.529
Aimless	.350	.051
Interesting	.459	.480
Sober	.233	.124
Prejudiced	.466	.375
Entitled	.701	.452
Selfish	.734	.367
Superficial	.716	.211
Hardworking	.557	.553
Competent	.335	.638
Motivated	.470	.505
Fragile	.063	.035

(Underlined loadings exceed .50 in absolute value)

The loadings in Table 2 indicate that the items loading above .50 in absolute value on Factor 1 include, in descending order of absolute value: selfish (.734); superficial (.716); entitled (.701); arrogant (.652); and hardworking (.557). Accordingly, this factor was named "self-centered and entitled." The items that loaded above .50 in absolute value on factor 2 included, in descending order of absolute value: competent (.638); hardworking (.553); self-reliant (.529); and motivated (.505). Therefore, Factor 2 was named "competent and self-sufficient." These factors represent the salient attitude dimensions along which the responding social workers conceptualized the clients they rated. It is clear that the items we selected to be included in the 15-item rating scale have captured two attitudes that are highly relevant to the issue of social class.

Factor scores were generated for each of these two factors, and a statistical procedure known as a three-way multivariate analysis of variance was performed. The acronym for this procedure is MANOVA. This analysis indicated, among other things, whether the respondents' attitudes toward the client described in the vignette varied on the basis of the family income level of the client, the gender of the client, and the gender of the responding social worker. The results of this analysis are presented in Tables 3 and 4. Table 3 contains the results of the actual statistical tests used to determine whether differences due to these factors were statistically significant, and Table 4 presents the mean scores on each attitude dimension for groups of respondents representing the different values of client income level, client gender, respondent gender, and the combinations of these factors.

The data contained in Table 3 include both multivariate and univariate tests of significance. The multivariate tests tell us whether the groups defined by a particular variable or combination of variables differ significantly across the two attitude domains, and the univariate tests tell us whether the groups differ significantly on a particular attitude domain. The multivariate tests are included primarily as a statistical control on false positive results, while the univariate tests tell us whether the variables of interest (client income, client gender, and respondent gender) actually make a difference in how the respondents regard the client described in the vignette.

Table 3 contains a significant univariate F-test for client income on Factor 1, the "self-centered and entitled" factor.[6] This means that respondents who read vignettes in which the client's family income was described differently tended to evaluate the client differently in terms of how self-centered they saw him. The mean scores presented in Table 4 indicate that when the client was described as coming from a family with an income over $400,000, the mean score assigned to the client on the self-centered dimension was .32 (sd = 0.95). In contrast, the mean score was .02 on this dimension when the client was described as coming from a middle-class family with an income of approximately $50,000; and the mean score was .36 when the client was described as coming from a family with an income of under

Table 3   Multivariate and Univariate Significance tests: MANOVA of Factor Scores Measuring Attitudes toward Adolescent Client by Client's Family Income, Client's Gender, and Respondent's Gender

	Multivariate Test		Univariate Test for:			
			Factor 1		Factor 2	
			Self-Centered		Competent	
Effect	F	p	F	p	F	p
Client income (A)	3.29^1	.011	5.14^3	.004	0.88^3	.417
Client gender (B)	0.54^2	.581	0.55^4	.460	0.51^4	.474
Respondent gender (C)	0.76^1	.471	1.27^4	.269	0.32^4	.570
A x B	1.12^2	.348	1.88^3	.154	0.32^3	.726
A x C	1.92^1	.106	3.70^3	.026	0.14^3	.873
B x C	0.30^1	.744	0.04^4	.852	0.56^4	.459
A x B x C	1.21^2	.305	1.84^3	.133	0.41^3	.667

^{1}df = 4 and 692.
^{2}df = 2 and 346.
^{3}df = 2 and 347.
^{4}df = 1 and 347.

$20,000. Thus, the wealthier the client's family, the more the respondents tended to view him or her as self-centered. Specifically, clients from wealthy families (over $400,000) were considered significantly more self-centered than clients from poor families (under $20,000).

The F-tests in Table 3 indicated no significant effect due to client family income level on the "competent" factor. Thus, although they tended to view a wealthier client as more self-centered, they did not necessarily see that client as either more or less competent than a middle class or poor client. In addition the F-tests in Table 3 indicated no significant main effects due to either client gender or to the gender of the respondent. Thus, overall, there was no difference in how self-centered or how competent the respondents viewed female and male clients, nor was there any overall difference in how self-centered or competent the client was, based on the gender of the either the client or the respondent.

There was, however, a significant interaction between client income and respondent gender on the self-centered factor.[7] This significant finding means that whatever the difference was between the ratings assigned to the wealthier and the poorer clients, these differences were not the same when the respondents were female from what they were when the respondents were male. The means shown in Table 4 for the ratings assigned on

Table 4   Cell and Marginal Means: MANOVA of Factor Scores Measuring Attitudes toward Adolescent Client by Client's Family Income, Client's Gender, and Respondent's Gender

Client Income	Client Gender	Respondent Gender	n	Factor 1 Mean	Factor 1 SD	Factor 2 Mean	Factor 2 SD
Under $20K	Both	Both	117	.36	0.96	.09	1.03
About $50K	Both	Both	120	.02	0.97	.01	1.02
Over $400K	Both	Both	122	.32	0.95	.10	0.95
All levels	Female	Both	175	.06	0.96	.08	1.00
All levels	Male	Both	184	.06	1.03	.08	0.99
All levels	Both	Female	295	.02	1.01	.01	1.00
All levels	Both	Male	64	.10	0.95	.06	0.98
Under $20K	Female	Both	60	.39	0.91	.03	1.09
	Male	Both	57	.33	1.02	.14	0.96
About $50K	Female	Both	59	.18	0.94	.07	1.02
	Male	Both	61	.13	0.98	.10	1.02
Over $400K	Female	Both	56	.42	0.86	.21	0.89
	Male	Both	66	.24	1.02	.00	1.01
Under $20K	Both	Female	98	.46	0.93	.07	1.04
	Both	Male	19	.13	0.95	.18	0.96
About $50K	Both	Female	100	.07	1.00	.01	0.97
	Both	Male	20	.20	0.84	.16	1.23
Over $400K	Both	Female	97	.32	0.94	.10	1.00
	Both	Male	25	.33	1.00	.10	0.76
All levels	Female	Female	143	.04	0.96	.12	1.99
		Male	32	.15	0.99	.08	1.06
	Male	Female	152	.08	1.06	.08	1.01
		Male	32	.05	0.92	.04	0.92
Under $20K	Female	Female	48	.48	0.89	.03	1.07
		Male	12	.03	0.91	.30	1.19
	Male	Female	50	.43	0.99	.17	1.01
		Male	7	.41	1.05	.02	0.35
About $50K	Female	Female	49	.26	0.93	.09	0.99
		Male	10	.22	0.95	.01	1.17

Cell and Marginal Means: MANOVA of Factor Scores Measuring Attitudes toward Adolescent Client by Client's Family Income, Client's Gender, and Respondent's Gender (continued)

Client Income	Client Gender	Respondent Gender	n	Mean	SD	Mean	SD
	Male	Female	51	.12	1.03	.06	0.95
		Male	10	.17	0.74	.29	1.01
Over $400K	Female	Female	46	.35	0.84	.23	0.91
		Male	10	.76	0.90	.13	0.89
	Male	Female	51	.31	1.03	.03	1.07
		Male	15	.03	0.98	.08	0.77

the self-centered factor to clients of various income levels by respondents who were female and by respondents who were male indicate that the female respondents tended to manifest greater discrepancies in their ratings of the wealthy and the poor clients than did male respondents. Among female respondents, the mean score on the self-centered factor assigned to clients with family incomes under $20,000 was .46 (sd = .93), compared to a mean of .32 (sd = .94) assigned to clients with family incomes over $400,000. In contrast, among male respondents, the mean score on the self-centered factor assigned to clients with family incomes under $20,000 was .13 (sd = .95), compared to a mean of .33 (sd = 1.00) assigned to clients with family incomes over $400,000. Thus the female respondents tended to view the poorer clients as much less self-centered than more affluent clients, whereas male respondents tended to view the poorer clients as only a little less self-centered than richer clients.

Respondents also rated the client described in the vignette they read in terms of their perceptions of the seriousness of the client's presenting problem, their self-perceptions of their ability to help the client, and their prognosis for the client. These ratings were cross-tabulated by the income level of the client as described in the vignette, and chi-square tests were performed to determine whether any of these ratings were related significantly to the family income level of the client.[8] These cross-tabulations and chi-square tests are presented in Tables 5, 6, and 7.

Table 5 presents the cross-tabulation of the respondent's rating of the seriousness of the client's presenting problem by the client's family income level. The data in Table 5 indicate a significant relationship between these two variables (chi-square (6) = 13.14, p = .041). Referring to the cell counts and column percentages in the table, we note that 8.6 percent of the respondents who read a description of a client with a family income under $20,000 rated that client's presenting problem as "extremely serious." Only 1.7 percent of

Table 5   Cross-tabulation of Perceived Seriousness of Client's Problem by Client's Family Income Level

	Client's Family Income					
Rating of Problem Seriousness	Under $20,000		About $50,000		Over $400,000	
	n	%	n	%	n	%
Not at all serious	1	0.9	2	1.7	2	1.7
Somewhat serious	55	47.4	53	44.5	56	47.5
Quite serious	50	43.1	62	52.1	59	50.0
Extremely serious	10	8.6	2	1.7	1	0.8

Chi-square (6) = 13.13, p = .041. (6 cells have expected frequencies less than 5.0)
When "not at all serious" and "somewhat serious" categories are collapsed into a single category, Chi-square (4) = 12.73, p = .013.

the respondents who read a vignette describing the client as having a family income of about $50,000 rated the client's presenting problem as extremely serious, and only 0.8 percent of the respondents who read a vignette describing the client as having a family income in excess of $400,000 rated the problem as extremely serious. This indicates a tendency among social workers to perceive the problems of a low-income client as more serious than those of an otherwise identical higher-income client.[9]

Table 6 presents the cross-tabulation of the respondents' ratings of how much they felt they could help the adolescent client described in the vignette by the family income of the client as described in the vignette. The data in Table 6 indicate that none of the respondents responded that they would

Table 6   Cross-tabulation of Perceived Degree to Which Respondent May Be Helpful to the Client by the Client's Family Income Level

	Client's Family Income					
Rating of How Much Respondent Might Help	Under $20,000		About $50,000		Over $400,000	
	n	%	n	%	n	%
Not at all	0	0.0	0	0.0	0	0.0
Very little	6	5.2	3	2.5	4	3.4
Quite a bit	90	77.6	88	73.9	95	79.8
A great deal	20	17.2	28	23.5	20	16.8

Chi-square (4) = 3.19, p = .526

Table 7   Cross-tabulation of Prognosis by the Client's Family Income Level

Prognosis	Client's Family Income					
	Under $20,000		About $50,000		Over $400,000	
	n	%	n	%	n	%
Very poor	1	0.9	0	0.0	0	0.0
Somewhat poor	9	7.8	4	3.4	9	7.6
Good	92	79.3	90	76.3	80	67.2
Very good	14	12.1	24	20.3	30	25.2

Chi-square (6) = 10.97, p = .089 (3 cells have expected cell frequencies less than 5.0)

When "very poor" and "somewhat poor" are collapsed into a single category, chi-square (4) = 9.39, p = .052.

not be able to help the client "at all," and very few felt that they would be able to help the client only "a little bit." Approximately three-fourths of the respondents indicated that they would be able to help the client "quite a bit," and approximately 20 percent indicated that they would be able to help the client "a great deal." The chi-square calculated for this contingency table was not significant (chi-square (4) = 3.19, p = .526). This suggests that the respondents' views regarding how much they might help the client are unrelated to the client's family income level.

Table 7 presents the cross-tabulation of the respondent's prognosis for the client described in the vignette by the family income of the client. The data in Table 7 indicate that nearly three-fourths of the respondents felt that the client's prognosis was "good," and nearly 20 percent felt that the client's prognosis was "very good." Somewhat fewer respondents who rated a client described as having a family income under $20,000 assigned the client a very good prognosis (12.1 percent) than did respondents who rated a client described as having a family income of about $50,000 (20.3 percent) or respondents who rated a client described as having a family income over $400,000 (25.2 percent). However, the chi-square test for the contingency table narrowly missed being statistically significant (chi-square (6) = 10.97, p = .089).[10] Thus we could not conclude with certainty that social workers tend to view the prognosis of a client described as having a high family income more favorably than that of an otherwise identical client described as having a relatively low family income. There is a trend in this direction, but the results are not conclusive.

In addition to these analyses, we ran a multiple regression analysis to determine how well scores on the self-centered and entitled factor could be predicted from the three major variables of interest in the study, client income, client gender, and respondent gender. Also included as predictors in this analysis were the respondent demographic and background variables noted above, including the income level of the responding worker's family of origin, the respondent's experience with pre-service and/or in-service training relative to the culture of affluence, and the extensiveness of the respondent's experience working with clients of various income levels. The results of this analysis were unremarkable. The overall regression was highly significant, as expected.[11] However, tests for the significance of the individual predictors yielded only one significant result, that pertaining to client income level.[12] None of the remaining predictors explained a significant proportion of the variability in scores measuring the perception of the client as self-centered and entitled. These findings suggest that the client's income level alone predicts the tendency of the social worker to view the client as self-centered and entitled.

This relationship does not appear to be mediated by any other predictor. Neither self-reported coursework on working with the affluent nor self-reported in-service training on working with the affluent was a significant predictor of the tendency to view the client in this manner.[13]

CONCLUSIONS

The results of the empirical study reported above were interpreted as indicating clearly that social workers tend to consider adolescents from high-income families to be more selfish and entitled than adolescents from families with lower incomes. The workers did not view the adolescents from affluent families as either more or less competent than adolescents from less affluent families. The respondents were also more likely to view the presenting problem of an adolescent from a low-income family as more serious than they were to view the same presenting problem in an adolescent described as coming from a high-income family.

The findings reinforce our earlier contention that some social workers may be limited with respect to the extent to which they can and do provide effective treatment to adolescents from high-income families. The findings do not prove, but certainly make us suspect, that some social workers may hold similarly negative attitudes toward affluent clients in general. These findings certainly support the need for affluent individuals who are contemplating treatment with a professional therapist to find out whether their potential provider has any preconceived notions or stereotypical views regarding the wealthy. Again, do not hesitate to bring up this question for fear that your raising the issue will prove the point that affluent clients are particularly demanding or even paranoid regarding how they may be treated. Our research has proved that some therapists do hold negative stereotypical views toward the affluent. Given this reality, it is only reasonable for you to take steps to insure that the therapist you hire to treat you or one of your family members does not fall into this group.

Notes

CHAPTER 1: THE AMERICAN DREAM AND THE MYTH THAT WEALTH BRINGS HAPPINESS

1. Luthar, S. S. (2003). The culture of affluence: Psychological costs of material wealth. *Child Development, 74*(6), 1581–1593. Luthar, S. S., & Becker, B. E. (2002). Privileged but pressured: A study of affluent youth. *Child Development, 73,* 1593–1610. Luthar, S. S. & Sexton, C. M. (2004). The high price of affluence. *Advances in Child Development and Behavior.* New York: Elsevier.

2. Capizzano, J., Tout, K., & Adams, G. (2002). Child care patterns of school-age children with employed mothers: A report from the Urban Institute. Retrieved from http://www.urban.org/publications/310283.html. Gilbert, S. (1999, August 3). For some children, it's an after-school pressure cooker. *New York Times,* p. F7. Rosenfeld, A., & Wise, N. (2000). *The overscheduled child: Avoiding the hyper-parenting trap.* New York: St. Martin's Griffin.

3. Pittman, F. S. (1985). Children of the rich. *Family Process, 24,* 461–472.

4. Capizzano, Tout, & Adams (2002).

5. Pittman (1985). Pollack, J. M., & Shaeffer, S. (1985). The mental health clinician in the affluent public school setting. *Clinical Social Work Journal, 13,* 341–355. Shafran, R. B. (1992). Children of affluent parents. In J. D. O'Brien & D. J. Pilowsky (Eds.), *Psychotherapies with children and adolescents: Adapting the dynamic process* (pp. 269–288). Washington, DC: American Psychiatric Press. Warner, S. L. (1991). Psychoanalytic understanding and treatment of the very rich. *Journal of the American Academy of Psychoanalysis, 19,* 578. Weitzman, S. (2000). *Not to people like us: Hidden abuse in upscale marriages.* New York: Basic Books.

6. Pittman (1985), 464.

7. Schwartz, B. (2000). Self-determination: The tyranny of freedom. *American Psychologist, 55*(1), 85.

8. Luthar & Becker (2002). Luthar, S. S. & D'Avanzo, K. (1999). Contextual factors in substance use: A study of suburban and inner-city adolescents. *Development and Psychopathology, 11,* 845–867.

9. Csikszentmihalyi, M., & Schneider, B. (2000). *Becoming adult: How teenagers prepare for the world of work*. New York: Basic Books.

10. Diener, E., & Seligman, M. E. P. (2004). Beyond money: Toward an economy of well-being. *Psychological Science in the Public Interest, 5*(10), 1–31.

11. Buss, D. M. (2000). The evolution of happiness. *American Psychologist, 55,* 15–23.

12. Diener, E., & Biswas-Diener, R. (2002). Will money increase subjective well-being? *Social Indicators Research, 57,* 119–169.

13. Sherman, B. (2006). The poverty of affluence: Addiction to wealth and its effects on well-being. *Graduate Student Journal of Psychology, 8,* 30–32.

14. Luthar (2003), 1589.

15. Whybrow, P. C. (2005). *American mania: When more is not enough*. New York: Norton & Company.

16. Myers, D. G. (2000). *The American paradox: Spiritual hunger in an age of plenty*. New Haven, CT: Yale University Press. Diener & Seligman (2004).

17. Nickerson, C., Schwarz, N., Diener, E., & Kahneman, D. (2003). Zeroing in on the dark side of the American Dream: A closer look at the negative consequences of the goal for financial success. *Psychological Science, 14*(6), 531–536.

CHAPTER 2: THE CULTURE OF AFFLUENCE AND THE UNRELENTING PRESSURE TO ACHIEVE

1. Luthar, S. S., & D'Avanzo, K. (1999). Contextual factors in substance use: A study of suburban and inner-city adolescents. *Development and Psychopathology, 11,* 845–867.

2. Kasser, T., & Ryan, R. M. (1996). A dark side of the American dream: Correlates of financial success as a central life aspiration. *Journal of Personality and Social Psychology, 22,* 280–287.

3. Diener, E., & Seligman, M. E. P. (2004). Beyond money: Toward an economy of well-being. *Psychologial Science in the Public Interest, 5*(10), 1–31.

4. Seligman, M. E. P. (2002). *Authentic happiness: Using the new positive psychology to realize your potential for lasting fulfillment*. New York: Free Press.

5. Diener & Seligman (2004).

6. Diener & Seligman (2004), 1.

CHAPTER 3: THE DISCONNECT BETWEEN AFFLUENT PARENTS AND THEIR CHILDREN

1. According to the U.S. Department of Labor, the proportion of all married couples in the United States in which both husband and wife worked in 2000 was 53.2 percent, and among couples with children under the age of 18, the corresponding proportion was 64.2 percent. Bureau of Labor Statistics (2002). Retrieved from http://www.bls.gov/opub/ted/2001/apr/wk4.

2. Two-career families typically require the services of a nanny, and that this labor need has fostered the growth of an informal economic network involving a large number of illegal immigrants to the United States from the West Indies and Latin America.

Sontag, D. (January 24, 1993). "Increasingly, 2-Career Family Mean Illegal Immigrant Help." *New York Times.* Retrieved from http;//query.nytimes.com/gst/fullpage.html?res.

3. Luthar, S. S. & Sexton, C. M. (2004). The high price of affluence. *Advances in Child Development and Behavior* (p. 143). New York: Elsevier.

4. Pittman, F. S. (1985). Children of the rich. *Family Process, 24,* 461–472. Shafran, R. B. (1992). Children of affluent parents. In J. D. O'Brien & D. J. Pilowsky (Eds.), *Psychotherapies with children and adolescents: Adapting the dynamic process* (pp. 269–288). Washington, DC: American Psychiatric Press.

5. Golden, L., & Gebreselassie, T. (2007). Overemployment mismatches: The preference for fewer work hours: The preference of workers for having either more or fewer hours has remained virtually unchanged since 1985; Rates of overemployment differ considerably by job type, workweek length, income level, gender, and stage of worker's life cycle. *Monthly Labor Review, 130,* 18–51.

6. Gallagher, R. (1999). Cited in PBS Online, *The lost children of Rockdale County. Is it isolated, or is it everywhere? Experts who work with teens and families offer their perspective on this FRONTLINE report.* Retrieved July 28, 2003, from http://www.pbs.org/wgbh/pages/frontline/shows/georgia/isolated/.

7. Capizzano, J., Trout, K., & Adams, G. (2002). Child care patterns of school-age children with employed mothers: A report from the Urban Institute. Retrieved December 20, 2002, from http://www.urban.org/publications/310283.html. Hochschild, A. R. (1997). *The time bind: When work becomes home and home becomes work.* New York: Henry Holt.

8. Casper, L. M., & Smith, K. E. (2002). Dispelling the myths: Self-care, class, and race. *Journal of Family Issues, 23,* 716–727.

9. Luthar, S. S. & Becker, B. (2002). Privileged but pressured? A study of affluent youth. *Child Development, 73*(5), 1593–1610.

10. Zucker, R. A., Fitzgerald, H. E., & Mosesd, H. D. (1995). Emergence of alcohol problems and the several alcoholisms: A developmental perspective on etiologic theory and life course trajectory. In D. Ciccheti & D. Cohen (Eds.), *Developmental psychopathology, Vol. 2: Risk, disorder, and adaptation* (pp. 677–711). New York: Wiley.

11. Luthar, S. S., & D'Avanzo, K. (1999). Contextual factors in substance use: A study of suburban and inner-city adolescents. *Development and Psychopathology, 102,* 187–196.

12. Rosenfeld, A., & Wise, N. (2000). *The overscheduled child: Avoiding the hyperparenting trap.* New York: St. Martin's Griffin. Shafran, R. B. (1992). Children of affluent parents. In J. D. O'Brien & D. J. Pilowsky (Eds.), *Psychotherapies with children and adolescents: Adapting the psychodynamic process* (pp. 269–288). Washington, DC: American Psychiatric Process.

13. Diener, E., & Seligman, M. E. P. (2004). Beyond money: Toward an economy of well-being. *Psychological Science in the Public Interest, 5*(1), 1–31.

CHAPTER 4: THE NEGATIVE ASPECTS OF HAVING WEALTH

1. Los Angeles Business Journal (2008). Flush, not plush: Contrary to stereotypes, many of the children of L.A.'s wealthy are living lives of moderation, preferring to

hide wealth rather than flaunt it. Retrieved April 23, 2008, from http://goliath
.ecnext.com/coms2.

2. Schwartz, B. (2000). Self-determination: The tyranny of freedom. *American Psychologist, 55*(1), 85.

3. Luthar, S. S. & Sexton, C. C. (2004). The high price of affluence. *Advances in Child Development and Behavior* (pp. 125–162). New York: Elsevier.

4. Peterson, C. & Seligman, M. E. P. (1984). Causal explanations as a risk factor for depression: Theory and evidence. *Psychological Review, 91*,347–374. Seligman, M. E. P. (1975). *Helplessness: On depression, development, and death.* San Francisco: Freeman. Seligman, M. E. P. (1994). *What you can change and what you can't.* New York: Knopf.

5. Klerman, G. L., Lavori, P. W., Rice, J., Reich, T., Endicott, J., Anderson, N. C., Keller, M. B., & Hirschfield, R. M. A. (1985). Birth cohort trends in rates of major depressive disorder among relatives of patients with affective disorder. *Archives of General Psychiatry, 42,* 689–693. Robbins, L. N., Helzer, J. E., Weissman, M. M., Orvaschel, H., Gruenberg, E., Burke, J. D., & Regier, D. A. (1984). Lifetime prevalence of specific psychiatric disorders in three sites. *Archives of General Psychiatry, 41,* 949–958.

6. Csikszentmihalyi, M. (1999). If we are so rich, why aren't we happy? *American Psychologist, 54,* 821–827. Diener, E., & Lucas, R. E. (2000). Explainign differences in societal levels of happiness: Relative standards, need fulfillment, culture, and evaluation theory. *Journal of Happiness Studies, 1,*41–78. Myers, D. G. (2000). *The American paradox: Spiritual hunger in an age of plenty.* New Haven, CT: Yale University Press.

7. Martin, J. (1981). Relative deprivation: A theory of distributive injustice for an era of shrinking resources. *Research in Organizational Behavior, 3,* 53–107. Williams, R. M. (1975). Relative deprivation. In L. A. Coser (Ed.), *The idea of social structure: Papers in honor of Robert K. Merton* (pp. 355–378). New York: Harcourt Brace Jovanovich.

8. Goff, B., & Fleisher, A. A., III (1999). *Spoiled rotten: Affluence, anxiety, and social decay in America.* Boulder, CO: Perseus Books Group.

9. Hagerty, M. R. (2000). Social comparisons of income in one's community: Evidence from national surveys of income and happiness. *Journal of Personality and Social Psychology, 78,* 764–771. Van Praag, B. M. S., & Frijters, P. (1999). The measurement of welfare and well-being: The Leyden approach: In D. Kahneman, E. Diener, & N. Schwarz (Eds.), *The foundations of hedonic psychology* (pp. 413–433). New York: Russell Sage Foundation.

10. Luthar & Sexton (2004).

Chapter 5: Promoting Class Envy and Class Warfare

1. John Edwards, Quote from 2004 stump speech. Retrieved fromhttp://en.wiki quote.org/wiki/John_Edwards.

2. Tax Foundation. (November 2000). Distribution of the Federal Individual Income Tax (Special Report No. 101).

3. Obama, B. (January 20, 2008). Speech entitled "The Great Need of the Hour. Quoted by Cary, L. (April 16, 2008). Obama, CEO pay, and the politics of class envy.

Retrieved from http://www.americanthinker.com/2008/04/obama_ceo _pay_and_the_politics.html.

4. Obama, B. (March 2008). Radio Ad used in Texas Democratic Primary Election. Quoted by Cary, L. (April 16, 2008). Obama, CEO pay, and the politics of class envy. Retrieved from http://www.americanthinker.com/2008/04/obama_ceo _pay_and_the_politics.html.

5. Obama, B. (April 11, 2008). Remarks made in Indianapolis. Quoted in *Reuters* article.

6. Cary, L. (April 16, 2008). Obama, CEO pay, and the politics of class envy. Retrieved from http://www.americanthinker.com/2008/04/obama_ceo _pay_and_the_politics.html.

7. Broder, J. M., & Zeleny, J. (February 19, 2008). Democrats make populist appeals before contests. *New York Times.*

8. Ibid.

9. Ibid.

10. Achenbach, J. (October 12, 2007). Clinton and Inequality. *Washington Post.*

11. Ibid.

12. Broder & Zeleny (February 19, 2008).

13. Killbuck Creek Politics (January 30, 2008). John McCain: "Class-warfare demagoguery used by Democrats." Retrieved from http://killbuckcreekpolitics .wordpress.com/2008/01/30/john-mccain-class-warfare-demagoguery-used-by-democrats/)

14. Ibid.

15. Eckholm, E. (May 6, 2006). America's "near poor" are increasingly at economic risk, experts say. *New York Times.*

16. Ibid.

17. Ibid.

18. Ibid.

19. Arr, E. (May 8, 2006). NYT finds new victim class: The "near poor." Retrieved from http://newsbusters.org.node/5258.

20. Ibid.

21. Irwin, N., & Kang, C. (July 10, 2006). Well-paid benefit most as economy flourishes: Trend is pronounced in Washington Area. Retrieved from http://www .washingtonpost.com/wp-dyn/content/article/2006/07/html.

22. Ibid.

23. Ibid.

24. Poor, J. (February 25, 2008). CBS plays class envy card over Countrywide event that didn't happen: Embattled mortgage lender cancels controversial Colorado event, but "Early Show" report spins it anyway. Retrieved from http://www .businessandmedia.org.

25. Ibid.

26. Tomcat (April 14, 2008). Signs of the times: Class warfare. (http://politics plusblogspot.com/2008/04signs-of-the-times-class-warfare-html.

27. Ibid.

28. Ibid.

29. Ibid.

30. Ibid.

31. Mitchell, D. J. (July 7, 2005). A brief guide to the flat tax. The Heritage Foundation, *Backgrounder #1866*. Retrieved from http://www.heritage.org/Research/Taxes/bg1866.cfm.

32. Ibid.

33. Ivins, M. (Dec. 22, 1994). Common sense shows a progressive income tax is just plain fair. *New York Times*.

34. Mitchell (July 7, 2005).

35. Hamm, E. (Jan 2, 1995). Liberals create class envy. *The Virginia Pilot*. Retrieved from http://scholar.lib.vt.edu/VA-news/VA-Pilot/1995.

36. Mitchell (July 7, 2005).

37. HR-1040, introduced by Representative Michael Burgess.

38. Mitchell (July 7, 2005).

39. Hamm, (Jan 2, 1995).

40. Quoted in Jeralyn, S. O. T. (March 21, 2005). A dorm cleaning service as class warfare? Retrieved from http://www.talkleft.com/story/2005.

41. Ibid.

42. Ibid.

43. Ibid.

44. Ibid.

CHAPTER 6: PROFESSIONALS' ATTITUDES TOWARD THE AFFLUENT

1. Warner, S. L. (1991). Psychoanalytic understanding and treatment of the very rich. *Journal of the American Academy of Psychoanalysis, 19,* 578.

2. Ibid., 579.

3. Ibid., 591.

4. Ibid., 591–592.

5. Wolfe, J. L. & Fodor, I. G. (1996). *Women & Therapy, 18,* 74.

6. Ibid., 75.

7. Ibid., 81.

8. Ibid.

9. Weitzman, S. (2000). *Not to people like us: Hidden abuse in upscale marriages* (p. 25). New York: Basic Books.

10. Ibid., 207.

11. Wakefield, J. C. (1988). Psychotherapy, distributive justice, and social work: Part 1: Distributive justice as a framework for social work. *Social Service Review* (June 1988): 188–210.

12. Rawls, J. (1971). *A theory of justice.* Cambridge, MA: Harvard University Press.

13. Wakefield, J. C. (1988). Psychotherapy, distributive justice, and social work: Part 2: Psychotherapy and the pursuit of justice. *Social Service Review* (September 1988), 353–382.

14. Ashbach, N. W. (2002, October). The elephant in the room: Why does nobody talk about the real problems with health care today? *American Family Physician*. Retrieved from http://www.aafp.org/fpm/20021000/15thee.html).

CHAPTER 8: RAISING CONFIDENT, COMPETENT, AND CONNECTED CHILDREN

1. Stein, B. (September 21, 2008). Commentary. CBS Sunday Morning.

CHAPTER 9: RELATIONSHIP ISSUES AMONG THE AFFLUENT

1. Irving, S., & Stoner, K. E. (2008). Prenuptial agreements: An obverview. Retrieved from http://www.nolo.com/asrticle.cfm/ObjectID.

CHAPTER 10: THE MID-LIFE CRISIS AMONG THE AFFLUENT

1. Center for Midlife Crisis of the San Francisco Institute for Personal Growth. (2005). What is midlife crisis? (http://www.midlifeskills.com).
2. Ibid.
3. Man of Action. (August 28, 2008). What I've learned from my wife's midlife crisis. Retrieved from http://lifetwo.com/production/node.

CHAPTER 11: SUBSTANCE ABUSE AMONG THE AFFLUENT

1. Drug and Alcohol Treatment Finder (2008). Drug Treatment for the Wealthy. (http://drugalcoholtreatmentfinder.com/information/drug-rehab-treatment-wealthy).
2. Wolfe, J. L., & Fodor, I. G. (1996). The poverty of privilege: Therapy with women of the upper classes. *Women and Therapy, 18* (3/4), 75.
3. Ibid., 83.
4. Luthar, S. S. (2003). The culture of affluence: Psychological costs of material wealth. *Child Development, 74*(6), 1581–1593; Luthar, S. S., & Becker, B. E. (2002). Privileged but pressured: A study of affluent youth. *Child Devlopment, 73,* 1593–1610; Luthar, S. S. & D'Avanzo, K. (1999). Contextual factors in substance use: A study of suburban and inner-city adolescents. *Development and Psychopathology, 11,* 845–867; Way, N., Stauber, H. Y., Nakkula, M. J., & London, P. (1994). Depression and substance use in two divergent high school cultures: A quantitative and qualitative analysis. *Journal of Youth and Adolescence, 23,*331–357.
5. Swanson, J. W., Linskey, A. O., Quintero-Salinas, R., Pumariega, A. J., & Holzer, C. E. (1992). A binational school survey of depressive symptoms, drug use, and suicidal ideation. *Journal of the American Academy of Child and Adolescent Psychiatry, 31,* 669–678.
6. Way, N., Stauber, H. Y., Nakkula, M. J., & London, P. (1994). Depression and substance use in two divergent high school cultures: A quantitative and qualitative analysis. *Journal of Youth and Adolescence, 23,* 331–357.
7. Hansell, S., & White, H. (1991). Adolescent drug use, psychological distress, and physical symptoms. *Journal of Health and Social Behavior, 32,* 288–301.
8. Hochschild, A. R. (1997). *The time bind: When work becomes home and home becomes work.* New York: Henry Holt.

9. Bogard, K. M. (2005). Affluent adolescents, depression, and drug use: The role of adults in their lives. *Adolescence, 40*(158), 281–290.

10. U.S. Department of Health and Human Services. (2001). *Trends in the well-being of America's children and youth.* Washington, DC: U.S. Government Printing Office.

11. Luthar, S. S., & Becker, B. (2002). Privileged but pressured? A study of affluent youth. *Child Development, 73,* 1593–1610.

12. Werner, E., & Smith, R. (1992). *Overcoming the odds.* Ithaca, NY: Cornell University Press.

Chapter 12: Problems with Inheritances

1. Kapor, J. R., Dlaby, L. R. & Hughes R. J. (2005). *Personal Finance,* New York: McGraw-Hill; Tyson, E. (2006). *Personal Finance for Dummies.* New York: John Wiley & Sons.

Appendix: An Empirical Study of Professional Social Workers' Attitudes toward the Affluent

1. In the language of research design, the respondents may exhibit "social desirability response set bias." This means that they do not wish to appear biased in their responses, so they consciously or unconsciously respond in a manner that makes them appear less biased than they actually are. In the study reported here, if respondents were aware that they were rating both more and less affluent individuals, they might discern that the purpose of the study was to compare their attitudes toward the more and less affluent. They might therefore tend to rate the individuals described in the vignettes similarly, so as to mask their biases.

See Kerlinger, F. (1973). *Foundation of empirical research.* New York: Holt, Rinehart, & Winston; Osgood, C. E., Suci, G., & Tannenbaum, P. (1955). *The measurement of meaning.* Urbana: University of Illinois Press; Snider, J. G. & Osgood, C. E. (1969). *Semantic differential technique: A sourcebook.* Chicago: Aldine Publishing Co.

2. For a description of the various methods of factor analysis and the statistical requirements for the use of the procedure, see Stevens, J. (1996). *Applied multivariate analysis for the social sciences.* Mahwah, NJ: Lawrence Erlbaum Associates. The specific factor analysis algorithm employed here was principal components analysis with varimax rotation The obtained sample of 359 was more than adequate for the use of factor analysis.

3. The calculation of factor scores is performed by the statistical program that performs the factor analysis. The factor scores are simply weighted sums of the respondent's ratings. The weights are derived from the factor analysis and reflect the extent to which each adjective rating contributes to the particular factor for which the scores is being obtained.

4. The multivariate analysis of variance procedure is also described in Stevens (1996). The analysis employed included a comparison of respondents rating clients described as having each of the three income levels. The numbers of respondents

who rated clients with each of the three income levels were as follows: (1) under $20,000, n = 177; (2) about $50,000, n = 120; and (3) over $400,000, n = 122. These numbers yielded a statistical power for the test for the significance of client income of .98, assuming a moderate effect size and the .05 level of significance (see Cohen, J. [1988]. *Statistical power analysis for the behavioral sciences*. Hillsdale, NJ: Lawrence Erlbaum Associates). This power means that if the three groups actually differ from each other by an average of one-fourth of a standard deviation on any dependent variable, then there is a 98 percent chance that the test will be significant, and we will conclude that attitude differences due to client income level do exist.

5. In conducting the principal components analysis of the adjective ratings, all the respondents' ratings were pooled, regardless of the manipulated descriptors of the client that were contained in the vignette each client received. Initially, all factors having eigenvalues greater than 1.00 were extracted (see Stevens 1966). Then the scree criterion was employed to aid in the determination of the number in factors that would be easily interpretable. The analysis yielded four factors having eigenvalues greater than 1.00. The eigenvalues were 4.01, 2.59, 1.19, and 1.03, respectively. The plot of these factors appeared to become asymptotic to the x-axis at Factor 3, and the loadings of the 15 items on each of the four factors extracted initially suggested that the first two factors were interpretable. Accordingly, the factor analysis was rerun specifying that two factors be extracted. It is the rotated factor matrix for this two-factor solution that is presented in Table 2.

6. $F = 5.14$, $df = 2$ and 347, $p = .004$.

7. $F = 3.70$, $df = 2$ and 347, $p = .026$.

8. One-item rating scales are most appropriately regarded as ordinal data rather than interval scale data. Chi-square statistics may be used appropriately to determine the significance of relationships between such variables. See Twaite, J. A. & Monroe, J. A. (1979). *Introductory statistics*. Glenview, IL: Scott-Foresman.

9. For readers who are conversant in statistics, note that in the initial cross-tabulation presented in Table 5 there were six cells in the table that had expected frequencies less than 5.0. These low expected cell frequencies render the significance probability of the obtained chi-square statistic somewhat unreliable. Accordingly, the two lowest categories for rated seriousness of the client's presenting problem were collapsed, and the chi-square was recalculated. The chi-square computed for the collapsed table was also significant (chi-square (4) = 12.73, $p = .013$). Thus, the significant result persists, suggesting the credibility of the reported relationship.

10. When the "very poor" and "poor" prognosis categories were collapsed, the chi-square remained nonsignificant (chi-square (4) = 9.39, $p = .052$).

11. ($F = 4.19$, df = 10 and 348, p < .001; R-squared = .107).

12. ($t = 5.31$, $df = 5.31$, $p < .001$).

13. Again, for the statistically sophisticated reader, we note that collinearity diagnostics indicated that potential multicollinearity was not a concern in this regression analysis, since no correlation between the predictors exceeded .60; and no condition index exceeded 30 (see Stevens 1996).

Index

About the Authors

ORLA CASHMAN is a doctor of clinical social work with degrees from New York University and Hunter College School of Social Work. She maintains a private psychotherapy practice in Greenwich, Connecticut, and Chelsea, New York City. She works with children, adults, and families and has extensive experience as a parent and community educator. Dr. Cashman speaks publicly on a variety of topics and provides consultation to clinicians, schools, and organizations.

JAMES A. TWAITE is a psychotherapist and statistician practicing in Tenafly, New Jersey, and Rowlan, Pennsylvania. He holds doctorates in psychology from Columbia University and in econometrics from the Fletcher School of Law and Diplomacy (Tufts/Harvard). He has authored or co-authored four previous books on topics in psychology and statistics.